UNPOPULAR CULTURE: TRANSFORMING THE EUROPEAN COMIC BOOK IN THE 1990s

In the last fifteen years or so, a wide community of artists working in a variety of western European nations have overturned the dominant traditions of comic book publishing as it has existed since the end of the Second World War. These artists reject both the traditional form and content of comic books (hardcover, full-colour 'albums' of humour or adventure stories, generally geared towards children), seeking instead to instil the medium with experimental and avant-garde tendencies commonly associated with the visual arts. *Unpopular Culture* addresses the transformation of the status of the comic book in Europe since 1990.

Increasingly, comic book artists seek to render un-popular a traditionally degraded aspect of popular culture, transforming it through the adoption of values borrowed from the field of 'high art.' The first English-language book to explore these issues, *Unpopular Culture* represents a challenge to received histories of art and popular culture that downplay significant historical anomalies in favour of more conventional narratives. In tracing the efforts of a large number of artists to disrupt the hegemony of high culture, Bart Beaty raises important questions about cultural value and its place as an important structuring element in contemporary social processes.

(Studies in Book and Print Culture)

BART BEATY is an associate professor in the Faculty of Communication and Culture at the University of Calgary.

Unpopular Culture: Transforming the European Comic Book in the 1990s

Bart Beaty

UNIVERSITY OF TORONTO PRESS
Toronto Buffalo London

© University of Toronto Press Incorporated 2007
Toronto Buffalo London
Printed in Canada

ISBN-13: 978-0-8020-9412-4 (paper)
ISBN-13: 978-0-8020-9133-8 (cloth)
ISBN-10: 0-8020-9412-0 (paper)
ISBN-10: 0-8020-9133-4 (cloth)

Printed on acid-free paper

Library and Archives Canada Cataloguing in Publication

Beaty, Bart
    Unpopular culture : transforming the European comic book in the
    1990s/Bart Beaty.

    (Studies in book and print culture)
    Includes bibliographical references and index.

    ISBN-13: 978-0-8020-9133-8 (bound)
    ISBN-13: 978-0-8020-9412-4 (pbk.)
    ISBN-10: 0-8020-9133-4 (bound)
    ISBN-10: 0-8020-9412-0 (pbk.)

    1. Comic books, strips, etc – Europe – History and criticism.   I. Title.
    II. Series.

    PN6710.B42 2007   741.5′9409049   C2006-903810-4

University of Toronto Press acknowledges the financial assistance to its
publishing program of the Canada Council for the Arts and the Ontario
Arts Council.

This book has been published with the help of a grant from the Canadian
Federation for the Humanities and Social Sciences, through the Aid to
Scholarly Publications Programme, using funds provided by the Social
Sciences and Humanities Research Council of Canada.

University of Toronto Press acknowledges the financial support for its
publishing activities of the Government of Canada through the Book
Publishing Industry Development Program (BPIDP).

Contents

Acknowledgments

Scholars who specialize in comics have frequently had to overcome institutional obstacles in order to complete their work. Inadequate library collections, a dearth of secondary sources, and a lack of institutional support for work in this interdisciplinary area are just some of the roadblocks I faced when undertaking this project. Thus, I would like to first extend my gratitude to the Social Sciences and Humanities Research Council of Canada for its ongoing commitment to inquiry-based research. Without its funding, I would never have embarked upon this project and this book would remain a series of uncollected thoughts in the back of my mind.

This book stems first and foremost from my interest as a reader of contemporary European comics. My awareness of this important cultural form might have remained casual were it not for the timely intervention of Tom Spurgeon, formerly of *The Comics Journal*. In 1997, Tom asked me to consider writing regularly on the topic of European comics for that magazine, and the result was an ongoing review column entitled 'Euro-Comics for Beginners.' Writing this column sparked my interest in investigating European comics more deeply, and I am grateful to Tom for placing me on this road. I would also like to thank Gary Groth and Kim Thompson for their continuing patronage of the column, and Darren Hick, Eric Evans, Anne Elizabeth Moore, Milo George, Mike Dean, and Dirk Deppey for their editorial guidance over the ensuing years.

In 1997, while still a graduate student, I visited the Festival International de la Bande Dessinée in Angoulême, France, for the first time. There I met many of the artists and publishers whose work I discuss in the pages that follow. My introduction to this world was aided considerably by the kindness of many friends who shared their knowledge and passion for European comics with me. A great deal of this book is born out of conversations that I have had over dinner at Le Passe Muraille with Christiane Markowitz, Uli Proefrock, and Kai Wilksen over the course of the past eight years. There is simply no way I can repay their kindness. The travellers at the Hotel Palme have changed from year to year, but they all contributed to this project in their own ways: Jessica Abel, Greg Bennett, Peter Birkemoe, Stephen Betts, Desmond Brice, Tony Davis, Tom Devlin, Alfred Eichholz, Sylvia Farago, Ben and Susan Katchor, Nadia Katz-Wise, Sean Lester, Ellen Lindner, Lisa Lippman, Jason Little, Matt Madden, Ana Merino, Paul Socolow, George South, Craig Thompson, and Ebi Wilke.

Some of the material presented in this book was developed at conferences, including the Canadian Communication Association, the Popular Culture Association, the International Comics Arts Festival, the History of French Graphic Narrative, Mapping the Magazine, the Comics Arts Conference, and the International Humanities Conference. I am grateful to the organizers of these conferences for allowing me to present my work in its early stages. I would particularly like to thank a number of specialists in comics scholarship whose comments I have found particularly useful: Peter Coogan, Cécile Danehy, Charles Hatfield, Craig Fischer, Thierry Groensteen, Gene Kannenberg, Pascal Lefèvre, Mark McKinney, Ann Miller, Mike Rhode, Mark Rogers, and Guy Spielmann. In particular, I would like to thank John Lent for the interest he has shown in this manuscript and for his insightful comments as editor of *The International Journal of Comic Art,* which published an earlier draft of the material that forms the basis for chapter seven of this book.

A number of good friends and colleagues have contributed to the shaping of this book. First among these is Mark Nevins, whose generosity of spirit knows no bounds. Mark has been involved in this book at every stage of its development, and he has been one of its staunchest supporters. He has my deepest thanks. Rusty Witek has been a supporter of this work for many years and in many important ways. I am truly grateful for his example of rigorous scholarship. Nick Nguyen has influenced my thinking on European comics more than he would likely admit, and I want to thank him for his insightful comments on an earlier draft of this manuscript. I would also like to thank Keith Logan for his friendship and his strong support of this project.

My family has been a tremendous support through the process of writing this manuscript, and I want to thank them for their loving support. My parents, Dianne and Harry Beaty, never wavered in their faith that this oddball project would come to fruition. I am deeply grateful to my grandfather, Don Beaty, whose generosity allowed me to travel to Angoulême as an impoverished student and who was a constant inspiration. Finally, Rebecca Sullivan has been so deeply involved in the creation of this book at every level that it would be impossible to enumerate all the roles that she has played. With all my love, I thank her.

Finally, this book would never have been written if I had not been able to share ideas with so many of the artists, critics, journalists, editors, and publishers whose work is discussed herein. I am exceedingly grateful to these men and women for the openness, receptiveness, and frankness they showed me on various trips to Europe. They tolerated my incessant inquiries with a patience that underscored their own enthusiasm for this project. Many opened up their ateliers, their collections, and even their homes to me, and I would like to thank each and every one who took the time to share their ideas: Cuno Affolter, Yvan Alagbé, Giovanna Ansechi, David B., Alex Baladi, Jens Balzer, David Basler, Edmond Baudoin, Jimmy Beaulieu, Charles Berberian, Martin Brault, Daniele Cauzzi, Eric Cartier, Christopher, Martin tom Dieck, Julie Doucet, Christian Humbert-Droz, Philippe Dupuy, Anke Feuchtenberger, Vincent Fortemps, Mira Friedmann, Christian Gasser, Frédéric Gauthier, Francesca Ghermandi, Dominique Goblet, Paul Gravett, Emmanuel Guibert, Markus Huber, Caroline Hui Phang, Jason, Jean-Paul Jennequin, Joan, Hansje Joustra, Ulf K., Killoffer, Reinhart Kleist, Kristiina Kolmaneinen, Batia Kolton, Erik Kriek, Knut Larsson, Olivier Marboeuf, Roland Margerin, Max, Jean-Christophe Menu, Rutu Modan, Fabrice Neaud, Uli Oesterle, Thomas Ott, Daniel Pelligrino, Marcos Pellojota, Yirmi Pinkus, Joost Pollman, Igor Prassel, Itzik Rennert, Stefano Ricci, Nicolas Robel, Johanna Rojola, Ria Schulpen, Joann Sfar, Joost Swarte, Thomas Thorhauge, Lewis Trondheim, Johannes Ulrich, Thierry van Hasselt, Pierre Wazem, and Sabine Witkowski.

UNPOPULAR CULTURE: TRANSFORMING THE EUROPEAN
COMIC BOOK IN THE 1990s

Introduction

Intention commune: réhabiliter la BD de création face au mercantilisme ambiant.
Antoine de Gaudemar, *Libération* (1996)[1]

At its heart, this is a book about oppositions – cultural, ideological, social, national, and aesthetic oppositions. Moreover, it is a book about how these oppositions structure our understanding of art and about how the declaration 'this is what I am not' has been mobilized in a particularly neglected cultural domain because the declaration 'this is what I am' has historically held little sway. The oppositions that most interest me here – fundamentally the tension that exists between comic books conceived as popular culture and comic books conceptualized as art – can be witnessed through a comparison of any number of works. For example, to choose not quite at random, in 1997 two Swiss cartoonists published two very different books. Zep authored the bestselling *Tchô, monde cruel* (Glénat). Nadia Raviscioni authored the lesser-known *Odette et l'eau* (Drozophile). The differences that exist between these works highlight the tension in the comic book field that I am interested in interrogating, specifically by forcing the question of what is meant by the term 'comic book' in the contemporary cultural landscape.

Zep's *Tchô, monde cruel* is a traditional comics album by an incredibly popular Swiss cartoonist and is published by one of the largest and most commercial of French comic book publishers, Glénat. The book is the sixth in the popular Titeuf series, which began in 1992. The star of this series, Titeuf, is a young boy who appears in a series of single-page gag strips in the magazine *Tchô*, where he is, by an overwhelming margin, the most popular character. Indeed, the Titeuf books are so popular that they regularly occupy as many as nine spaces on the list of the top ten bestselling comic books in France. For example, in 2000 the eighth book in the series (*Lâchez-moi le slip*) sold 370,200 copies in France, with each of the previous seven selling more than 100,000 copies in that year as well.[2] Over the course of a decade, each volume has sold millions of copies in the French-speaking world, although they remain significantly less popular in other languages. Titeuf is also the star of an animated television program, episodes of which are collected on DVD, and is featured on dozens of toys, games, and licensed trinkets of all sorts. It is indisputable that Titeuf is the most popular French comic book character since the creation of Astérix in the 1960s.

Typically, the Titeuf strips focus on the character's interactions with his friends and family, and deal with the prepubescent boy's confusion about an increasingly accelerated world. The strips often include sexual overtones, but it is clear that Titeuf and his friends have no clear understanding of sexuality beyond an ambiguous sense of fascination with a classmate named Nadia. Other strips focus on sports, practical jokes, and skateboarding. The popularity of the strip owes much to the writing style, which is quickly paced and filled with slang. Indeed, Zep is widely credited with (or blamed for) the creation of new slang terms in the French language, and the young often imitate Titeuf's patterns of speech. In short, *Tchô, monde cruel* is a quintessential album in the classic format, featuring a recurring character whose exploits unfold in a series of bestselling volumes. Its Swiss author fits seamlessly within the Franco-Belgian cartooning tradition, and its popularity is of the type that tends to guarantee a lengthy career.

Odette et l'eau, by Nadia Raviscioni, could not be further removed from the world of Titeuf. Published in the same year, and also by a Swiss cartoonist, this is a fifteen-page soft-cover book that was hand-printed by Christian Humbert-Droz on 20 June 1997 outside of Geneva, the first single-artist book published by Drozophile. Unlike the mass-market Titeuf volume, *Odette et l'eau* was limited to 150 signed and numbered copies. The book is printed on coarse brown paper that retains a pulpy quality. The brief work is not a narrative but a short description of a woman who dislikes water and refuses to go swimming. The book largely eschews the type of panels that are associated with comic books and instead is composed of a series of illustrations that incorporate textual elements. Transitions generally lack narrative rationales, and images reside in relation to each other in an oblique fashion. The book's title page has a tiny hole in the paper through which it is possible to see a small portion of the third page, specifically Odette's shoe, an effect that creates a voyeuristic sense akin to looking through a peephole. In short, *Odette et l'eau* has much more in common with the traditions of the artist's book than with the traditions of comic book publishing.

Yet, at the same time, Raviscioni is commonly regarded as a comic book artist – albeit not a tremendously popular one – and her work participates in many of the logics of the field. This tension exists in her biography, as she specialized in comics at an art school at which the form was not taught: 'When I arrived at art school, I already wanted to make comics and the professors wanted abstraction. I made prohibited works, and when I started to include colors, one said to me: "One color, it's enough already."'[3]

The question arises: How can works as disparate as these, even when created roughly contemporaneously and by artists from the same culture and nation, be reconciled under a common rubric? Indeed, the differences threaten to overwhelm the similarities. Physically, the objects little resemble each other. *Odette et l'eau* is wider than the Titeuf album, but considerably shorter – giving it a horizontal orientation in contrast to Titeuf's vertical. *Odette et l'eau* is clearly constructed by hand, while Zep's book is clearly machine-made. While Zep's name is minuscule in comparison to Titeuf's on the cover of his book, Raviscioni's name is almost invisible, appearing simply in a small hand-written note (upside-down) on the image of an umbrella that reads 'par Nadia.' The name of the publisher is entirely absent from *Odette*, whereas it figures prominently on the Titeuf album, suggesting that one is legitimated through reference to the market and the commercial importance of its publisher, while the other functions as an art object that seeks to efface such material concerns. Indeed, the Titeuf volume signals its participation in the marketplace in several important ways: an ad for *Tchô* magazine on the inside-back cover; reproductions of the eight additional volumes in the series on the back cover that place the book in sequence and alert the reader to further consumption possibilities; the presence of a bar code and ISBN number. *Odette et l'eau*, on the other hand, carries neither ISBN number nor bar code because it presents itself not as a book but as an art object. The text does, however, include the direct contact information for the publisher – including a phone number – on the title page, suggestive of a more immediate interaction between publisher and consumer that can be mediated at the level of direct interpersonal communication.

These physical and presentational differences are related to several other more important distinctions. One of these would be price. Despite the fact that it is considerably shorter in length, *Odette et l'eau* is a significantly more costly book than is the Titeuf volume, selling for about six times the price of a traditional bestselling album. This price difference is partly a function of scale, as Zep sells millions of copies and Raviscioni sells 150 if her entire print run sells out. Yet, more than this, the price difference marks a significant ideological distinction as each book appeals to a differing conception of legitimacy. For Zep, what Pierre Bourdieu terms the heteronomous principle of the marketplace, in which bestseller status is a guarantor of quality (one million readers can't be wrong), is central. For Raviscioni, on the other hand, the autonomous principles of artistic creation are mobilized in relation to artisanal creation long associated with cultural fields other than comics. For adherents of the autonomous principle, Zep is a non-artist, a cultural hack with no credibility, churning out repetitive product for a lowest-common-denominator audience. For those who subscribe to the heteronomous principles of the marketplace, on the other hand, Raviscioni and her 150-copy-selling book simply do not exist as a factor at all, not even as the most remote blip on the radar.

This book focuses its attentions on those tiny blips. Specifically, it is interested in how artists like Raviscioni have, since 1990, steadily chipped away at the heteronomous principle of the marketplace and championed autonomous principles of artistic production in one of the most neglected of cultural fields. This book is about a revolution in progress. Certainly, it is clear that the revolution has yet to succeed – the bestseller logics of comics production are as central to the field today as at any time in history. Yet it is also clear that for the first time it is possible to conceptualize within the field of comic book production a space for innovative and avant-garde cultural practices. As early as 1996, the French daily *Libération* asked:

> After a serious identity crisis marked by an unquestionable academicism and a bending of the market, is a new comics being born in France? One is tempted to believe it considering the number of initiatives undertaken in recent years on the margins of the traditional circuits. A new generation of artists and illustrators gathered around magazines with small print runs – while not actually fanzines – like *Lapin, Cheval sans tête,* and editorial structures that are as light as they are rudimentary, such as l'Association, Cornélius, les Requins marteaux or Amok.[4]

Although the space that *Libération* described is not yet dominant, and may never achieve a dominant position, it is revolutionary nonetheless.

For adherents of the bestseller logics of the market, the period that this book most concretely addresses, the 1990s, is an era of failure. For example, in his book about comic book script writers, *Avant la Case*, Gilles Ratier titles his chapter on this epoch 'The Agony of the Press: 1990–1999.' Following, as it does, a chapter celebrating 'The Triumph of the Album: 1979–1989,' the sense of decline in Ratier's narrative is palpable.[5] For Ratier, and others interested in the prolongation of the classical traditions of European cartooning, the era of innovation that this volume charts is an aberrational break with history, punished through declining sales. Ratier's book, with its focus on the importance of comic book writers rather than artists, is a celebration of the literary aspect of comic book production. This model did, as the author suggests, reach a zenith in the 1980s, with the emergence of serious literary comics that operate according to a graphic novel ideal. The 1990s, on the other hand, reversed the polarity of the comic book. Without entirely abandoning the well-written literary tendency, comic book artists of this era increasingly drew inspiration from the visual arts. A generation of cartoonists raised in art schools saw in postmodernism's erosion of high/low distinctions the possibility of creating avant-gardist work in the comic book form. The turn to the visual in comics, which was in point of fact simply an exaggeration of the existing visual plane through the incorporation of techniques borrowed from the fine arts, transformed the field of comic book creation in Europe by announcing an end to the existing paradigm. No longer would comic book artists seek legitimacy in relation to literature, but in relation to the visual arts. This shift in orientation meant abandoning the novelistic ideal for one more closely related to the traditions of the artist's book.

Through the seven case studies included here, this book argues that the evolution from a criterion of value with its basis in the novel to one rooted in the artist's book is the most significant shift in the orientation of the comics field in the past century. The idea of the book, and in particular the 'comic book,' has been fundamentally altered over the course of the past fifteen years of comics production in Europe. Beginning from a position in which nearly all comics were produced as hardcover, full-colour, forty-six page albums by commercial presses – a tradition still very much alive today in the work of artists such as Zep – the concept of the comic book has been radically splintered by a variety of forces and actors. The rise of the small press, which was, first and foremost, the rise of a publishing model based on the artist-run cooperative and a struggle for creative autonomy, recast the shape and look of the comic book as a defiant statement of aesthetic and commercial independence. Increasingly, these artists and publishers challenged the heteronomous logics of the bestseller by creating limited-edition works that did not circulate in the mass market, a publishing model more akin to arts presses than to the large publishing houses that were themselves subsidiaries of international media conglomerates.

The conflation of artist-run cooperatives and new publishing forms inevitably gave rise to new visual techniques. Departing from the traditions of the Franco-Belgian illustration schools, the new comics artists incorporated fine arts techniques, including linogravure, etching, photography, collage, and sculpting, in an effort to find new expressive means within the comics form. As this tendency spread from the French-speaking nations of France and Belgium to other parts of Europe, they were subtly altered by local tendencies and necessities. New genres emerged, most notably autobiography, which gave voice to the quest for legitimacy. At the same time, the largest and most commercial publishing houses acted to solidify their market dominance by recruiting from this new movement and transforming the most commercially promising of the young artists into *la nouvelle bande dessinée*. Some of these artists became bestselling stars within the established traditions of the comic book field because of the way they successfully bridged the divide between old and new traditions, revitalizing a moribund comics format with new energies. Throughout it all, the tendency that has united the work of disparate artists working in a wide range of genres, nations, and techniques has been a focus on the transforming power of the image to reshape popular conceptions of the book.

In many ways this volume is itself a departure from traditions of its own. The dominant thread in the scholarly study of comic books has always been the literary and the textual. Since many scholars of the comic book, a small pool to be sure, find their institutional homes within literature departments, this is not surprising. One result of this tendency has been to root the study of comic books squarely in textual traditions, with detailed, theoretically informed (in the best cases) readings of key texts being the order of the day. Many of these readings tend to be more evaluative than critical and analytical, arguing for the importance of certain writers, artists, or books. The other major trend in comics scholarship has been broadly historical and sociological. These works tend to suggest that certain comics mirror key attitudes of the time in which they were produced, and the scholarship mines the texts for the light they can shed on society, past or present.

This volume, while containing elements of both tendencies, probably contains so little of either that it is all but guaranteed to disappoint both schools. My work here borrows heavily from that of Pierre Bourdieu, who placed the question of the creation of value squarely on the table. Despite their importance in the field of French popular culture, comics are virtually absent from Bourdieu's analyses of the interrelationship between restricted and wide-scale cultural creation. While Bourdieu's colleague Luc Boltanski addressed the subject of comic books in 1975, the field has evolved a great deal since that time. My effort here is to come to terms with the transformation of the field of comic book production in Europe since 1990, not to highlight seminal works nor to uncover a submerged history of this period, but to reflect upon increasingly fluid notions of what constitutes a 'legitimate culture.' By charting the way in which various communities of artists have positioned themselves in relation to the dominant traditions of the comic book field, I am able to suggest the way that a historically marginal form of culture has moved closer to the field of power, represented by cultural legitimacy.

My argument about the transformation of the comic book field is advanced in this book in seven chapters, each of which addresses a key issue in the development of European comic books since 1990. The first chapter focuses on the French artist-run publishing cooperative L'Association as the most important single industrial player in this transformation and as the model for much of what would transpire. Founded in 1990, L'Association radically restructured the popular conception of the comic book. Beginning from a punk-inspired do-it-yourself aesthetic, L'Association has, in the intervening period, emerged as the most important trendsetter in comics. Works by L'Association's founders have been widely translated across Europe and around the world, and, moreover, the associational model has served as an inspiration for cartoonists in a number of European nations. Indeed, it is fair to say that in many ways the small-press comics movement of the past decade and a half has become synonymous with L'Association as an organization. Chapter 1 begins by considering the explicit ways by which L'Association has come to occupy a specific location within the field of production and, more important, how that position exists in terms of both rupture and continuity with the heritage of European cartooning, particularly as it has been defined in France and Belgium. Specifically, L'Association and other small-press comics publishers have taken up their work against a historical background of the development of European comics in the twentieth century, which has been especially interested in the creation of an 'adult' sensibility in comics and the attendant benefits. Since at least the 1960s, artists like Jacques Tardi and Moebius have sought to create possibilities in magazines (*Pilote, Métal Hurlant*) and publishing houses (Futuropolis) for serious-minded literary comics that pushed the boundaries of the medium. With few exceptions, in the 1970s and 1980s these efforts existed within a structuring framework of genre-based storytelling and a corporate production method. L'Association, on the other hand, broke with both the corporate and generic model of comics production in the 1990s, repositioning the serious (or 'high') comics model as a function of visual rather than literary predispositions. By considering the specific tendencies mobilized by L'Association in their anthology (*Lapin*), their book collections, and, most important, in their 2000-page millennial anthology *Comix 2000*, I argue that L'Association represents not so much a unified style of comics production but a particular disposition towards the field that is rooted in the possibility of visually defined books.

The second chapter extends from the first by considering the relevance of the changes brought to the comic book form by small-press publishers in the 1990s. Central to the notion of novelty created by the small press has been a challenge to long-held definitions of what constitutes comics and what constitutes a 'comic book.' The renunciation of the traditions of the comics field has necessitated a concomitant rejection of the conventional form of the comic book. Small-press publishers in the 1990s and after have worked to denormalize the popular equation of comic books with forty-six page albums, initially by privileging works that were longer, physically smaller, and printed in black and white. Nonetheless, a tremendous diversity of approaches has come to dominate the field as a result of the innovations of the small press, and this chapter considers the relevance of form as it relates to both norms of storytelling and the creation of distinction within the field. The origins of the small-press movement reside in the realm of fan publishing and fanzine creation, with its attendant reliance on photocopied production rather than offset printing. Yet, the increasingly 'professional' look of many fanzines calls into question understandings about the distinctions between amateur and professional comics creation, with many artists struggling to redefine themselves in light of this divide. Indeed, some publishing groups have explicitly sought to mimic non-professional works as a counter-discourse to official comics policies. At the same time, however, a number of commercial publishers have adopted traditionally artisanal methods in order to borrow legitimacy from the consecrated arts by creating special-edition books that are artificially scarce. These volumes of *tirage-de-tête* and *ex libris* editions depend on notions of specialness that are central to the conception of comic books as collectibles and fetish objects. These volumes place the issue of comic book form firmly at the forefront of the field, where small-press publishers, such as Switzerland's BüLB and Drozophile, have provided a counterdiscursive model of production that exists in opposition to the dominance of the largest commercial publishing houses.

Chapter 3 outlines the visual aesthetics of the contemporary European small press, with a particular emphasis on the way in which avantgarde and experimental styles have contributed to a new awareness of the possibilities of visuality in the medium. The adoption of radical publishing arrangements and the embrace of new formats have been equally matched in the small-press comics renaissance by a reliance on non-traditional aesthetics. Indeed, it is impossible to disregard the fact that cartoonists have increasingly turned to aesthetic advances made by artists working in non-comics media, such as painting, photography, and sculpture, for inspiration. To this end, it is possible to suggest that comics are only now moving through a modernizing period but that they are doing so against a larger cultural backdrop of postmodernism. This presents a particular disconnect for cartoonists, who struggle to legitimize their work within a field that has been traditionally disregarded by the so-called high arts. Nonetheless, a large number of artists have adopted non-traditional expressive means in the comic book field, and many of those are explored in this chapter. Specifically, this chapter considers the work of the OuBaPo group of cartoonists, whose goals include the deliberate testing of formal boundaries relating to the comics form in a modernist manner. For the most part, these boundaries exist around issues of sequentiality, and those questions are considered here. Other artists, particularly those associated with Franco-Belgian publisher Frémok, have explored the boundaries of comics through a reliance on non-traditional visual media. The specific ways in which these artists rely upon unusual comic book aesthetics in order to comment upon questions of politics, philosophy, and personal aesthetics are discussed in this chapter in relationship to the aestheticizing and politicizing tendencies of the new comics producers. Ultimately, this chapter explains how avant-gardist visual techniques have come to replace literary pretensions as the hallmark of artistic seriousness within the field of comics production.

Chapter 4 extends the argument advanced by the first three chapters by specifically addressing the divergent and similar ways in which the small-press comics culture has been conceptualized as an international project. The small-press comics movement has developed differently across Europe, often as a function of the histories of indigenous comics publishing prior to the 1990s. Thus, the movement is strongest in France and Belgium, the two countries with the most developed comics industries in Europe since at least the time of the Second World War. Large, national comic book industries have resulted in structures that support artistic experimentation, such as festivals and comic book specialty stores. In countries where the comic book industry was small or virtually non-existent, the small-press movement has developed at a more tentative pace. Nonetheless, it has developed across almost every European country, to at least some degree. By focusing on a few of the nascent national scenes, it is possible to suggest how the metropole does and does not structure the development of culture in the hinterlands. Specifically, this chapter focuses on comic book festivals in Switzerland and Portugal as examples of important spaces in which various voices are allowed to collide and cross-pollinate. Further, it examines the specificities of a number of non-francophone comics scenes (Switzerland, Spain, Portugal, Italy, and Finland) through reference to the most important local alternative comics anthologies in each country (*Strapazin, Nosotros Somos los Muertos, Quadrado, Mano,* and *Napa,* respectively). The question of how certain authors circulate in differing national contexts is addressed in order to demonstrate the internationalization of the small-press disposition. Further, the relative success – and lack of success – of certain talented authors from the periphery is investigated to suggest the structures of the comic book field as they have been redefined by recent developments.

The fifth chapter begins the reorientation of the book away from a focus on the organization of the field and towards a consideration of the products of that field. Chapter 5 addresses the significance of autobiography as a genre in contemporary comic book production. Largely conceptualized by its practitioners as a rejection of genre, this chapter will demonstrate that autobiography has in fact become the dominant genre of independent comics itself, owing particularly to the influence of Edmond Baudoin. The success of Marjane Satrapi's *Persepolis* and the ongoing viability of Ego Comme X as a publisher specializing in autobiographical comics are testament to the importance of the turn towards the real and towards the self. This chapter focuses, to a greater degree than the previous chapters, on close readings of major works by leading autobiographical cartoonists. Specifically, the ways in which various authors depict the process of comic book production will be examined to reveal how these moments are used to construct a discourse of authenticity. Three works are central here. First, David B.'s six-volume autobiography, *L'Ascension du Haut Mal*, is discussed in relation to his fictional comics production, particularly relative to the dynamic that exists between his work in the two modes. The chapter then looks at *Journal d'un album* by Philippe Dupuy and Charles Berberian and how it conceptualizes the process of artistic production within the confines of the large French publishing houses and offers a commentary on the status of comic book authorship as a legitimate career. Finally, Fabrice Neaud's *Journal* series of autobiographical comics are examined in light of the author's philosophical understanding of the significance of creation within the field. Each of these books points to the way in which cartoonists associated with the small-press renaissance conceptualize creation as an affirmative action that contributes to a sense of personal identity. Further, autobiography is seen as a genre in which the differences in the visual register – rather than the textual – structure personal identities and inform expressions of authenticity.

Chapter 6 borrows from the sociology of popular music to examine the increasingly frequent charge that many of the artists associated with the small-press comics movement have 'sold out' by creating genre-based works for the established publishing houses. Since the mid-1990s, the largest publishers of comic books in Europe (including Dargaud, Casterman, Humanoïdes Associés, Dupuis, and Delcourt) have aggressively recruited many of the stars of the small-press comics movement. Offered increased exposure and greater financial remuneration, many of these artists have chosen to set aside more 'personal' works in the small-press arena and have turned to the creation of genre works in the traditional album format and the use of recurrent characters. For some, this represents a betrayal of the small-press comics movement, which was rooted in a rejection of mainstream traditions that are represented by contemporary comic book stars like Zep. For others, however, these works represent a logical changing of the guard and are a natural evolution within the field. The question of how an oppositional cultural practice is co-opted and diverted, and, further, whether this is still a relevant way of conceptualizing cultural change, is central to this chapter. The case studies focus on three authors whose works reflect different positions in relation to the large and small publishers. First, Joann Sfar is discussed as an artist whose origins are in the small press but who has risen to become a small-scale media celebrity in France by producing a wide variety of comic book series, many of which examine the influence of Judaism on popular culture. Emmanuel Guibert, a frequent collaborator of Sfar's, is an example of a cartoonist who has successfully transferred a small-press realist aesthetic – rooted in the autobiographical tradition – to genre-based work. Finally, Christophe Blain, another collaborator of Sfar's, has been long associated with the small press despite the fact that he has never worked for the small publishers in any significant fashion. These artists are contrasted with the more normative tendencies in contemporary European comic book production in order to demonstrate how the so-called *nouvelle bande dessinée* serves as a partial re-inscription of the literary tendency enabled by distinctions from tradition activated at the level of the visual.

The final chapter summarizes many of the arguments in the book by examining in detail the career of the single artist who best stands for the particular developments I have been discussing. Lewis Trondheim, a founder of L'Association who has done amateur comics, experimental comics (OuBaPo), autobiographical comics (*Approximativement, Carnets*), genre comics for large publishers (*Lapinot, Donjon*), and whose work is widely translated throughout Europe, Japan, and the United States, is the ideal case study for a book like this. This chapter provides a close reading of his works in relation to each other in order to determine the specific ways Trondheim manipulates his image to be at once a 'serious alternative artist' and at the same time 'a crowd-pleasing genre writer.' This is, I would argue, the central tension in the field of contemporary comics production. As a medium with a long association with large-scale mass-market production, comics have generally been neglected by the public and by scholars of culture. The drive to legitimate the medium, a desire widely shared among small-press cartoonists of the current generation, has often taken an oppositional stance that has driven comics towards unpopular aesthetics. Trondheim represents an effort to balance the extremes of both poles within a single career – a daunting task. His relative success or failure in this endeavour goes a long way to establishing the current shape of the field of comic book production in Europe.

While this brief overview provides a précis of what I have attempted to accomplish with this book, a word is perhaps required to note what I have not taken on. First, this book is in no way a comprehensive overview of the development of European comic book industries since 1990.

Significant trends are omitted, important artists are neglected, and entire genres are forgotten in this book. For example, the issue of the translation of Japanese comics (manga) throughout Europe, inarguably the most important economic driver of the comics industry in the period which I am discussing, is touched upon only in passing, despite the fact that it corresponds with many of my own arguments (including the dismantling of a notion of a Franco-Belgian heritage, and the resizing of the comic book). Nonetheless, despite some small degree of mutual interest, for the most part the independent comics revolution and the manga invasion have proceeded unconnected to each other. Indeed, even within the limited purview of my argument I have been forced through want of space to ignore a large number of artists whose work I find illuminating and whose efforts would bolster my own argument. Nonetheless, were I to cover all of the material that contributed to the development of my thinking on these subjects, the resulting book would be ridiculously overlong and unwieldy. Second, I have not attempted to approach the works that I consider as a catalogue of the best or most interesting books being published. In short, while I greatly admire many of the works discussed in these pages, it is not my intention to act as a reviewer or to judge the qualities of the works. Since 1997 I have published a regular column reviewing European comics in *The Comics Journal,* and readers hoping that this book will be an extended version of those commentaries are bound to be disappointed.

Finally, a note on the title of this book. *Unpopular Culture* stems from a description of my research that I have frequently used. In claiming that I study unpopular culture, I have hoped to signal the fact that I study an area of popular culture in which few researchers are interested. Comics, which have lengthy roots predating film and television, are among the least-studied communicative forms and are among the aspects of popular culture that are the least enjoyed by a wide public. Many of the artists discussed in this book have struggled with this legacy. Working in a field commonly derided as merely popular, but reaping few of the benefits that accrue to producers of genuinely popular culture, these artists are caught in a double bind. The reaction of many of the cartoonists discussed here has been an attempt to erase the popularity of comics through the assumption of dispositions more frequently associated with the traditional fine arts. In a sense, therefore, comic book artists working to transform the image of the comic book in light of new concerns with visuality are interested in making the form un-popular or bringing it into the realm of high culture. This process of un-popularizing culture is that which most interests me about these works. As Pierre Bourdieu has pointed out generally about culture, the field is marked by the tension between those who have made their mark and those who are attempting to do so.[6] In the case of European comics in the 1990s this tension existed primarily between those who wished to mark the field as a site of popular entertainment and those who wished to mark it as a space for autonomous cultural production akin to other, more legitimate, fields. This is the story of how one of the last bastions of pure popular culture was made unpopular.

Chapter 1

L'Association and the '90s Generation

Merci à Van Hamme et Ted Benoît qui nous font détester *Blake & Mortimer* encore plus qu'avant.

L'Association editorial[1]

Étienne Lécroart's 2003 book *Le Cycle* (L'Association) (figure 1) provides a particularly interesting encapsulation of much of the activity that characterizes the small-press European comics renaissance. The thirty-eight-page book tells the story of a scientist and his two assistants. The scientist has developed a new theory about the structure of reality, and his hypothesis is tested in a number of manically comedic ways. Of course, because he is a comic book scientist, his reality is that of the field of comics. This is to say, reality for the scientist is an ongoing series of spatially contained boxes arranged in sequence. Time unfolds in spatial units, and particular spatial units exist only in relation to others of the same type. Thus, when the scientist attempts to crawl through the left-hand boundary of a panel on the left-hand side of the page, he exits the page entirely. Yet, when he subsequently attempts to exit that same boundary from a panel on the right side of the page, he re-enters the previous panel, which is now to his left. Written out, these observations sound confusing, but actualized in the narrative they seem perfectly clear and precise. Lécroart's book establishes a scientific rationale for the examination of the comic book form that is rendered comedic because the participants lack the external awareness of the fact that they are themselves characters bound within that form. More important, Lécroart suggests not only that the reality of the comic book page is now fixed at the level of abstract form but that comics exist as a social and aesthetic field.

1 In Étienne Lécroart's *Le Cycle*, M. Marmouset visits the world of Lewis
Trondheim's *Lapinot et les carottes de Patagonie*.

When the professor's assistant M. Marmouset vanishes from the 'reality' of his comic book universe he finds himself, over the course of nineteen pages, in a series of different comic book worlds. In this space, Lécroart recreates the social milieu of the small-press comics movement of the 1990s by bringing it aggressively to the fore. Marmouset finds himself on each successive page living in the work of a different cartoonist. Beginning with Ivars, Joann Sfar, and François Ayroles, Marmouset moves through a vast array of comic book pages. On each page, several important transformations take place. First, the narrative is restructured. While Lécroart is careful to build narrative cohesion by relying on scenes that share common visual elements (such as vast libraries), the beginning of each new page disrupts the flow of the story by shifting diegetic worlds. This disruption is further a function of the second transformation, which finds Marmouset depicted in a new visual style on each page as Lécroart blends his character into the representational mode of the artist whose work he is borrowing. Finally, in most of the new pages Marmouset takes on the role – temporarily – of a better-known character. On each page, Lécroart has erased a key figure to make room for his own gatecrasher, and, as a consequence, Marmouset becomes some of the best-known figures in the small-press comics world, if only for a page. Thus, Marmouset becomes Lewis Trondheim's Lapinot and, in an autobiographical dream story, the cartoonist David B. As he takes on each character he retains his unique characteristics, and Lécroart changes only the dialogue of the character usurped by Marmouset. In this way, each new story disrupts the narrative of *Le Cycle* with its distinct conventions – from fantasy to autobiography – and tone, but at the same time *Le Cycle* disrupts our understanding of these works as completed texts that exist on their own.

The world enacted by *Le Cycle* depicts comic books as a particular social scene. The nineteen artists that are invoked by the book are, presumably, friends and colleagues of the artist, or at least sympathetic enough to his take on their work to allow his sampling of it. In weaving these artists together, Lécroart demonstrates similarities in their approaches and unites the artists under a common rubric. That rubric is the contemporary European comics small press. Indeed, of the artists present here, seventeen are European (primarily French), while the remaining two (American Robert Crumb and Canadian Julie Doucet) have lived in Europe for extended periods of time. The works utilized in *Le Cycle* are from a similarly delimited set of publishers, including ten works from L'Association, two from Seuil, and one each from the likes of small-press publishers Zéhu, Square, Cornélius, and Les Mal Élevés. Only one traditional publishing house has a work included (Delcourt), and that is for one of its least typical books. Moreover, L'Association has published the vast majority of the artists represented in the work, and many are almost entirely known for their work with that group. Ultimately, therefore, *Le Cycle* structures its commentary on the nature of comic books as a medium of communication by locating comics almost exclusively at the level of the small press generally, and L'Association specifically. By dramatically reducing the field of expression, Lécroart creates what is at once an extended in-joke of circular references and self-references which can also be understood as a sort of small-press manifesto that lays claim to important stylistic and structural ground.

One way to read *Le Cycle* is as a particular form of what Pierre Bourdieu has termed position-taking. In his essay 'The Field of Cultural Production, or; The Economic World Reversed,' Bourdieu argues that the artistic field is defined by the constant struggle that exists between proponents of two divergent principles of cultural hierarchization, the autonomous and the heteronomous.[2] The autonomous principle of legitimacy refers to degree-specific consecration, or the prestige that is accorded to artists by other artists. The heteronomous principle, on the other hand, rests on the logic of financial success, measured primarily through sales or performances.[3] Bourdieu suggests that the field of cultural production is the arena in which the struggle to impose the dominant definition of the artist, and thereby delimit admittance into the field, takes place.

Insofar as Lécroart's book creates a sub-group that, it is suggested, represents those works that are the most important – in the logic of the story, the most worthy of scientific investigation – he articulates a point of view that celebrates autonomous values. Indeed, in *Le Cycle*, Lécroart seems to seek only the approval of other artists, whose work he samples and celebrates. The construction of an autonomous viewpoint by the total exclusion of the heteronomous would not be surprising in any cultural sub-field except, perhaps, for comic books. Indeed, until the 1990s, it was difficult to even imagine the European comic book industry operating along any principle other than that of the market. The consecrated artists in this field, whose degree of legitimation is always minimal relative to the more established fields of drama, literature, painting, and even cinema, have always been those whose works sold particularly well: Hergé, Uderzo and Goscinny, Jacques Tardi, Enki Bilal. Nonetheless, a book like *Le Cycle* signals the presence of a different logic, and a counter-discourse; *Le Cycle* announces the existence of an autonomous logic that the book did not create but which it nonetheless draws upon for narrative coherence.

The radical restructuring of the comic book field in Europe that Lécroart suggests fully emerged only in the 1990s. As early as 1975, Luc Boltanski, a colleague of Pierre Bourdieu, had diagnosed the beginning of a transformation in the French comic book industry, but the autonomous principle of art for art's sake only emerged in the field in a significant way following the rise of small artist-run presses.[4] Of these, the most influential has certainly been L'Association.

It is not my intention in this volume to offer a comprehensive overview of the history of European comic book production. Many admirable histories of this sort exist already, and there is no need to duplicate those efforts. Nonetheless, a brief précis of the construction of the field will prove useful in the long term. While contemporary historians now trace the development of the comics form to the inventions of Rodolphe Töpffer in the 1820s, comic books did not emerge as a significant industrial form until the twentieth century. In France, for example, the appearance of popular strips such as *Bécassine* and *Les Pieds nickelés* in the first decade of the century provided the foundation for much of what would follow. Throughout Europe at this time, comics began to be widely diffused through magazines, from *Sondags-Niss* in Sweden to *Charlot* in Spain. While some American newspaper comic strips of this period, appearing as they did in the 'mature' print form of the newspaper, appealed largely to an adult readership, at the time European comics were almost exclusively targeted at a primary audience of children and were published in children's magazines.

In the 1920s, two influential strips – Alain Saint-Ogan's *Zig et Puce* and Hergé's *Tintin* – made their debut, extending the popularity of comics to a broad public and shifting the emphasis of the industry away from a disposable model based in magazines and towards the greater permanence of books. An influx of American comic books and strips in the Depression-era 1930s negatively impacted indigenous production in many European countries, with national specificities returning to the comics pages only after the end of the Second World War. At this time, a number of new comics publications were launched, including, in France, *Coq Hardi* and *Vaillant,* and, in Belgium, *Tintin* – magazines that helped establish the standard for French-language comics in the golden age.

At the end of the Second World War the most advanced comics-producing countries in the world were the United States, which continued to export material across Europe with the assistance of the Marshall Plan, and Belgium, which launched two magazines that defined a trans-European comic book style for generations. *Spirou*, launched in 1938, defined the Charleroi style as lively, cartoonish, and inflected with humour. This style was found in the work of André Franquin in the humorous adventures of the titular hero, and particularly in the work of Morris and René Goscinny on the extremely popular western-comedy series *Lucky Luke*. *Spirou*, which included besides humour comics genres such as the police thriller (*Valhardi*) and the straight adventure series (*Buck Danny*), expanded considerably in the 1950s and 1960s, adding a number of new series across genres. By the end of the 1960s, *Spirou* was publishing many of the best-loved comics series in the world by artists such as Peyo (*Les Schtroumpfs*), Will (*Tif et Tondu*), and Tillieux (*Gil Jourdan*).

Many of the others, however, were published by its greatest rival, *Tintin*. Launched in 1946 as a new home for the adventures of Hergé's intrepid boy reporter, *Tintin* established the so-called Bruxelles School in opposition to the Charleroi style. Dominated by a hyper-stylized realism that favoured flat colouring, the elimination of shading, and the suppression of extraneous detail, the 'clear line' style of the Bruxelles School was practised by Hergé, E.P. Jacobs, Jacques Martin, Willy Vandersteen, and others. Unlike *Spirou*, *Tintin* strongly favoured adventure stories, including, aside from the title strip, classics such as Jacobs's *Blake et Mortimer* and Martin's *Alix l'Intrépide*. In the 1950s and 1960s the magazine added a wide roster of new talents, including Greg, Bob de Groot, Dany, and Hermann. The competition between these two magazines for dominance of the Belgian comics market – which extended into France and the Netherlands – standardized the economics of the industry in the postwar period and defined the normative visual aesthetics of the comic book medium. Rooted in line drawings that varied from cartoonish to realist depending on the genre, the postwar Belgian comics magazines lay the foundation for a comics culture that extended across western Europe.

The success of the postwar Belgian comics had the effect of consolidating the industry in French-speaking nations and established a business model that continues in somewhat altered form to this day. The postwar mass-market model of comics production was two-pronged, seeking to sell the same material to an audience twice. Stories were serialized in comics magazines, of which *Tintin* and *Spirou* were only the most popular, over the course of weeks or months, with new installments appearing a few pages at a time. This had a significant impact on the development of narrative structures, requiring frequent cliffhangers in adventure stories or self-contained gag sequences in comedies.

The heteronomous principle and the logic of the market were enshrined in the field as only the most popular series from these magazines were collected into forty-six-page hardcover books, called albums, with the intention of reselling an endurable copy of the material to an audience that had already read and enjoyed it. The large scale that is required for newsstand and bookstore distribution, complete with its potentially crippling return system, favoured large publishing houses. These houses could afford staff to conduct readership surveys so that editors could make informed decisions about audience preferences. The process of producing magazines like *Tintin* and *Spirou* was a constant effort to please the largest possible readership and to convert magazine readers into book buyers when the opportunity arose.

Lombard, the publisher of *Tintin*, was extremely tentative on this front, publishing only seventy-eight albums between 1950 and 1965.[5] Newer comics publishers, such as Casterman (a long-established book publisher), eventually pushed the comics industry more aggressively towards a book model of production, a shift that culminated in the 1970s with the first inklings of the serious comics novel. Nonetheless, the industry as it was established in the postwar period consisted of a relatively small number of specialist publishing houses emphasizing mass-market magazine publishing with an eventual goal of consolidating a back catalogue of bestsellers in book form.

By the 1960s, a new generation of cartoonists was poised to shake the foundations of the comic book industry by seeking to appeal to audiences of all ages. The flagship of this movement was undoubtedly *Pilote* magazine. Launched in 1959 by Radio-Luxembourg and purchased by Dargaud in 1960, *Pilote* was the product of René Goscinny, Jean-Michel Charlier, and Albert Uderzo. The magazine was anchored by Uderzo and Goscinny's extremely popular Gaulish humour adventure series *Astérix*, which was coupled with other well-liked series such as *Tanguy et Laverdure* (Uderzo and Charlier) and *Barbe Rouge* (Hubinon and Charlier). In 1963, *Pilote* added *Lieutenant Blueberry* (Giraud and Charlier), a realistic western series that would adopt an increasingly anti-authority tone as the decade wore on. In 1968, the magazine welcomed Marcel Gotlib's nonsensical *La Rubrique-à-Brac*, a popular strip among students. Other well-regarded cartoonists added at this time included Fred (*Philémon*), Druillet (*Lone Sloane*), Cabu (*Le Grand Duduche*), Greg (*Achille Talon*), Mandryka (*Concombre masqué*), and Claire Bretécher (*Cellulite*). Throughout the last years of the 1960s, and particularly in the wake of the events in Paris of May 1968, these artists pushed *Pilote* increasingly towards more adult themes and issues. At the same time, new magazines such as the American underground comics-inspired adult humour journal *Hara-Kiri* helped to end the traditional association between comics and children's literature. If the legacy of the 1950s was a publishing model and a visual code, the 1960s is often regarded as a transition period in which new magazines bridged the divide between child and adult readers, dragging the comics form towards maturity.

Boltanski argues that it was in the 1970s that European comics broke decisively with childish stories and entered the adult realm for the first time. Several influential new magazines were launched in this period, signalling a break from the past and the creation of an arena for what he terms 'symbolic expression,' or a space in which comics could be enacted as a legitimate art form for the first time.[6] Frustrated with the editorial direction of *Pilote,* Bretécher, Mandryka, and Gotlib founded *L'Echo des savanes* in 1969, a mixture of sex, subversion, and psychoanalysis that functioned as a radical departure from the Franco-Belgian comics heritage. In 1975, Gotlib launched another humour magazine for adults, *Fluide glacial.* At the same time, Philippe Druillet, Moebius (Jean Giraud), Jean-Pierre Dionnet, and Jean-Pierre Farkas began *Métal hurlant,* an adult-themed science-fiction comics magazine. Here, Moebius created the wordless comics epic *Arzach,* and Druillet presented innovative works like *Salammbô.* These stories, freed from the aesthetic traditions of the Franco-Belgian school and from limiting narrative structures, marked a turn towards new models of comics storytelling. With large, expansive, and bold imagery, *Métal hurlant* clung to the often marginal genres of science fiction and fantasy adventure but imbued the material with an expressionism that was at odds with the heritage of the field. For the first time, it seemed, cartoonists were creating work with a cultivated disposition that they explicitly hoped would be recognized as art.[7] Moreover, this sentiment was widely shared, even across international borders. In Italy, Guido Crepax and Hugo Pratt were creating serious-minded and sexually charged adventure work, while Spanish cartoonists struggled to define an adult sensibility despite the censorship of the Franco regime.

The success of the turn towards adult content in the comics field of the 1970s was significantly bolstered by the possibility of reprinting popular works as books. Historically, not all comics series had been collected into book form. One consequence of this was that the distinction between a series in a magazine and one in books became a clear demarcation of status in the field, entirely defined by the heteronomous principle. Indeed, it is clear that the collection of an artist's work in book form significantly impacted that artist's reputation. Jacques Laudy, for example, was one of the pioneering cartoonists associated with *Tintin*, but because Lombard did not collect his work, it remains under-appreciated relative to that of his peers. Clearly, because nostalgia plays such a key role in the historiography of popular culture, these economic choices have had a structuring impact on our understanding of the development of the comics form in the postwar era. Moreover, the distinction between ephemeral comics for magazines and more permanent comics for books – a distinction reinforced by Hergé's postwar decision to redraw and rewrite his prewar *Tintin* books so that they more closely adhered to the aesthetics and politics of his later work – impacted the development of the form.

Working in a neglected medium, one in which prestige was exceedingly difficult to acquire, cartoonists in the 1970s adopted the novel as a model of artistic ambition and cultural seriousness. In a field in which books marked the intersection of prestige, popularity, and financial success, book-length material became increasingly conceptualized as a significant goal. The success of Hugo Pratt's *La Balada su il mare salato* in 1967, which featured the exploits of the tremendously popular Corto Maltese, opened the possibility of conceptualizing comics as novels for the first time. In the 1970s and 1980s, this idea was taken up by a variety of publishers who created book series targeting specific types of readers and who launched new artists as stars. In 1978, Casterman (who translated the French edition of Pratt's book) launched a new magazine *(À Suivre)*, specifically to serialize works that would be eventually collected as graphic novels – comic books that exceeded the forty-six-page standard that had existed for decades.

The cartoonist-as-star phenomenon was a reversal of the traditions of the European comics market that had existed to that point. While it is true that some individual artists had become famous because of the extreme popularity of the characters whose stories they told – Hergé for Tintin, Goscinny and Uderzo for Astérix – these artists were rarities. Moreover, it was always clear that the character was far more popular and better known than its creator, a relationship signalled by the small size of the author's name relative to the character's name on the covers of the various books. This relationship shifted as cartoonists began to increasingly regard themselves as artists and to treat their work as artistic creations rather than the product of the mass market, even while working within the conventions of commercialized genres that were most often associated with B movies (science fiction, the western, the *péplum*, the police thriller, soft-core pornography).[8] Jacques Tardi's historical fantasy series *Adèle Blanc-Sec* featured a proto-feminist adventurer who battled pterodactyls in post–First World War Paris. Tardi's work visually recalled the Franco-Belgian heritage but merged it with serious political themes explored within fantastic narratives.

Enki Bilal's science fiction *Nikopol* trilogy, on the other hand, placed political commentaries in a futuristic setting. Bilal's work highlighted the shift towards direct-colour comics, or comics that are coloured directly on the original art page with watercolours or gouache rather than in a separate process. Direct colour, whose connection to the traditions of painting emphasized the contribution of the single artist rather than a penciller/inker/colourist team, became a hallmark of serious cartoonists in the 1980s, including Miguelanxo Prado, Lorenzo Mattotti, and Jacques de Loustal. This particular aesthetic, adopted by a wide array of cartoonists with novelistic or serious ambitions and by very few doing work for children, helped to shift the terrain of 'literary' comics production. By adopting a visual style that would be associated with artistic seriousness – and coupled with literary ambitions – these cartoonists helped to establish the terms by which their own work would be supplanted by the 1990s generation. Placing an emphasis on the visual composition of the individual comics page through the creation of comics manuscripts that could be welcomed in galleries and museums shifted European comics production towards the predominantly visual for the first time, rupturing the word/image balance and creating new spaces for innovation.

Of course, other genres were also mined for their adult potential as the comics reading audience aged. The historical comic series became popular with the work of François Bourgeon (*Les Passagers du vent*) and André Juillard (*Les 7 Vies de l'épervier*). Humour comics remained a constant, with new authors such as Frank Margerin (*Lucien*) and Vuillemin addressing an adult sensibility. Erotic comics, long a submerged tendency, came to the fore in the work of Milo Manara (*Le Déclic*) and Philippe Bertrand (*Linda aime l'art*). Finally, realism emerged as a significant tendency for the first time, finding expression in works by artists like Baru (*Quéquette Blues*) and Ferrandez (*Arrière-Pays*). The star cartoonist phenomenon of the 1980s was built largely around the idea that the traditions of the industry could be bent enough to allow individual voices to flourish. Thus, artists like Tardi and Margerin continued to work largely, and often exclusively, within generic constraints while at the same time carving out particularly individual voices as unique artists. This sensibility contributed to a tradition of quality that was particularly evident in France and Belgium, whose comics cultures increasingly stretched to incorporate many of the most personal and idiosyncratic cartoonists from around Europe and the rest of the world.

This process was so hegemonic that Argentine cartoonists José Muñoz and Carlos Sampayo were often characterized as 'French' simply by virtue of the fact that their work was primarily distributed in that market. Indeed, the dominance of the Franco-Belgian publishing empires in the field of European comics at this historical moment cannot be understated. An obvious analogy would be to the cinema of North America, where the impact of Hollywood productions greatly outstrips the significance of Canadian and Mexican filmmaking and has completely eradicated the output of most Central American countries. In the field of European comics, France and Belgium are Hollywood, and the largest comics publishers (Glénat, Dupuis, Dargaud, Casterman, Delcourt, Soleil, and Humanoïdes Associés) correspond to the Hollywood studios, turning out huge commercial successes and award-winning dramas but little that could be termed truly revolutionary in relation to a genuine avant-garde.

In the 1980s, these large publishing houses – themselves often part of much larger publishing and media conglomerates – found themselves facing a crisis. Pressed by the demands of short-term profitability and the need to generate shareholder return, the largest publishers increasingly reduced potentially risky investments by eliminating opportunities for cartoonists with novel approaches to the medium. The tradition of quality in the European comics industry accounted for only a small percentage of all works published and a smaller percentage of gross profits. A bestseller mentality took over the market, with publishers seeking artists who could emulate the visual styles of popular cartoonists like Moebius. The ongoing series and the beloved character once again became increasingly important as a way of predicting future sales. At the same time, however, competition from cinema, television, and video games as visual entertainment stymied the industry. Publishers turned to new formats, including pocketbook-sized editions, and to new revenue streams, including licensed products such as toys and collectible statues, in order to staunch the red ink.

The first victims of the industrial crisis were the long-established comics magazines. During the late 1980s *Pilote* and *Tintin* and other comics magazines ended decades-long runs. In 1993, *Pif,* the spin-off magazine from *Vaillant,* published its last issue, and in 1997 *(À Suivre)* ceased publication, marking the end of the golden age of European cartooning, the end of an aesthetic era, and the end of a business model that had existed for almost fifty years. This is not to say, however, that the field of large-scale comics production had evaporated entirely; far from it. As Thierry Groensteen notes, '*Largo Winch, Joe Bar Team, Petit Spirou, Lanfeust de Troy* or, again, *Titeuf* have attested, in this decade [the 1990s], that the comics industry has maintained its ability to manufacture *les bestsellers.*'[9] Nonetheless, the limits of the traditional comics model were exposed by the crisis of the late 1980s, which opened up the possibility for new industrial models.

For many cartoonists, the most appealing model was that offered by Futuropolis. Begun by comic book storeowner Étienne Robial in 1972, Futuropolis was one of an increasingly large number of small commercial publishers that built a space for themselves in the market of the 1980s almost exclusively through sales to comic book specialty stores. Such stores had arrived in France in the early 1970s, and the first edition of *Répertoire professionnel de la BD francophone* (1989) indicated that by the end of the 1980s there were 39 comic book stores in Paris, 128 in the rest of the country, and 62 in Belgium. Catering to the most devoted fans of the medium, these stores could be used to promote innovative and non-traditional material. Futuropolis made its mark with the publication of works by consecrated 'serious' artists from the 1970s generation, most notably Jacques Tardi, Joost Swarte, and Robert Crumb. Moreover, Robial sought to shift the relationship between comic book artists and their characters, placing emphasis for the first time on cartoonists as significant artists in their own right. While publishers at that time minimized the names of the artists on their books, stressing instead the name of the characters or series, Robial bucked tradition. In 1974 he released three oversize books (30 × 40 cm – the same size as an original comic book page) titled simply *Calvo, Gir* (for Jean 'Moebius' Giraud), and *Tardi.* These massive names across the tops of exceptionally large books triumphantly announced the arrival of cartoonists as legitimate artists.

At the same time, Robial began aggressively promoting works by non-traditional and new artists, including Edmond Baudoin, Charlie Schlingo, and Jean-Claude Denis. The Collection X series of half-sized albums, launched in 1985, was specifically intended to bring the works of young cartoonists to market, taken to a self-parodying extreme in the case of Julien's *Après-Midi torride* (1986), published when the cartoonist was only eleven years old. Futuropolis combined this interest in young authors with a comprehensive reprinting tradition. The Collection Copyright resurrected works by Alain Saint-Ogan and Calvo, and translated the best of American prewar comic strips, including *Dick Tracy, Krazy Kat, Terry and the Pirates,* and *Bringing Up Father.* The dissolution of Futuropolis in 1994, as the company became part of Gallimard, is often cited as the true end of the adult comics revolution that had begun in the early 1970s. It was the inheritors of the tradition exemplified by Futuropolis that would revitalize the European comics industry at the start of the 1990s.

One of the last Futuropolis publications, *LABO* (1990), can be seen as the end of one model of comic book publishing and the birth of another precisely at the beginning of the new decade. Dated January 1990, and edited by Jean-Christophe Menu, *LABO* represented an attempt to launch a new magazine featuring a number of artists who had made names for themselves in the non-professional French fanzine-publishing scene of the late 1980s. Menu himself was a product of this scene, having published *Le Lynx à tifs* since 1982. In 1984, Menu created, with Stanislas and Mattt Konture, the Association pour l'Apologie du 9e Art Libre, which continued to publish *Le Lynx* in a new album-inspired format. Menu, Stanislas, and Konture all published early books through Futuropolis in 1987 and 1988, and in 1990 *LABO* was released to accompany an exhibition at the Musée du Papier in Angoulême.

In May of that year, the participants opted to leave the increasingly endangered Futuropolis and create their own independent publishing group, calling it L'Association (à la Pulpe). The founding members were Menu, Stanislas, Konture, David B., Killoffer, Lewis Trondheim, and Mokeït (who left the group shortly after its creation to return to a career in painting). Of these, only David B. and Stanislas could have been properly termed comic book industry professionals at that time. As an artist-run cooperative to which individual patrons could subscribe, L'Association adopted a policy of paying artists royalties of 10 per cent of the cover price of their books, nothing for contributions to their anthology (*Lapin*), and 'the common labour, like the manual assemblage of limited edition albums, are remunerated in the form of a meal in a restaurant to be consumed on that same day.'[10] Their artistic practice, defined in opposition to the dominant tendencies of the market, was summarized by *Libération:*

> L'Association asserts to be 'a shared space' and establishes its brand: works
> of immaculate fabrication, forsaking glazed paper for thicker paper, and

colour for black and white, characterized by a smaller format and by more literary themes (notably autobiography) or experimentalism (in the graphics).[11]

In November 1990, L'Association released its first publication, the anthology comic book *Logique de Guerre Comix,* officially launching the publishing house that would become most closely identified with the European new comics renaissance of the 1990s.

L'Association's first bulletin, which followed the release of *Logique de Guerre Comix,* announced the new paradigm of comics production, which was rooted in an opposition to the heteronomous state of the market and a celebration of autonomous principles. First, L'Association explicitly disdained the commercial comics culture of the era. Jean-Philippe Martin suggests that L'Association, and similar publishers that originated around this time, were 'resolutely alternative to the established comics.'[12] Indeed, this was signalled as early as *LABO,* in which Menu's editorial expressly addressed this question: 'Concerning this rotten context, we will not reconsider the fact that the 1980s seem to have been catastrophic for comics.'[13] Menu's condemnation of the crassly commercial comic book industry set the stage for a philosophical shift towards avant-gardism and art for art's sake. The first communication of the new group, in January 1991, outlined the fundamental principles of their new organization: 'Our long engagement in the defence of an expression of the High idea in comics could not wait any longer for this second breath. L'Association will be the new independent structure within which this adventure will continue. A structure whose guiding principles will be: Integrity and the Long Term.'[14]

The emphasis on independence, integrity, and the defence of a 'high' conception of comics all point to the arrival of a fully articulated sense of comics as a legitimate cultural form operating beyond the demands of the market. Indeed, in that same newsletter, L'Association explicitly declared their break from a commercial comics industry when they announced to bookstores and readers that 'we are above all authors, and we consider the publishing house to be an additional creation. We are not really professionals in management and public relations.'[15] The expressed opposition between artistic creation and the demands of the market is the hallmark of the autonomous principle, so rarely expressed in European comics up to this time.

L'Association's stated principles – integrity and the long term – read as if they were directly lifted from Bourdieu's writing on the autonomous principle. Indeed, Bourdieu notes a distinction between the economic structures of the cultural field that are rooted in short-term bestsellers and those works that are created in a more restricted fashion and with an eye towards the accumulation of cultural and symbolic, rather than economic, capital over the long run.[16] For L'Association, cultural capital is derived by publishing only important books and never by publishing simply to increase revenues. 'L'Association does not have the intention of publishing too many books, but only the books that continue to be indispensable.'[17] To this end, L'Association positioned themselves simply as one part of a larger struggle against the dominant traditions of the comic book industry. They routinely indicated their kinship with similarly minded small publishers, including, in the first issue of their newsletter (*Le Rab de lapin*), Automne 67 and Éditions Cornélius.

In 1995, when L'Association was reasonably established, they encountered a potential problem with regard to Seuil, the French book publisher who had recently launched a comics line and who seemed to be infringing on their cultural space. L'Association noted that the books in Seuil's comics line bore a strong resemblance to their own collection Ciboulette, particularly the covers. This was exacerbated by the fact that the authors of three of the first six books in the series (Lewis Trondheim, with two books, and Fabio), were associated with L'Association and had published in the collection Ciboulette. While noting that 'L'Association is no longer the only player in the field publishing creative and intelligent comics' and that this would cause them problems as a publisher insofar as it was possible that they would lose a number of interesting projects to competitors, ultimately this did not pose a problem. 'It is probably better to be in healthy competition with other talented editors defending the same ideas (as is the case with Le Seuil, Cornélius, or Amok) than to be eternally the only one tilting at windmills.'[18] This expression of solidarity and shared values in the face of financial competition from a rival is core to the self-image of the European small-press movement of the 1990s. The sense that the movement is united against the dominant principles of hierarchization stands as central to the logic of the restricted production and a long-term economic outlook as an artist-run cooperative rather than a publisher. Nonetheless, this solidarity did not extend to large comics publishers a decade later. In a lengthy essay entitled *Plates-bandes* (2005), Jean-Christophe Menu criticized Casterman's Écritures book series as a cheap knock-off of the type of work published by L'Association.[19]

Despite their solidarity with the small press in general, by the end of

1994 even L'Association was forced to reluctantly admit, 'Finally, in short, everything is damned well beginning to resemble a real publishing house.'[20] In that year the group hired its first full-time employee to deal with the office and expanded the print runs of their books from one thousand to two thousand copies. In 1995, works by some of their artists were translated into German (*Strapazin*) and Finnish (*Suuri Kurpitsa*). By this time, it was suggested by one of the subscribers that the very identity of the organization was threatened by its success, which was, at best, relative.[21] The publisher was clearly growing rapidly. Revenues for 1995 (1,200,000FF) were more than double those of 1994. In 1996, revenues rose 66 per cent to more than 2 million FF. In 1997, the group recorded a profit of 183,000FF.[22] By this point, all signs pointed to the fact that L'Association had fully emerged as a genuinely flourishing agent in the French comic book industry. The group had passed five hundred sub-scribers in 1995 and doubled that number by the end of 1996. By 2002, they had a number of large-scale financial successes, including the four volumes of Marjane Satrapi's autobiography *Persepolis*, which had sold more than 100,000 copies, including 30,000 copies of the fourth volume within a month of its publication. Nonetheless, it must be borne in mind that this success was still limited and that the publisher continued to operate with less than a half-dozen employees.

The relative financial success of L'Association as a publisher has gone hand in hand with the rise of the small-press comics movement over the past decade and a half, and their ability to maintain an autonomous disposition while negotiating this success has been a balancing act. The question of whether they continue to publish only those books that are 'indispensable' is, of course, largely a question of personal taste. None-theless, the collective publications of L'Association, now numbering more than 230 titles, are among the most visible accomplishments of the small-press comics movement, and they stand as the benchmark against which claims to editorial independence and autonomy are measured.

As for the books published by L'Association, it is important to bear in mind how these works both draw upon and break from prior traditions of comic book publishing. In *LABO*, Jean-Christophe Menu asked, 'where is the *Spirou* of our childhood, where is the *Métal* and *l'Echo* of our youth, where is the adult comics magazine of our maturity that never existed?'[23] As originally conceived, *LABO* was intended to be an ongoing anthology comic featuring the best young cartoonists in the industry. When L'Association was formed, however, this role fell to *Lapin*. Because it of-ten pre-serialized works that would later be collected, *Lapin* (figure 2) is

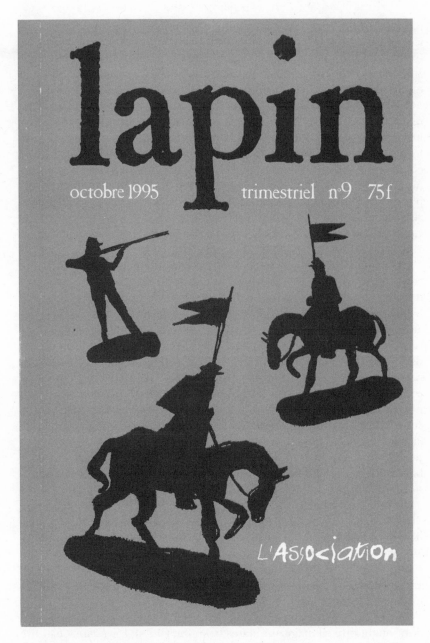

2 Vincent Vanoli's cover for *Lapin* #9.

part of the long tradition of comics magazines in the Franco-Belgian comics industry; however, its particular form was, in fact, a radical departure from that tradition. *Lapin* was formatted not as a traditional comics magazine but as a literary journal. Printed in a small size, square-bound, and on high-quality paper, the anthology more closely resembled *Granta* than *Métal Hurlant*. This packaging served as a shorthand introduction of the magazine's aspirations, which were to advance the status of the comics medium by placing it on equal footing with more consecrated cultural forms. Thus, *Lapin* fell somewhere between the literary review and the comics magazine as it clung to aspects of each. Indeed, the tension between tradition and innovation is something that L'Association explicitly played upon with *Lapin,* particularly insofar as they positioned the magazine as the heir of *Pilote* when the magazine ran into a problem with the Commission Paritaire des Publications et Agences de Presse (CPPAP) in 1995.

In October 1978, *Pilote* appeared on magazine stands with an all-white cover upon which was written '*Pilote* n'est plus un journal.' This cover drew attention to a decision by the CPPAP to withdraw magazine status from the magazine. The CPPAP is a French governmental agency created in the postwar period to foster French cultural production by reducing taxes on magazines and providing them with advantageous mail rates. The implications for *Pilote* were severe. Aside from making it more expensive to run the magazine because of increasing costs, the commission had also ruled that the contributors to the magazine were not journalists, which resulted in a loss of professional standing for the contributors. Writing in *Pilote* #53, Guy Vidal, the editor-in-chief, stated, 'a small group of unknown functionaries have been given the power to decide what is a form of expression and what is not? And these judges have decided in September 1978 that comics are not a form of expression.'[24] He also raised the question of censorship. *Pilote* noted that it lost its licence immediately after having published a cover image depicting then French prime minister Raymond Barre as a baby. The close connection of the two events – the attack on Jacques Chirac's prime minister and the loss of the licence occurring in the space of a month – gave the appearance of political motives. In the ensuing scandal the CPPAP announced that they were re-examining their regulations, and within six months *Pilote* once again had its licence.[25]

In 1996, five years after they had launched it as a magazine, L'Association sought official magazine status from the CPPAP for *Lapin*. Over the course of two years, *Lapin* was rejected by the CPPAP on four separate occasions for three different reasons: twice because the committee ruled that the magazine was a '*fin en soi*,' an end in itself, and not a true periodical; once because it was not published four times per year; and once because it lacked the requisite news content that characterized a general-interest magazine. In an angry response to the committee, L'Association president Jean-Christophe Menu lashed out at the rejections, arguing that the definition of *Lapin* as a '*fin en soi*' was arbitrary, bureaucratic, and nonsensical. The term, he noted, had absolutely no legal basis, was nowhere to be found in the actual law governing the CPPAP, and was intellectually dishonest. How, Menu wondered, could bureaucrats who had so little basis in the work of culture make cultural decisions? He argued that the case bordered on plain censorship, wondering 'After the *Pilote* scandal, the *Lapin* scandal?' Nonetheless, despite their outrage, L'Association was never granted the dispensation they sought.[26]

Ultimately, one could argue that the disputes between the CPPAP and *Pilote* and *Lapin* magazines point to a commonality between the two magazines, and between two generations of French comics artists struggling to push the medium towards artistic respectability. Certainly, linking the magazines seems to have been the intention of L'Association, who deliberately recalled the *Pilote* controversy in commentaries on their own affair. This teleological reading of the situation, however, fails to accurately account for many of the complexities of French comics production, which can be better regarded as a series of strategies of self-identification and distinction-making. So, for instance, *Pilote* organized its argument around the topic of political censorship and positioned itself as opposed to the government and in favour of art. *Lapin* recalls *Pilote* under similar circumstances to exploit one part of *Pilote*'s legacy while rejecting other attributes of the magazine as commercial. This is not a straightforward history but a complex set of strategies on the part of comics publishers attempting to win certain points at certain historical moments. It is interesting to note, following this logic, that the one-shot revival of *Pilote* in a 2003 *Spécial Été*, published as a tribute to late editor Guy Vidal, includes works from L'Association founders David B. and Lewis Trondheim. To this end, the revived *Pilote* claims to be the legitimate heir to *Lapin*, which had positioned itself as the legitimate heir to the original *Pilote*, which itself was the arbiter of all that was serious and adult in the French comic book industry. By 2003, therefore, it was clear that *Lapin* represented the standard of artistic seriousness in French comics to which a more commercial publication might aspire.

While L'Association claimed, at least rhetorically, a connection between

Lapin and *Pilote*, drawing such a line seems highly suspect. *Pilote* was a mass-market magazine, sold on newsstands, constantly tailored to match the interests of its changing readership. *Lapin*, on the other hand, is only available through comic book specialty stores and by subscription. Moreover, its focus is almost entirely different from a magazine like *Pilote*, and this is reflected in its design sensibility and contents. Until it was reconceptualized in January 2001 (#26) as a bimonthly magazine, *Lapin*'s similarities to the literary review structured its editorial direction. Stories published in the magazine were a mixture of short works and serials contributed by the six founding members of the group, along with their friends and colleagues. Subject matter was wide-ranging, although the works tended to shy away from genre-based material or stories based on regular, ongoing characters. For the most part, *Lapin* is conceptualized as a workshop for ideas that might not work as full-scale books or as a showcase for young or under-exposed artists. To this end, *Lapin* serves a vital purpose in exposing new and innovative cartoonists to French comic book audiences. Among the many international talents who publish in the magazine's pages are Milorad Krstic, Tobias Schalken, Ulf K., Pennti Otsamo, and Renée French. The effect of bringing together artists from a variety of nations has been to place L'Association at the crossroads of the new comics movement by establishing *Lapin* as the most important and influential comics magazine being published anywhere in the world.

The influence of L'Association, however, has also been historically constructed by the breadth and diversity of their catalogue. The publisher has five primary book collections, as well as a line of books that are *Hors Collection*. Each of these lines has been defined in different terms, and each shapes the perception of L'Association – and the small-press aesthetic in general – in a different way. Arguably the most notable of these collections are the various iterations of the *Patte de mouche*. These comics are physically small (10.5 × 15 cm) and short (twenty-four pages), and the collection itself is the most obvious link between L'Association and its mini-comics heritage. Indeed, the first *Patte de mouche* collection, which predated the formation of L'Association by five years, was printed on photocopiers and assembled by hand. The second collection, from 1986 and 1987, included ten photocopied editions with colour-photocopy covers. These were assembled by hand in editions of two hundred and included works by Mattt Konture, Stanislas, Jean-Christophe Menu, and other artists who would come to be associated with L'Association. In 1991, the first L'Association-produced *Patte de mouche* books were released, totalling twenty-one volumes. These editions had colour covers that resembled book jackets. Printed in editions of five hundred, these books were still assembled by hand. According to an editorial in *Le Rab* #9, this became increasingly prohibitive as it meant that more than 10,000 books had been hand assembled.[27] In 1995, a new line of professionally printed *Patte de mouche* books was launched, featuring high-quality, off-white paper and two-colour printing on the covers.

In many ways, these books, more than sixty in total, are a succinct definition of the space occupied by L'Association. By featuring professionally produced mini-comics, the publisher signals its own history in the fanzine movement and its own liminal status between fandom and the large professional publishing houses. The books themselves, which range from short-form experimentation to complex narratives, highlight the diversity of the L'Association approach. Indeed, the publisher is so closely associated with the format and aesthetic of the *Patte de mouche* books that when, in 1999, a Dutch publisher (de Plaatjesmaker) copied the format by releasing books with an identical aesthetic down to the paper stock and colour scheme, L'Association stepped in to complain about the infringement. In short, the *Patte de mouche* books, at least one of which has been produced by every founding member of the group, as well as by most of their closest associates, is emblematic of the publisher's position as a transition away from fanzines and towards professional credibility.

L'Association's approximation of the professional album standard took the form of the *Collection Éperluette,* launched in late 1991. The *Éperluette* series – named for the typographic symbol for 'and' – takes the dimensions of the traditional Franco-Belgian album, although it is produced with soft covers rather than hard and, with a few recent exceptions, in black and white rather than colour. The series suggests at once that it is both a pale imitation of the traditions of European comic book publishing and the movement that will supplant that tradition by abandoning superfluous elements. Ranging in length from 32 to 304 pages, books in the *Éperluette* series fall primarily in the range of 40 to 64 pages. While some books in the series take a novelistic approach to telling a single story, for the most part the books in this line are collections of short works or strips, including works like Dupuy and Berberian's *Les Héros ne meurent jamais* (1991), Jean-Christophe Menu's *Le Livre du Mont-Vérité* (2002), and the anthologies *L'Association en Égypte* (1998) and *L'Association au Mexique* (2000). This tendency hearkens back to the earliest days of the Franco-Belgian comics industry when albums were based on material collected from magazines.

Nonetheless, not all books in this line are reprints, and several serve as important interventions into the publishing conventions of the field that are worth noting here. For example, Aristophane's 304-page epic about a war in Hell, *Conte démoniaque* (1996), signalled with its girth the importance of the novelistic as a key to L'Association's conception of the field. Jacques Tardi and Daeninckx' *Varlot Soldat* (1999), a sequel to their Casterman-published book *Le Der des ders* (1997), helped to solidify the reputation of the publisher as a space for artistic production free from commercial restraints. Casterman, Tardi's primary publisher, had rejected this work. By taking it to L'Association, one of the most consecrated of the previous generation of cartoonists showed his support of the new small press and affirmed L'Association as a publisher known for its creative freedom.

Finally, with the *Éperluette* series L'Association has moved most sharply towards the traditions of traditional album publishing. With Guy Delisle's *Aline et les autres* (1999), they took their first tentative steps towards publishing with colour, producing a work with more than simple black-and-white line art. Mahler's *Flaschko* (2003) took this tendency further, utilizing spots of orange and blue in an otherwise black-and-white volume. Finally, the reprint of Massimo Mattioli's *M le magicien* (2004; originally published in *Pif* magazine from 1968 to 1973), represented the first full-colour book published by L'Association. Given the centrality of the black-and-white aesthetic to the small-press comics movement as a means of distinguishing the work from the large presses, books such as these increasingly highlight the fact that distinctions between amateur and professional, large press and small press, restricted production and large-scale production, are deployed selectively as tactics rather than marking fixed positions in aesthetic and social space.

While the *Collection Éperluette* draws attention to L'Association's proximity to the established traditions of the Franco-Belgian comics industry, the *Collection Ciboulette* – from the typographic symbol for 'or' – highlights a new direction. These books, which are physically smaller than the *Éperluettes* but often longer in page length, privilege the novelistic rather than the short work. Resembling trade paperback novels, the *Ciboulette* collection played a central role in announcing the importance of the non-serialized long-form comics in L'Association's publishing strategy. Typically running more than one hundred pages, the *Ciboulettes* have reached as high as five hundred pages with Lewis Trondheim's *Lapinot et les carottes de Patagonie* (1991). The resemblance to novels has helped L'Association to position themselves as significantly different from other comic book publishers, and the conception of the comic book as novel has resulted in the books being regarded as akin to literature. Certainly, Marjane Satrapi's four-volume autobiography *Persepolis* (2000–3) benefits from the perception that it is simply a novel with pictures. Other volumes dealing with serious social and historical issues, such as Emmanuel Guibert's *La Guerre d'Alan* (2000–ongoing) or Guy Delisle's *Shenzhen* (2000) and *Pyongyang* (2003), display a desire to be read along similar lines. The centrality of novel-length black-and-white books to the L'Association project was so clear to the largest publishers of French comics that the line was imitated by Dargaud (*Roman BD*), Les Humanoïdes Associés (*Tohu Bohu*), Casterman's *Écritures*, and Seuil's untitled comics line. These collections, which met with varying degrees of success, were so clearly derivative of L'Association's series that two of Dargaud's books – David B.'s *Le Tengû Carré* (1997) and Joann Sfar's *Paris-Londres* (1998) – were reprinted as *Ciboulettes* when Dargaud allowed them to go out of print; the catalogue noted that David B.'s book had 'found its definitive place today.'[28]

In 1999, L'Association launched a fourth comics line, the collection *Mimolette*. Featuring blue and orange covers and sized to resemble the traditional shape of American comic books, the *Mimolette* line was produced in an 'ésprit Comix' – thirty-two- to forty-four-paged books created quickly and with a semi-disposable sensibility. The *Mimolette* books are not laboured masterworks but are intended as casually created experiments that do not necessarily strive to reach the same heights as other L'Association-published books. While some notable exceptions exist in the line, particularly Joann Sfar's multi-volume biography of the painter Pascin, for the most part books in this series are more akin to the traditions of American independent comics than they are to distinctly European ways of creating comics. This line, therefore, expands the aesthetic reach of L'Association into new areas of comics that are considered culturally relevant in other contexts, a globalizing move whose results suggest empire-building. In particular, works by Mattt Konture (*Krokodile Comix II* [1999]) and Julie Doucet (*Monkey and the Living Dead* [1999]) suggest the affinity of L'Association with the revolutionary energies of 1960s-era American undergrounds. By adopting this style of comics production and rebranding it in their unique fashion, L'Association seeks to present itself as the most inclusive comics publisher in the world, operating in almost every format and with a collection for virtually every type of work.

While the first four L'Association collections have specific resonances of prior comics traditions, the final collection, *Côtelette*, is almost entirely

unprecedented in the field. These books, occupying a physical space between the *Patte de mouche* and the *Ciboulette*, but with vastly expanded page
counts, are highly personal works told in an informal manner. Specifically, the line is dominated by diaristic comics, which are distinct from
the more polished autobiographical works, such as David B.'s *L'Ascension
du Haut Mal*, that are included in the other collections. Thus, Lewis
Trondheim has published four volumes of his *Carnet de Bord* (2001–3) in
this series, and Joann Sfar has also published five volumes of his journals.
In 2004, Julie Doucet published a year-long drawn diary entitled, simply,
Journal. In each of these cases, the artists are essentially publishing sketchbook material. Indeed, Trondheim's books explicitly point to the fact
that he is drawing directly for the finished page, using no erasures and
making no corrections to the work to polish it – misspelled words are
simply crossed out and written in again. In many ways, the *Côtelette* series
can be read as the culmination of the L'Association project. While each
of the previous collections draws on a specific tendency of comics publishing – the *Patte de mouche* series recalls fanzines, *Éperluette* recalls the
Franco-Belgian album tradition, the *Ciboulette* has an affinity with 1970s-
era comics novels, and the *Mimolette* is a gloss on the American underground and post-underground comix tradition – the *Côtelette*'s connection
to the sketchbook or diary is a new direction for comics publishing. Further, the highly personal nature of many of the works in the series can be
regarded as the logical outcome of the publisher's celebration of personal expression and unconventional publishing formats.

In addition to the five main book collections, L'Association has also
published a number of books outside the confines of these series. These
include non-comics books, such as Thomas Ott and Gila's photo collection *La Grande Famiglia* (1998) and Aleksandar Zograf's first-person
reporting of the NATO bombings of Serbia, *E-Mails de Pancevo* (1999).
Comics in the collection include the oversize editions of Killoffer's *Six
Cent Soixante-Seize Apparitions de Killoffer* (2002) and Matti Hagelberg's
Holmenkollen (2002), as well as Lewis Trondheim's undersize (and full-
colour) experimental comic, *Bleu* (2003).

Nonetheless, the most famous of L'Association's special publications
is undoubtedly *Comix 2000*. Published in 1999 in anticipation of the
millennium, *Comix 2000* is a single-volume collection of two thousand
pages of comics by 324 cartoonists from twenty-nine different countries.
Each of the works in the volume ranges from three to twenty-seven pages
in length, and each is entirely wordless. The mute stipulation, suggested
by Lewis Trondheim and Jean-Yves Duhoo, mitigated the necessity of

translating stories and allowed the same edition to be sold around the world. The book, designed by Futuropolis publisher Étienne Robial and edited by Jean-Christophe Menu, contained a prologue in ten languages and arranged cartoonists in alphabetical – rather than thematic or national – order. While French-speaking nations France, Belgium, and Switzerland – countries where L'Association books are widely available and the publisher is relatively well known – were the best-represented nations, cartoonists from Holland, Spain, the United States, and Canada also contributed a number of works. Thematically, the book was structured around a broad theme of 'the twentieth century,' although the real theme of the book seems to be the distillation of a contemporary small-press comics aesthetic.

Pierre Bourdieu has noted that in the field of publishing, 'the manuscripts a publisher receives are the product of a kind of pre-selection by the authors themselves according to their image of the publisher who occupies a specific position within the space of publishers.'[29] Following this logic, it seems probable that a massive book project by a leader in the small-press comics movement of the 1990s like L'Association would attract works primarily from cartoonists who identify themselves as part of that movement. Indeed, in the introduction to *Comix 2000*, Jean-Christophe Menu writes, 'if some of the mainstream styles may export poorly to other countries (the Franco-Belgian school, American superheroes, commercial mangas), their independent alternatives stem from a truly international culture.'[30] Menu is correct to point out the absence of artists whose work has been primarily characterized by mainstream traditions. L'Association, as a publisher, has fundamentally defined itself in opposition to the established currents of the international comics market, and *Comix 2000* solidifies that repudiation. At the same time, however, the book also structures absences in other important ways. Thus, while the *Collection Mimolette* recalls the energy of the American underground comix movement, only one American underground artist (Skip Williamson) is represented in the book, and figures central to the underground movement such as Robert Crumb, Gilbert Shelton, and Jack Jackson are absent. Further, the *Collection Éperluette* recalls the more serious trends in the Franco-Belgian cartooning heritage, but names like Claire Bretécher, Jacques Tardi, Enki Bilal, Loustal, Mattotti, Daniel Goossens, and Moebius are not to be found.

While absences such as these may disappoint readers hoping for a comprehensive or encyclopedic anthology of 'the best' cartoonists at the turn of the millennium, they more accurately point to the manner in which, in ten years, the small-press comics scene had consolidated to generate a project of this scope. Indeed, while many consecrated names are absent from the work, the two thousand pages include almost every artist who had published a book with L'Association and most of the artists associated with other independent comics publishers around the world. Further, in publishing a work of this magnitude, L'Association marked a generational transformation in the field, indicating that they could fill a two-thousand-page comic book anthology without drawing upon the old guard. Moreover, they indicated defiantly that they now no longer needed or desired a connection with the groundbreaking cartoonists who came before them.

A project as vast as *Comix 2000* does little to suggest the prevalence of a single visual mode and in fact demonstrates the heterogeneity of the contemporary small-press comics movement. Nonetheless, a few similarities suggest themselves. One of the most important would have to be the importance of the cartoonist as an artist working individually to create art. While the vast majority of comics in the so-called golden age were the products of collaborative teams, creators who both write and draw their own works dominated the small-press comics movement of the 1990s. In *Comix 2000,* for example, fewer than ten stories were created collaboratively, and many of these were the product of two cartoonists who frequently or exclusively work alone joining forces for this single project (as with Julie Doucet and Max).

Second, the prevalence of narrative as a central form within comics is brought to the fore. In a review of the book, Vincent Bernière argues, 'certain pages are not that figurative – I want to say infra-narratives – like the work of the painter Ricardo Mosner or that of Carlos Nine.'[31] Yet, I would argue that both of these pieces contain strong narrative elements, though Mosner's is almost inexplicable and Nine's is revealed as a narrative only by the final image, which creates the context for the images that precede it. Further, the insistence on mute comics highlights the centrality of sequence in the construction of comics as a distinct visual medium, irrespective of the presence of text. The mute requirement is met by certain cartoonists – Mattt Konture and Stéphane Blanquet, for example – by the utilization of nonsensical words composed of entirely new alphabets, and strips such as these particularly highlight how unnecessary the linguistic element is in comics.

Indeed, based on the fact that an exhibition of original art from *Comix 2000* toured comics festivals in Angoulême, Bastía, Luzern, Lisbon, Haarlem, Sierre, and elsewhere, it seems clear that L'Association has created a book manuscript not so much to be read as to be toured. In creating this mammoth conceptual book as a possible museum piece, the publisher solidified the connection of the 1990s generation of cartoonists with visual – rather than textual – innovation. Ultimately, this would be the most important accomplishment of this generation of cartoonists, and *Comix 2000,* with its festival exhibitions and the heft of the actual volume, was the most public – if not necessarily the best – presentation of this transformation in the field.

As a publishing agent in the field of comic book production, L'Association both diverges from many of the established tendencies of European comic book publishers and reinforces others. Nonetheless, the most significant challenge to the established modes of the field stem from L'Association's status as an artist-run publishing cooperative – specifically, the emphasis on long-term publishing plans that privilege the 'indispensable' at the expense of short-term, profit-driven undertakings. While the expansion of L'Association's publishing efforts makes clear the fact that they are as profit-oriented as any other comic book producer, it is clear from both their rhetoric and practice that their business model is significantly different from their larger competitors. Bourdieu has noted that it is the publisher, promoter, or agent who is the creator of value, not the artist. It is the cultural businessman who exploits the labour of the creator by bringing it to market. Following this logic, it is necessary to come to terms with the fact that L'Association, as an organization working with other similarly oriented publishers, has done more to transform the field of comic book production than have individual artists. This has been accomplished through an ideology of independence, autonomous production, and selection that privileges an idea of creation as founded exclusively in the arena of personal expression and individual style. Nonetheless, as the slowly increasing intrusion of colour into L'Association's books seems to indicate, the distinction between restricted and large-scale production is a narrow one. Bourdieu points out that every major art gallery was, at one time, an avant-garde gallery, known for a particular style that it championed.[32] In the case of L'Association, the intimate and the personal, which exist in distinction to the generic and popular productions of the established publishing houses, have dominated that style. The efforts of the 1990s generation activated by L'Association have been largely focused on the expansion of the visual component of the comic book. They have succeeded in promoting this idea through a variety of strategies, many of which have resulted in a reconceptualization of what exactly constitutes a 'comic book.'

Chapter 2

The Shifting Terrain of the Comic 'Book'

Central to the small-press comic book renaissance of the 1990s has been a reconceptualization of the notion of the comic book. L'Association and other publishers greatly expanded the shape and size of the comic book and have made distinctive, non-traditional packaging a signature of the small-press style. The reasons for this tendency are varied, yet one element that seems to unite small-press design tendencies is a focus on an appeal to established norms of elegant or beautiful design that exist beyond the field of comics. Thus, while the vast majority of comics albums published by the largest and best-established publishing houses announce their status as comic books through format and cover design choices, small-press efforts, following L'Association's lead, have tended to recall the design schemes of a more literary model.

This attention to non-comics notions of 'the beautiful' in book design have a tendency to more fully position small-press comics within the traditions of art history, a field that has been concerned with the identification and theorization of the beautiful since the eighteenth century. Kant's introduction of the notion of the sublime, the overwhelming, awe-inspiring, and, importantly, masculine, as a category distinct from the more decorative, graceful, and feminine notion of the beautiful, has helped to hierarchize aesthetic judgments, generally to the detriment of cultural objects such as comic books. Further, the arguments of scholars like David Hume, who suggested that, with regard to those who might argue Ogilby to be the equal of Milton, that it was natural and commonsensical to 'pronounce, without, scruple, the sentiment of those pretended critics to be absurd and ridiculous,'[1] had necessarily negative implications for critics who might champion comic books relative to better-established art forms, such as painting, poetry, and literary fiction.

For art historians captured by the Kantian beauty myth, there are few possibilities that comics will come to reside within the canons of legitimacy.

Yet, if one dissents from Hume's presumption, finding value in Ogilby and other disparaged cultural producers, it is possible to see that accepting a broader notion of the theory and history of art opens up an extremely heterogeneous space for cultural expression. Noël Carroll has pointed to the significant way in which art history has been captured by a focus on the beautiful and by attempts to locate and theorize it. He points to Monroe Beardsley's emphasis on unity, complexity, and intensity as the defining characteristics of the beautiful as having created a blind spot within art history, making it incapable of recognizing the avant-garde as art. Noting that Beardsley's categorization excludes a work like Marcel Duchamp's *Fountain* from the domain of art, because the artist did not produce it with the intention of satisfying an aesthetic interest, Carroll observes that works intended to defy traditional senses of beauty remain unaccounted for in an aesthetics rooted in the concern for the beautiful. The problem, according to Carroll, is that as the theory of beauty has been transformed into a general theory of art, the test for beauty – disinterestedness – has come to be erroneously seen as the very purpose of works of art.[2] Nonetheless, the fact remains that the transition from the theory of beauty to a general theory of art, whatever its theoretical and philosophical shortcomings, has had a tremendous impact upon the way that visual culture is understood in contemporary society. Further, historically it has played an important role in marginalizing not only the avant-garde, as Carroll observes, but nonconsecrated cultural practices such as comic books. One result of this history has been, since the early 1990s in the field of comic books, an attempt to acknowledge the hegemony of the beauty ideal by remaking comic books along the lines of more consecrated art objects.

The small press has, over the course of a decade and a half, aggressively attempted to reframe the notion of beauty within the field. While beauty was once supposed to have existed almost exclusively on the printed page – in the linework, composition, and balance employed by the artists – the current generation of cartoonists has extended visual appeal to include the design and shape of books themselves, which grew longer, thinner, taller, shorter, and fatter all at the same time. It is not uncommon in the contemporary comics scene to encounter comics as objects whose design has been meticulously laboured over and which are printed in non-traditional formats intended to separate them from the conventions of the field. Shifts in the content of comic books – away from children's material and adventure stories – had resulted in new forms as early as the 1970s, particularly with regard to the comics novel undertakings of that era, but the trend accelerated quickly throughout the 1990s as new formats became almost *de rigueur*. At the same time, however, a counter-movement privileging an anti-aesthetic has also arisen. Challenging both the mainstream heritage of the field, as well as some of the more precious elements of the small-press movement, the hand-made, photocopied fanzine, often with aggressive punk-inspired graphics and a DIY sensibility, offers a critique of professionalism and a celebration of expressiveness. Both traditions are equally part of the contemporary small-press comics movement, and both seek to displace the hegemony of mass-market albums as the marker of comic book excellence. These new formats were explicitly linked to the transformation of comics content occurring at the time and existed as an external signifier of an increasingly autonomous sensibility in the field.

In questioning the status of the book, contemporary European cartoonists have sought to integrate the comics form more closely within the traditions of the visual arts. In particular, the small press has drawn upon the invigorated category of the artist's book. This tradition, which dates from the beginning of the Third French Republic in the 1870s, was a return to the form following the mechanization of printing in the fifteenth century that largely divorced the artist from the process of book production. *Livres d'artiste* began to appear in France during the last quarter of the nineteenth century, a protest against the shoddy production of illustration in the text-heavy traditional book publishing industry. By the twentieth century, a number of prominent artists began to create engravings and etchings specifically for book publication. Pablo Picasso, for example, who owned his own etching press, illustrated 156 books over the course of sixty-eight years.[3] The artist-created book was a form that was similarly used by the Russian avant-gardists, who were attracted to the potential for creating small, inexpensive booklets announcing new revolutions in design. In the 1930s, the surrealist movement, which depended on the intersection of artists and writers, found in the book an able outlet for their collaborations. In the late 1950s and 1960s, the international group of Fluxus artists, such as George Brecht, self-published small editions of offset books. Ed Ruscha took this tendency further with his *Twenty-Six Gasoline Stations* (1962), an artist-produced work intended to circumvent the gallery system wherein the book would provide the primary vehicle for the artist's work. Ruscha's books, which were often reprinted when they sold out, were, as Donna Stein points out, 'instrumental in launching and publicizing inexpensive, antiliterary, large-edition publications made with photomechanical techniques that contain a sequences of images and ideas.'[4] Crucially, the innovation of the artist's book that Ruscha spurred stemmed, as Lucy Lippard argues, from a 'new awareness of how art (especially the costly "precious object") can be used as a commodity by a capitalist society, new extra-art subject matter, and a rebellion against the increasing elitism of the art world and its planned obsolescence.'[5] The attack that minimalism and conceptualism launched on the uniqueness of the art object in the 1960s and 1970s was well suited to the book form. Moreover, it inadvertently opened a potential space for comics artists in the traditional domain of fine arts by helping to undermine elitist divisions within that field.

Nonetheless, the turn to the artist's book as a separate category of cultural production did not simply break down traditional barriers to the legitimation of comics in the fine art world. The definition of the artist's book, generally undertaken by art historians, has often functioned as a means through which comic book artists are excluded. This definition, like the definition of art itself, is circular and fraught with the power issues that are a consequence of the legacy of art history. Dick Higgins, for example, defines the artist's book as 'a book done for its own sake and not for the information that it contains,' an admittedly ambiguous definition that rests on questions of intentionality.[6] Richard Kostelanetz notes that the key distinction between presenting an artist's work in book form (a retrospective collection of reproductions) and an artist making a book is, essentially, the honorific *art book* that is applied to the latter, which defines the work by the profession of the author, rather than by qualities of the work itself.[7] An example of this tendency is provided by Steven Bury, who, in the first paragraph of his catalogue *Artists' Books,* eliminates books, such as Jacques Derrida's *Glas* (1974), that resemble artists' books but are not because 'they were not made by artists.'[8]

This type of boundary policing has been the primary means by which comic books have been excluded from the traditions of the artist's book and, consequently, one of the chief ways in which comic book artists have been erased from the traditions of art history. Clive Phillpot, one of the most noted historians of the artist's book, rationalizes the exclusion of comic books from the field in this way: 'The status of comic books in the world of artists' books is awkward, because comic books are arguably the most successful verbi-visual book form with which artists of one sort or another are associated, and yet they have a quite separate existence. The comic books that have achieved a presence in the art world, such as Art Spiegelman's *Maus,* do not stand out as prominently in the world of comic books.'[9] Phillpot offers no further elaboration on this point, indicating that he either considers his argument to be self-evident or realizes that the distinction that he is drawing is capricious and arbitrary.

A number of valid arguments suggest that comic books are an important, indeed central, sub-genre of the artist's book phenomenon. One of these would surely note the roughly contemporaneous rise of the artist's book movement and the comics form as a mode of visual narrative storytelling. Alternately, one could note that the overwhelming visual narrative components of so many artists' books place them in extremely close formal proximity to comic book traditions. Indeed, Robert C. Morgan divides what he terms 'systemic books' by artists into two categories, the narrative and the concrete, a distinction that highlights the important role of narrative, a central element of most comics, in the artists' books medium.[10] Similarly, in discussing artists' books as a form of visual literature, Shelley Rice points to the fact that, like comic books, 'a number of artists' books are straightforward narratives, which juxtapose words and images in relatively direct relationships.'[11] Rice makes the connection to comic books explicit when she compares the work of Michael Smith with that of Lynda Barry, Gary Panter, and Mark Beyer, three central figures in the early 1980s American comics new wave that was associated with Art Spiegelman and Françoise Mouly's avant-garde comics anthology *RAW.* Rice's observations highlight how artists' books and comic books overlap in many important respects and how the presumed distinction between the forms resonates only insofar as it is possible to maintain that cartoonists are not artists.

The status of the cartoonist as an artist has been central to the small-press comics revolution of the 1990s in much the same way that the idea of the cartoonist as writer informed so much experimentation and change in the 1970s. Many contemporary European small-press comics artists have explicitly sought to redefine their cultural practice through reference to the book as a form of material culture that is constructed as an art object. From this standpoint, the shift to the longer form of the comic book – as opposed to the hardcover album – was not so much an undertaking with renewed novelistic aspirations but a visual strategy intended to delineate comics as a unique art form. In attempting to redefine the field of comic book creation in the 1990s, publishers like L'Association adopted a series of novel formats for their books in order to announce, through the physical form of the art object, the fact that these publishers had adopted new business practices that were ideologically aligned with new aesthetic approaches to the medium. L'Association began with a series of hand-made photocopied mini-comics before graduating to machine-produced books as the organization became increasingly professionalized. Nonetheless, other publishers – such as the Geneva-based silk-screen book publisher Drozophile – have resisted machine-printed works in order to focus exclusively on hand-made, artisanal products. At the same time, however, other publishers have adopted non-traditional formats as a means of both creating a unique and identifiable space for themselves in the marketplace and developing a counter-aesthetic outside of the mainstream of comic book production. These works draw on a long tradition that has sought to elevate the status of comic books by adopting elements of the fine arts – artisanal production, limited editions, artificial scarcity – that have been traditionally more consecrated than the mass-produced and bestselling hard-cover album.

Since at least the 1970s, the production of comic books in non-traditional formats has been used to signify that an artist's aspirations are distinct from the traditions of the field. Centrally, the production of non-traditional books has been a key signifier of a cartoonist's intention to have the work understood in visual rather than textual terms. Futuropolis's 30 × 40 Collection, launched in 1974 with individual volumes whose titles were also the names of the artists, announced a specific type of production centred on the notion of cartoonist as legitimate visual artist. The oversize 30 × 40 cm format was chosen because it precisely matched the dimensions of the standard page of original comic book art and could therefore reproduce a facsimile of the art as it was originally drawn rather than at a reduced size. The promise of this collection, therefore, was the reproduction of the art with a near-precise match to what the artist produced on the drawing table without mediation.

Subsequently, the oversize comic book has become a standard trope in European cartooning, as well as in North America, where Art Spiegelman and Françoise Mouly's *RAW* had formally cemented the equation of oversized comics with high graphic and literary aspirations by the end of the 1980s. Around the same time, a similarly sized avant-garde colour anthology was produced on newsprint in Italy, called *Dolce Vita*. L'Association mimicked the format for the first edition of Edmond Baudoin's *Chemin de Saint-Jean* (L'Association, 2002) and for Killoffer's *Six Cent Soixante-Seize Apparitions de Killoffer*.

The short-lived German anthology *Boxer* took the trope of largeness to its logical conclusion, using it to signal an affinity with fine art traditions. Published between 1989 and 1992 in limited editions by Edition Kunst der comics, *Boxer* regularly combined various traditions, including modernist painting, classic American comic strips of the pre-war period, and cutting-edge contemporary European cartoonists. In four issues, for example, the magazine published works from artists that included David Hockney, Öyvind Fahlström, George Grosz, Jean Dubuffet, Benito Jacovitti, Max Beckmann, Raoul Hausmann, and Pablo Picasso alongside comics by Eric Lambé, Jean-Claude Goetting, Thomas Ott, Gary Panter, Lorenzo Mattotti, Hendrik Dorgathen, Martin tom Dieck, Atak, Cliff Sterrett, and George Herriman. *Boxer* utilized its size to denote its significance, to suggest by its physical presence the idea that it was more important than similar anthologies. The magazine's contents, which freely roamed between eras and aesthetic possibilities, were united by a modernist sensibility that sought to build a bridge between comics and more legitimated art forms by including both on equal footing and by modelling itself on the look of contemporary arts periodicals.

Stakhano, a small-press French comics group run by the cartoonists Eric Cartier and Joan, took the opposite approach. Stakhano, named for the mythic hero of Soviet propaganda, Alexei Stakhanov, produced full-colour albums in the Italian piccolo format, which has the same width as a traditional album but only one-third the height. These horizontally oriented books are often used to reprint comic strips (as with German daily strip artist ©Tom's 512-page collections of *Touché*). Stakhano, which produced more than a dozen books in this format in the mid-1990s, focused on the creation of wordless humour works that could circulate internationally because of the lack of translation requirements. The smaller format utilized here, with its longstanding relationship to children's and humour comics, marked the Stakhano books as humorous as quickly as their cartoony visual style.

Yet, needless to say, not all small comic books are associated with humour. In Sweden, for example, the comics culture has increasingly turned to the pocketbook format for works of all types, which allows the works to be sold easily by bookstores that do not need to accommodate the material with special shelving. Similarly, many mini-comics creators rely on small formats for their inexpensiveness and the sense of intimacy that the delicate format creates. Indeed, it is clear that the undersize format, because of its connection to the mini-comics and fanzine movements of the past twenty years, is far more prevalent and well established than is the over-sized comic book.

More innovative comic book formats have also characterized efforts to redefine the state of the art since the beginning of the 1990s, some in particularly unusual ways. The spiral-bound comic book, for example, remains a rarity but has been mobilized in a number of international contexts, including Holland (*Eumefius* by Nicolas Marichal [1999]) and Germany (*Some Dirty Littul Storries* by Steffen Haas [1998]). The 2002 book *Atak vs. Ahne* (Avant Verlag), by the authors of the same names, reprints in full colour more than 140 daily newspaper strips and is bound at the top of the page rather than the side. Atak has also taken his comics production in other unusual directions, producing *Box of Wonder* in 2001, a collection of postcards reproducing his artwork in a cardboard box with hand-printed covers. Similarly, boxes of mini-comics that together comprise a single anthology have been produced in Slovenia (*Mini-Burger*, 2000) and Switzerland (*Töpfferware*, 1998).

No publisher has pushed innovation in the comics format to the same extent as the German group Moga Mobo. Specializing in themed series, Moga Mobo has used a wide array of strategies to mark their comics as distinct from the norm. In December 1997, for instance, they created an Advent calendar consisting of two dozen miniature (5 × 7 cm) stand-alone comic books, each by a different German cartoonist. This format was recycled two years later for a series of thirty-one comics about the millennium. Other formats, however, have included a pocketbook anthology that reduces one hundred masterworks of world literature to a single black and white wordless comics page (*100 Meisterwerke der Weltliteratur*, 2001), and a series of ten 15 × 15 cm booklets addressing potential cures for bad luck, including sex, cars, and football (*10 wege zum glück*, 2003). A classically oriented publisher would regard the unpredictability of the Moga Mobo format as dangerous, particularly insofar as it mitigates against both brand recognition and ease of sale. Collections of easily misplaced – or shoplifted – micro-comics, for instance, represent a potentially bad business model. Nonetheless, Moga Mobo has used innovative packaging as a means of rendering their work distinct within the marketplace, and the publisher uses their unique take on the formal properties of the medium as a branding strategy.

In *Le Rab de lapin* #14, L'Association explained to their readers that Aristophane's *Conte démoniaque* would be published in a format that was three centimetres shorter than the other books in the Collection Éperluette because the book would be 'more beautiful adapting itself to the smaller square format of the originals, rather than with disproportionate white space at the top of the each page.'[12] This logic, which regards the work of the publisher to adapt the presentation of the work to a form that best suits it, rather than imposing a particular format (forty-six pages, hardcover album) upon the creative process, is a hallmark of the small-press ideology that regards comic book creation as particularly autonomous. As Pascal Lefèvre has pointed out, the size of the comic book page alters the fundamentals of the form in a manner that does not occur in a field like literature. While a smaller page in a printed book might result in a need for a greater number of pages to present the manuscript or a change to a differently sized font, changes to the size of the comic book page radically structure the representational possibilities. Greater flexibility is available to the artist working in the comic book format than in the comic strip, simply by virtue of page design. Similarly, as Lefèvre demonstrates through reference to the work of Edmond Baudoin, shifts in the size of the page drive the construction of narrative by enabling or restricting visual elements, including dialogue and narration.[13]

The work of Anke Feuchtenberger (figure 3), for example, especially highlights the equation of changing formats with artistic seriousness in the small press. Feuchtenberger's work, which draws more heavily on a fine arts tradition than almost any cartoonist in Europe today, has been presented in Germany in an extremely varied array of books. *Mutterkuchen* (Jochen, 1995), for example, is a collection of short works presented in a 16 × 23 cm softcover book. *Die Biographie der Frau Trockenthal* (Jochen, 1999) is both wider and shorter, a hardcover, full-colour book that reproduces a number of illustration projects. *Somnambule* (Jochen, 1998) and *Der Palast* (Jochen, 2000) are both horizontally oriented, although the former is a smaller softcover book, while the latter measures 30 × 22 cm and is a hardcover volume printed in full colour. *Die Skeletfrau* (Büchergilde Gutenberg, 2002) is a colour mini-comic complete with a slipcover, while *Das Haus* (Reprodukt, 2001) is a tall, thin (11 × 30 cm) hardcover, bound at the top of the page, which reprints a number of newspaper strips across the 60 cm of the open two-page spread, the same size as a full newspaper column. In the case of *Das Haus,* the unusual format is necessary in order to reproduce the works in a manner similar to their unusual presentation in February 2000 issues of the news daily *Frankfurter Allgemeine Zeitung,* where they ran vertically down the side of the page. Nonetheless, what is common among Feuchtenberger's books is the fact that they do not resemble each other and that they confound market logics because they cannot be easily placed alongside each other on a shelf at a bookstore. Exploring similar mythological, bodily, and

3 Die Hure H encounters a mysterious, older woman. From *Die Hure H Zieht ihre Bahnen* by Anke Feuchtenberger and Katrin de Vries.

feminist themes in a variety of styles, Feuchtenberger's books – whether hardcover or soft, black and white or colour – highlight the importance of presentation for the construction of a counter-discourse rooted in the concept of artistic autonomy.

The comic book artist's demand for a format that best fits her work is necessarily akin to the desire of a painter for a canvas sized appropriately for the scale of the painting, because, in essence, the cartoonist has conceptualized the work as art, not as a book or a product of the mass market. Different sizes and different formats convey competing values and represent different ideologies in the comics form, as they do in other fields of culture. From the intimate to the epic, the format of the comic book is bound to its position within the field and its interpretation by audiences.

Nonetheless, because the dominant tradition of European, particularly Franco-Belgian, comics publishing has been the hardcover album, almost every other format imaginable has been co-opted by the small-press movement as counter-hegemonic. This has enabled small-press artists and publishers to mobilize book design in such a way that any deviation from the norm is regarded as less commercial than the album tradition, despite the fact that the books that they publish are self-evidently commercial enterprises. This rhetorical sleight of hand is dependent on the ability of small-press artists to present their work as legitimate art, rather than as an example of what Clement Greenberg termed kitsch. This ability is reliant on the artists' skill in presenting their work as art objects, imbued with an aura in the sense that Walter Benjamin described it, rather than simply as commercial properties. Indeed, it is possible to suggest that the entire drive of the contemporary European small-press comics movement has been one of reinscribing the aura of the work of art into a form that has been virtually synonymous with mechanical reproduction.

Central to the process of reconsecrating the aura of the comic book has been a renewed emphasis on modes of visuality. While the mature comics works of the 1970s and 1980s were primarily conceptualized as comic book novels that sought to be on a par with high-end literary productions, in the 1990s the ground shifted to favour the visual realm, with stronger connections to the fine arts. One result of this tendency was the creation of comic books that highlighted unique visual features, in opposition to the normative tradition in which each *Tintin* book, for example, is presented in a manner intended to visually recall all other *Tintin* books. Unique or innovative presentation styles, therefore, signal artistic seriousness and a desire to be read as distinct from the traditions of the field. Indeed, in bookstores across Europe, the comic book with a non-traditional shape or format is an invocation, recognized by certain readers, that a comic book is seeking to hail them in their role of connoisseur of difficult comics texts.

If the distinction between consecrated and non-consecrated artistic forms rests, as it has for much of our history, on the distinction between the auratic and the mass-produced, how can comics be art? Some, following the modernist art theories of Clement Greenberg or Theodor Adorno, would likely argue that they cannot be, that the very act of printing comics renders them not-art. It is possible, of course, to resolve the distinction by suggesting that original comics pages are themselves art, and it is typical of European comics festivals to display original art in museums and galleries around town. Indeed, the exhibitions are one of the central attractions for the festival, or possibly the central attraction. This rhetorical sleight of hand, however, is neither particularly convincing nor particularly fulfilling and does little to rectify the larger issue.

Another possibility, of course, is suggested in the rhetoric of difference itself. A shift in the discourse accomplishes much. Indeed, theories of postmodernism – particularly theories of postmodern aesthetics – have done much to erode, while not completely vacating, the traditional distinctions between high and low art, between the auratic and the mass-produced, or at the very least the limited production. Theories of photography, for example, emphasize not the unique negative but the importance of the artist-drawn print, usually in a limited edition. Photography offers one example to the field of comics insofar as it demonstrates that a mass-mediated object can find consecration when it adheres to certain terms. These terms still require an obeisance to the distinction between wide-scale production and restricted production. Art may no longer mean unique, but it also does not mean widely available to the public in a mass-produced form. The photography orientation, limited production of artist-created works, has been adopted in the comics field by a number of practitioners.

Mass-produced books, of course, are only collectible in a limited fashion. While first editions are highly desirable long after their publication, the value that accrues to a first edition does not benefit the publisher or artist/writer, but rather the book collector with the well-maintained edition and the book dealer who brings it to market. Mass-produced books are sold at a price point that offers the surest return on investment and consequently rarely generate significant value in the secondary market. Indeed, the vast majority of used books are not sought-after first editions but are deeply discounted by second-hand bookshops. Comics are no exception to this rule. Nonetheless, publishers and artists have developed strategies to create artificial scarcities in the book market, generally through the creation of special editions of books that are otherwise published on a large scale. In this way, publishers seek to turn their works into fetish items, attractive to a small but extremely loyal subset of all comic book readers. This strategy relies on two different but complementary notions of the fetish. Freud's conception of the fetish as a substitute object that helps to ward off anxiety and restore emotional well-being instructively highlights the desire that many comic book readers have for limited editions of mass-produced books and, in particular, for copies that have been signed by the authors. Similarly, Marx's notion of commodity fetishism spotlights the way in which certain types of books, particularly artificially limited editions, are imbued with substantially more value than other types, despite the obvious strategies of market manipulation that are involved in the construction of scarcity.

In Europe, two traditions particularly structure the practice of artificial scarcity intended to stimulate a desire among readers for a limited edition: the *tirage-de-tête* and the *ex libris*. The *tirage-de-tête* is a form of the mass-market book that has been reprinted, generally by a specialist publisher other than the book's original publisher, in an enhanced edition. These special editions are produced in limited runs and are signed and numbered by the authors. This category of collectible comics is so important within the fan culture of European, particularly Franco-Belgian, comics that it has its own category on the French version of the online auction house eBay, where books regularly sell for more than €100. The movement towards the *tirage-de-tête* and other deluxe editions of popular comics originated in the 1980s as specialist stores sought new ways to stave off a widescale industry decline. Popular books were issued in new editions at inflated prices, specifically intended to appeal to the most devoted comic book connoisseurs. A deluxe edition of Pierre Christin and Enki Bilal's *Partie de chasse* (1983) by Éditions Rombaldi, for example, sold out its 1200 copy run on the day of its release.[14]

Specifically, the deluxe edition of the mass-market comic book seeks to attract fans through the inclusion of rare or unpublished production material, similar to the extras that have become so ubiquitous on the DVD releases of Hollywood movies, though more collectible because they exist on a smaller scale. For instance, the deluxe edition of Marc-

Antoine Mathieu's *La Fin du début/Le Début de la fin* (Book-Maker, 1995)
differs significantly from the edition published in the same year by
Delcourt, despite the fact that they are essentially the same book. The
book, which is extraordinary for the fact that it tells a single story in
mirrored images, is ripe for the deluxe treatment. The story begins with
Le Début de la fin, in which the hero, Julius Corentin Acquefacques,
investigates a reality where everything is inverted. At the midpoint of the
work, however, the reader is obliged to flip the book over and begin
again from a second beginning, *La Fin du début*, where the same images
are presented, but this time with inverted colours. The two stories
combine in a middle sequence in which Julius passes through a broken
mirror, completing the doubling theme that is evident throughout the
text.

The Delcourt edition of this book, which, as the fourth in the
Acquefacques series, adopts the traditional textual position associated
with mainstream French comics, is produced as a standard hardcover
album, save for the fact that the book has two apparent front covers and
seemingly no back cover. The Book-Maker edition, however, is different
in several ways that seek to place the object closer to a pole associated
with visual art. First, while it too is a hardcover album, the production
quality is significantly better, and the cover consists of white ink em-
bossed on black cloth, rather than full-colour production printed on
glossy boards. Second, the book includes a print, signed and numbered
by Mathieu, in an edition limited to 333 examples. Each side of the book
also includes a text piece, one an essay and the other a two-page interview with the artist, with examples of some of his illustration work.
Additionally, there is a one-page story, 'Début de l'autre côté du miroir,'
that is positioned as an early inspiration for the book, and a two-page
story, 'Monsieur Hamid,' whose relationship to the main text is less
evident. Finally, the book includes a series of reproductions of Mathieu's
breakdowns, pencilled pages, and inked pages. Further, two sets of these
images are printed on thick transparent acetates that allow the reader to
see the same image from both sides of the page, a central motif in the
book. The remainder of the book is simply a reproduction of the same
material as the Delcourt edition. In short, therefore, the appeal of the
limited edition of Mathieu's work lies primarily in the sense that the
reader derives of obtaining some small amount of additional knowledge
of the book, its artist, and the manner in which it is produced. More
importantly, however, the reader obtains the artist's signature and an
assurance that this edition of the book, because of its limited print run, is

more akin to a restricted-scale production, even though it is simply a version of a large-scale production. Essentially, the deluxe edition seems more valuable because it is presented as if it had more to do with visual art than with literary commerce, although arguably the opposite is the case.

A similar, though more circumscribed, version of the deluxe edition exists as the *ex libris*. Made popular by certain comic book specialty shops, the *ex libris* simply takes the extant printing of a book – whether popular or not – and adds a signed and numbered serigraph bookplate created by the artist. In terms of the European small-press comics movement, this tendency has been particularly developed by the Parisian comic book shop Super-Héros, which developed a relationship with L'Association to produce editions of this type in 1994.[15] Super-Héros has continued to produce *ex libris* editions of books since that time, including books from publishers both large and small. Thus, for example, Nicolas de Crécy created a serigraph for three hundred copies of *Priez pour nous* (1998), the third book in the *Léon la came* series from the large publisher Casterman, while Ludovic Debeurme drew one for eighty copies of *Ludologie* (Éditions Cornélius, 2003), a book with far more modest sales expectations. The primary appeal of these editions, which are not more costly than the standard printing of the book available at any bookstore, is the idea of receiving a special hand-signed insert into a mass-manufactured product. For the bookstore, of course, it is a marketing opportunity stemming from positive ongoing relationships with a large number of cartoonists, as the possibility of getting a bonus with the purchase of a book will impel some customers to purchase the book from that store rather than from a competitor. In both cases, the illusion is that the buyer of the special edition is somehow closer to – or more connected with – the artist than is the person who simply picks up the book at the local media superstore. This sense is rooted in a logic of scarcity that itself has its origins in the notion of the art object as auratic, as artists, publishers, and retailers seek to minimize the aesthetic distance imposed by the mass production of comic books through signatures in special editions.

While a number of mass-market comics attempted to reposition themselves specifically as consumer collectibles by the adoption of artificial scarcity, a much more common form of scarcity existed on the fringes of European comics culture. The comic book fanzine – or amateur magazine – had long been a staple of comic book culture, dating back at least to the 1960s with the creation of the first fan-produced commentary and opinion journals. In the 1980s, fanzines became increasingly more important as the number of comic book specialty shops grew to the point that it could sustain a micro-network of amateur publications directed towards hardcore comic book readers. Indeed, by the 1980s the fanzine was so entrenched in the culture of European cartooning that the Salon International de la Bande Dessinée in Angoulême, France, the largest and most significant comic book convention in the world, created a category in their awards (the Alph-Arts) for the best amateur publication, the Alph-Art Fanzine. The creation of this category performed a dual function, legitimizing amateur production on the one hand, but also separating it from traditional publishing forms on the other. Thus, while the prize granted some significance to the movement that would ultimately spawn groups such as L'Association, it remained clear that the Salon considered non-professional works secondary and ultimately distinct from the traditions of the industry as it existed at that time.

Since the beginning of the 1990s, the Alph-Art Fanzine has structured the seemingly 'natural' divide between amateurism and professionalism in European comics. Primarily a distinction between large- and small-scale production, the mobilization of logical arguments regarding these definitions has often been abrogated by a tendency of the committee to simply reward the best work from an exhibitor in the Espace Fanzine of the Bulle New York, a selection of exhibitor booths that are sold at reduced rates to small-press publishers by the festival.

The winners of the prize have been largely of two types. First, magazines such as *Rêve-en-bulles* (1995) and *Tao* (1997) recall the long-established traditions of fanzine publishing, mixing reviews, interviews, and amateur comics into a single package. *Rêve-en-bulles*, for example, published from 1991 until 1997, featured a series of portraits and commentaries on established cartoonists such as Jacques de Loustal and Denis Lapière, as well as news features and book reviews. The magazine also included occasional original comics by artists like José Parrondo. Similarly, *Tao* featured lengthy interviews and dossiers on cartoonists such as David B. and Alejandro Jodorowsky. For many, these magazines, which were produced by and for fans interested in a larger comics culture, neatly conform to the expectations of the term fanzine. At the same time, however, other winners of the prize raise more serious questions.

Typically, the Alph-Art Fanzine is awarded to an anthology comic. Since 1995, for example, with the exception of fan journals such as *Rêve-en-bulles* and *Tao*, the award has always been presented to an anthology of one sort or another. The privileging of anthologies in this award is another key factor that the festival uses to distinguish fanzines from 'professional' works. The primary Alph-Arts, for best album and best foreign album, are awarded to stand-alone books, whether albums or some other format, generally by solo artists, but sometimes by a writer–artist tandem. Thus, the awards privilege the individual long-form works as the standard mode of production and confine short and collaborative projects to amateur status. At the same time, however, many of the contributors to the winners of the Alph-Art Fanzine are themselves not amateurs but simply professionals whose work is, in this particular instance, presented by a publisher working on a smaller scale of production. For instance, the 1996 winner, *La Monstrueuse,* is an anthology published by Stéphane Blanquet's Chacal Puant. Known for its emphasis on disturbing post-underground imagery, *La Monstrueuse* includes the work of Jean-Christophe Menu, Julie Doucet, Paquito Bolino, and Mike Diana in its first issue, all of whom were working as professional cartoonists at that point. Nonetheless, each creates work that exists on the periphery of the traditions of the field, focusing on particularly visceral topics and utilizing non-traditional graphic styles akin to *art brut* tendencies. It is clear, however, that *La Monstrueuse* is not an amateur publication, but simply a small-scale endeavour far removed from the mainstream of French cartooning at that time.

Similar confusions arise when the prize is awarded to foreign publishers. In 1999, for example, the prize went to *Panel,* a German small-press anthology regularly featuring the works of such professional cartoonists as Reinhard Kleist, Uli Oesterle, and Ulf K. The magazine, which is professionally printed on glossy paper and which contains ads, is impossible to logically characterize as an amateur production and can be regarded as such only insofar as the German comic book industry is seen as a non-element within the French-speaking comic book field. Similarly, 2004's winner, the British anthology *Sturgeon White Moss,* featured the work of English-language alternative comics mainstays such as Charles Burns, Dave Cooper, Ron Regé, and Tom Gauld. Again, these artists can hardly be classified as amateur, and the professionally produced, though limited-scale, magazine defies that label. Clearly, therefore, the fanzine label does not define amateur production but something else entirely. The fanzine label is mobilized by the festival to demarcate an exotic Other.

This tendency is particularly pronounced if one considers the work of the *Stripburger* collective, winners of the Alph-Art Fanzine in 2001. *Stripburger* is the name of a comics anthology created in 1992 in Ljubljana,

Slovenia, by the Stripcore group. Having published more than three dozen issues, *Stripburger* focuses on a mixture of comics news, reviews, essays, and original comics production, with a particular emphasis on comics produced in the former Eastern bloc nations. The magazine is professionally printed, averaging more than eighty pages of material in each issue. *Stripburger* is a unique comics anthology not only because it collects the work of a large number of artists from Eastern Europe that might otherwise receive little attention internationally, but also because of a policy of printing works without translating them. Thus, works in Czech are printed in Czech, while works in Slovenian are printed in Slovenian. Many issues contain added inserts that translate all of the texts into English. *Stripburger*'s broad focus on internationalism extended its reach to western Europe and also to Canada and the United States. The magazine frequently presents special issues that include the works of cartoonists who are better known than their core contributors. This has the effect of both exposing western European comics traditions in the east and positioning the comics production of Eastern Europe as akin to the work that is being undertaken by the small-press comics renaissance.

A typical non-themed issue of *Stripburger* presents a wide variety of comics by both professional and amateur creators. Issue #34, for example, includes works from relatively unknown Eastern European artists David Krancan and Tomaz Lavric alongside works by well-known American cartoonist Joe Sacco; Israeli cartoonists Batia Kolton, Itzik Rennert, Mira Friedmann, Rutu Modan, and Yirmi Pinkus (all published in English); and short works by Anke Feuchtenberger, Kati Rapia, Dominique Goblet, and Caroline Sury created at a Slovenian City of Women festival at which they were guest artists. Specially themed issues, however, are more focused on the integration of the work of Eastern European cartoonists with works from around the world. Regionally themed issues have included: #25's focus on Italy (including Stefano Ricci, Gabriella Giandelli, and Francesca Ghermandi), #27's focus on Finland (including Petteri Tikkanen, Matti Hagelberg, and Katja Tukiainen), and #31's examination of Montreal (with Richard Suicide, Eric Braün, Julie Doucet, and Henriette Valium). More recent issues, however, have narrowed the focus to national scenes within Eastern Europe, including issue #37, which deals with New Russian Comics. In the case of an issue like #37, it is clear that many of the contributors are, in fact, amateur artists who make their living in another field. Yet, in all of the other issues mentioned here, it is clear that there is a mixture of well-established professionals and relative newcomers. What characterizes the magazine as a non-professional fanzine, therefore, seems to be the fact that it is exotic both for its mixed languages of creation and publication and for the fact that it does not widely circulate within the French comics marketplace, of which the festival in Angoulême is the most public face.

One additional winner of the Alph-Art Fanzine highlights many of the issues that are raised by the small-press comics movement's emphasis on form as a distinguishing characteristic of difference, particularly the relationship between limited-scale production and claims to art status. When the Swiss anthology comic book *Drozophile* won the prize in 1998, the announcement was met with a curious dissatisfaction, not because *Drozophile* was not seen as good enough to win, but the contrary – it was seen as *too* good to win. The anthology, some argued, was too professional to be a fanzine. It was too well produced, too slick, possibly too artistic to win an art prize intended for fanzines. This immediately raises the question of definition central to my discussion here: what is a fanzine? Is it defined by its form, by its mode of circulation, by its disposition? Those who would deny the Alph-Art to *Drozophile* seemed to be drawing an allegedly commonsensical distinction between amateurism and professionalism, despite the fact that these terms have been long troubled by just such a prize. Nonetheless, *Drozophile* problematizes the distinction between mass production and auratic culture in interesting ways. Specifically, their focus on artisanal production methods challenges the modernist distinction between art and not-art through the self-conscious, even postmodern, use of *pre*-modern sensibilities.

Drozophile is a publishing concern run by Christian-Humbert Droz in Thônex, a suburb of Geneva on the French border. In 1991, Droz organized a counter-exhibition focusing on young artists of the political left in opposition to the official choices of illustrators marking the 700th anniversary of the city of Geneva. Five years later, he published an anthology featuring the work of these illustrators. The initial intention was to have artists submit a work that they had created in just forty-eight hours, 'but, as they had prepared all of the work in advance, the result was too good, so they made a deluxe magazine.'[16] Thus, since 1996 Drozophile has specialized in publishing the work of the new wave of Franco-Swiss cartoonists who have emerged in the past dozen years, including Helge Reumann, Frederik Peeters, Tom Tirabosco, Pierre Wazem, Nadia Raviscioni, and about a half-dozen others, in deluxe editions.

Specifically, what most distinguishes Drozophile's productions from those of other publishers is the fact that they are all produced by hand in silk-screened editions, rather than mass-produced. To date Drozophile has published seven issues of its eponymous anthology, as well as a number of both short and long stand-alone books, all of which have been produced by hand. Until the sixth issue, each edition of *Drozophile* was printed at an exceedingly large size (30 × 40 cm) on heavy paper with light cardboard covers. Each of the interior pages was hand silk-screened in up to five colours. The comics themselves were produced in editions that ranged from between 400 and 600. Because of their high production qualities and low print run, *Drozophile* typically sold at a significantly higher cost than similar comics anthologies that had been mass-produced. The anthology, therefore, was distinct from traditional comic books in four important respects: first, it was physically larger than normal; second, its production was deliberately restricted in scale; third, it was costlier than a comparable anthology; and, most important, it was made entirely by hand. Indeed, the marks of the artisan – in this case the silk-screen puller Christian Humbert-Droz, were evident on the comics themselves. These marks align Droz's work with the traditions of William Blake. As Betsy Davids and Jim Petrillo have observed, Blake was the kind of book printer 'whose remarkable technical innovations rejected the trade aims of uniformity, consistency, and infinite reproducibility in favor of a process whereby each print of each page was virtually unique.'[17] The result of this process is an edition in which pages vary slightly, a distinct difference from the standard four-colour separation process that produces an edition that is uniform. By restructuring the printing process along these lines, Droz functions as a kind of artist working in collaboration with the artists who contribute to the anthologies that he edits.

In describing the production of *Drozophile* as artisanal, I use the term artisan deliberately. The books published by Drozophile recall a distinction between mass production, the method that has characterized almost all comic book production throughout history, and premodern artisanal methods celebrated by writers like Alexis de Tocqueville. In his book *Democracy in America,* Tocqueville argued that democracy had weakened the artisanal impulse and replaced it with a drive towards mass production and cheapness:

> In an aristocracy [the artisan] would seek to sell his workmanship at a high price to the few; he now conceives that the more expeditious way of getting rich is to sell them at a low price to all. But there are only two ways of

lowering the price of commodities. The first is to discover some better, shorter, and more ingenious method of producing them; the second is to manufacture a larger quantity of goods, nearly similar, but of less value.[18]

Tocqueville's distinction between the artisanal and the mass-produced has long structured the understanding of comic books as a cultural form, and indeed comics are virtually the textbook definition of a large quantity of goods of less value as far as the general public is concerned. By reactivating an artisanal mode, *Drozophile* signals its desire to be understood according to different aesthetic and financial logics. As an expensive, handcrafted limited edition, for example, it clearly announces the intention to be sold 'at a high price to the few,' a tendency that Tocqueville suggests is indicative of an aristocratic age. Thus, from a production standpoint, *Drozophile* challenges our understanding of comics as a cultural form. Further, the consequences of this shift in form play themselves out in significant ways at the level of content.

Narratively, *Drozophile* is not avant-gardist, relegating its innovations almost entirely to the level of visual presentation. Indeed, while many of the artists involved have unique graphic or storytelling styles, the comics themselves are very recognizable as comics – they do not push the boundaries of the form in terms of storytelling potential in the way that many avant-gardist cartoonists do. Each issue is organized around a central theme ranging from football to trains. Most of the stories unfold in a conventional manner despite their graphic innovations. For example, Helge Reumann's stories, which are characterized by crudely drawn figures within a complexly rendered social space, challenge only the traditional representational strategies of comics, not the narrative component. Similarly, Sylvain Victor's work expands the visual possibilities of the medium without impacting our understanding of formal organization. Exem's work in issues #3 through #5 even goes so far as to parody our understanding of the construction of traditional adventure books, particularly the *Blake and Mortimer* series of E.P. Jacobs. Exem's 'La Gabelle Jaune,' which metamorphoses over the course of three volumes from sketches to roughs to proofs, goes so far as to foreground the way comics are produced as a sort of indirect commentary on the distinctiveness of the anthology in which the stories appear. This conventionality, mediated as it may be by the challenge to traditional notions of illustratorly skill, is central to the position occupied by *Drozophile* and to the characterization of it as artisanal rather than avant-garde.

Drozophile is a work that seeks, through a very specific challenge to tradition, to move marginal cultural production – that is, the new wave of Franco-Swiss comics production – to a position of centrality within the larger confines of the *nouvelle bande dessinée*. As a publisher, Drozophile is careful not to challenge too many cultural assumptions about comics at once, preferring to focus specifically and uniquely on the issue of production by hand. In a book like Ibn al Rabin and Frederik Peeters's *Les Miettes*, for example, a traditional western – albeit with strong poetic realist overtones – is presented as a hand-made traditional album (the book had originally been commissioned by L'Association, who subsequently rejected it), again as a limited edition. Drozophile consequently occupies a very narrow distinctive space against publishers like L'Association, but this distinction is absolutely central in the ongoing discursive organization of comics as a consecrated form.

BüLB, which offers a more sustained challenge to traditional definitions of comics, occupies a much different space. BüLB, a publishing house owned and operated by Geneva-based cartoonist Nicolas Robel, has produced a series of objects that challenge the notion of the comic *book*. BüLB's two-watt collection (figure 4) is not, in fact, a collection of books. Each entry is a collection of five miniature fan-folded strips, compiled into a cardboard box that recalls a light bulb container. A different artist produces each strip, many from the Franco-Swiss new wave but others from as far away as Belgium (Thierry van Hasselt, Vincent Fortemps), Austria (Nicolas Mahler), and the United States (Archer Prewitt, Chris Ware). Each of these strips consists of eleven two-sided faces comprising twenty-two possible images (though many have far less), bound with an elastic band. They are printed in two colours and set in grey cardboard boxes that have also been printed in two colours, although the colours are rarely the same. Although they are machine printed, each of the strips is folded by hand in an artisanal fashion and the boxes are similarly assembled by hand. This task was once undertaken exclusively by Robel, but he was later able to employ art students to do it for work-study credit. Thus, the boxes are produced in an artisanal manner – as with Drozophile – but they also offer a far more intensive challenge to the comics form than does the anthology.

The comic strips in the BüLB boxes can be roughly characterized in three or four distinct types, ranging from the relatively traditional use of the comics form to unique hybrids actualized by the specific form of these particular folded strips. The most traditional of the strips are those that present a single panel on each folded face in order to tell a single narrative. These strips proceed in a linear fashion, offering either a

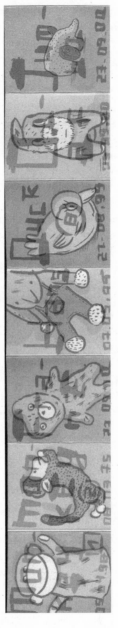

4 A portion of Nicolas Robel's horizontally scrolling 'My World.'

twenty-two-panel strip (reading front to back) or two eleven-panel strips. Examples of this first type would include 'Le Fond du jardin' by Stéphane Blanquet, which tells a fairly straightforward narrative using the artist's cutout approach to visuals. Nicolas Mahler's 'Action Man/Boring Bob' modifies this approach somewhat, using wider panels accomplished by placing the art in a two-panel spread across the folds. Mahler's strip makes extensive use of the two-colour printing process, with the green images depicting the mundane life of Boring Bob and the orange embellishments depicting the fantasy life of Action Man. Both of these strips could easily be presented in a more traditional format and thus offer only a slight difference from traditional conceptions of the comic book.

A second type of strip activated by the BüLB boxes are those that make sense only when unfolded. '3 × 3 Flowers and Robots' by the Berlin-based cartoonist Atak, for example, makes little sense as a series of individual panels. When unfolded and turned vertically, however, the strip is revealed as a non-narrative portrait of three robots (on one side) and three flowers (on the other). Similarly, Vincent Fortemps's 'Campagne' explains little in terms of individual panels and only makes visual sense when unfolded to reveal two farm scenes. In this work, Fortemps challenges both the typicality of cartoonists' drawing implements and the centrality of narration and figuration. The opposition of discrete panels telling a linear story and unfolded strips presenting non-narrative images is not entirely fixed by the BüLB boxes, however. Typically, the pieces included in the boxes work through a more complicated sense of hybridity, utilizing both methods at once. 'In Cold Blood,' again by Nicolas Mahler, is a good example of this tendency. His strip makes narrative sense as a series of two-panel images and also as an unfolded strip. Through the strategic placement of figures, Mahler opens up the possibility of a strip that reads initially as crime fiction, only to be unfolded in order to reveal the interconnectedness of all of the elements in the fiction. Xavier Robel challenges the closed nature of the panel border with his untitled strip, whose panels bleed beyond the folds in the paper and thus serve to link the panels in space even while the central figure moves through time. This type of hybridity seems to be a function of the folding of the paper, unavailable in a more traditional comic book format. Similarly, Helge Reumann's 'Super Peurs' mobilizes the image of a man on a roller coaster, moving through a terrifying fairground space. Each panel in Reumann's strip can be read as an individual moment in time, or the entire strip can be unfolded to reveal the coherence of the social space depicted in the fiction. Finally, Nicolas

Robel's 'undying' breaks from a traditional narrative construction only at key moments, extending the panel across the fold in order to create a triptych that emphasizes a crucial moment of loss. The experimental hybridity of the particular fan-folded form, therefore, can be seen as crucial to the challenge that these boxes represent to the traditional comics form.

This hybridity reaches its apex in a strip called 'addition/subtraction' by Hamburg-based cartoonist Markus Huber. Huber's strip has two similar images. In the first a woman covers her eyes and counts backward from eight to one. In each subsequent panel more detail is removed from her image, until she is virtually eliminated. On the reverse, the same happens to the image of a man. On the one hand, this is a typically hybrid pair of strips. Each can be read as a narrative of unbecoming, that is, as a series of single panels, or, when unfolded, as a single design piece. What makes this work particularly striking, however, is the fact that when the strip is held up to the light it takes on an entirely new meaning. The images of the man and woman are mirror images of each other, both with the same shape on the page. Because they are printed back to back and left to right the most complete image of the woman matches the least complete image of the man, and vice versa. This means that the dark lines from the woman are visible through the paper on the erased image of the man. Using erasure as both a technique and metaphor, therefore, Huber's strip becomes a commentary on gender relations that is activated only by the combination of the comic strip form and the particularistic printing associated with the BüLB boxes. From this standpoint we could suggest that the BüLB boxes have pushed the artisanal comics mode into the realm of avant-gardist experimentation, challenging the received status of the comics form at the level of both production and aesthetic innovation.

The cases of Drozophile and BüLB create some slippage between the notions of amateur, artisanal, and experimental – all of which have been held at different times to be antonyms of the mass-produced. These terms, however, are not equivalencies but distinct positions within the discursive field with no necessary correspondence. As the differing cases of BüLB and Drozophile demonstrate, artisanal comics production can be either traditional or avant-garde at the level of content. What is unique about these two publishers, however, is the return of a premodern sensibility as a means of distinguishing cultural production in an ostensibly postmodern age. Further, it is important to stress that the works privileged by these publishers – short pieces that are more poetic than novelistic – emphasize the visual to a far greater extent than the literary. Indeed, the emphasis that the contemporary small press has placed on the artisanal art object is almost exclusively rooted in the visual domain and has helped to separate the verbal and visual in the comics form rather than integrate it.

Gary Kornblith has argued 'like the myth of agrarian self-sufficiency, the ideal of artisanal independence shimmers with nostalgic appeal in the postmodern age.'[19] Certainly, it is true that some contemporary comic book artists are drawn to this particular appeal. Indeed, the logic of the artisanal comic book publishers is pushed to the extreme by Aymeric Hainaux, whose *Les Passeurs* (Les six berberes sont douze, 2000) was limited to only seventeen copies. The hand-made comic book has become a genre itself, bringing with it an entirely new set of assumptions about the status of the object and the structure of the field. At the same time, however, shifts in the structure of the comic book format have accelerated changing aesthetics. Thus, format can be seen to drive aesthetics, just as aesthetics drive format. The two are not only mutually dependent, but, ultimately, structuring. Indeed, it is difficult to conceptualize contemporary avant-garde comics practices independent of the possibilities created by atypical production practices. In the contemporary comic book small press, form and meaning are integrated to a much more deliberate degree than was ever the case in the traditions of album publishing that dominated European comic books for generations.

Chapter 3

The Postmodern Modernism of the Comic Book Avant-Garde

L'idée, je pense, c'est de défendre une bande dessinée assez difficile.

Thierry van Hasselt[1]

The catalogue for an exhibition entitled *Self-Service*, curated by Belgian university professor and comics theorist Jan Baetens at the Casa Fernando Pessoa in association with the 2001 Salão Lisboa de Ilustração e Bande Desenhada, highlights the particular intersection of modernist comic book practices and the contemporary avant-garde. The book is a collection of twenty-seven single-page comics inspired by classic works in the field. Each page is augmented by a poem, written by Baetens, and presented in three languages (Portuguese, English, and French). The exhibition brought together virtually every author associated with the Belgian avant-gardist comics collective known as Fréon, in addition to a number of artists with similar aesthetic leanings. These artists appropriated a large number of works, recreating them in their own unique styles. Thus, for example, Vincent Fortemps produced a *Prince Valiant* story using grease pencil, Exacto knife, and a transparent page, and Pedro Nora created an expressionistic and mute take on Art Spiegelman's *Maus*. Writing in the French daily *Libération*, Eric Loret noted that the structure of the work, in which the written poetic component was designed to replicate the receipts printed by electronic cash registers, was 'an ironic response, poetic and *bédéistique*, to the market and to globalization.'[2]

Given the text of the exhibition, the notion that the material is poetic is perfectly evident. The irony of the work stems from the aesthetic dislocations that are the result of refashioning the works of consecrated comic book modernists such as Winsor McCay, George Herriman, E.P.

Jacobs, Hugo Pratt, Joost Swarte, and Lorenzo Mattotti, in a more contemporary avant-garde visual style. Loret's contention that the exhibition is a challenge to the market and globalization, however, is not as clear-cut.

On the one hand, the work touches on the internationalizing tendency of the Franco-Belgian comics market through its utilization of artists from around the comics world (France, Belgium, the United States, Canada, Italy, Argentina), who are widely translated into French, though far less available in a Portuguese context. At the same time, the exhibition not only focuses on the work of consecrated modernists but also turns an eye towards artists far less well known in the world of comics. Contemporary cartoonists, such as Chris Ware, are appropriated in the exhibition, as are some of the Fréon mainstays. Thus, the themes of Fréon's Dominique Goblet are appropriated by Fréon's Sache Goerg, and similarly Eric Lambé recreates Olivier Deprez's adaptation of Kafka. By placing contemporary avant-garde cartoonists on the same level as more celebrated practitioners of the form, *Self-Service* confuses the hierarchies of taste that dominate the market logic of comic book publishing. In its place, Baetens substitutes an international avant-gardism that is newly emergent in the field of comic book production.

In this chapter, I would like to return to Pierre Bourdieu's notion, introduced in the first chapter of this volume, that it is through the struggle for a monopoly on the imposition of legitimate categories of appreciation that the history of a field is made. In particular, Bourdieu argues

> The ageing of authors, works or schools is something quite different from a mechanical sliding into the past. It is engendered in the fight between those who have already left their mark and are trying to endure, and those who cannot make their own marks in their turn without consigning to the past those who have an interest in stopping time, in eternalizing the present state; between the dominants whose strategy is tied to continuity, identity and reproduction, and the dominated, the new entrants, whose interest is in discontinuity, rupture, difference and revolution.[3]

In the field of European comic book production during the 1990s those actors who were most interested in discontinuity, rupture, difference, and revolution were those whose work constituted the first genuine avant-garde in the comics realm. In the previous chapter I argued that the distinction between the Swiss publishers BüLB and Drozophile can be articulated as the difference between traditional and avant-garde narrative construction within the confines of artisanal cultural production. In this chapter I would like to extend that analysis by examining the work of a relatively small number of comics authors who have quite consciously sought to reclassify the boundaries of comics, particularly in relation to traditional, legitimated art practices such as painting, dance, and sculpture. Bourdieu notes 'the struggles over definition (or classification) have *boundaries* at stake (between genres and disciplines, or between modes of production inside the same genre) and, therefore, hierarchies.'[4] In the specific example of contemporary European comic book production, the boundaries at stake are not only the definition of the 'comic book' but also the traditional conception of the avant-garde.

Taken from a term coined to characterize the shock troops of an army, 'avant-garde' implies a number of presuppositions about texts, audiences, and artists. Avant-garde works are traditionally conceptualized as difficult works or works that challenge or exceed the perceptual procedures of educated people. Sally Everett suggests that 'avant-garde art affronts the sensibilities of the popular culture by showing distorted images in unnatural colors,'[5] while Richard Kostelanetz argues that avant-garde works 'forbid easy access or easy acceptance, as an audience perceives them as inexplicably different, if not forbiddingly revolutionary. In order to begin to comprehend them, people must work and think in unfamiliar ways.'[6] Key to both of these understandings is the notion that avant-garde works are difficult because they are non-traditional and exist outside of common frames of reference.

Art historian Donald Kuspit extends the discussion of the avant-garde to include the mythologizations of the avant-garde artist, who is presented as 'uniquely authentic in an unauthentic society.'[7] From this standpoint, the avant-garde work is the product of the avant-garde artist, a circular logic that facilitates the construction of difference in the field of cultural production generally. Indeed, Bourdieu notes that the development of an avant-garde – or, as he terms it, an autonomous sector – simply signals the birth of a new discursive tension in the field of production as 'each of the genres tends to cleave into a research sector and a commercial sector, two markets between which one must be wary of establishing a clear boundary, since they are merely two poles, defined in and by their antagonistic relationship, of the same space.'[8] Nonetheless, despite Bourdieu's admonition that positions are not entirely fixed, the avant-garde has been so characterized throughout the twentieth century.

Diana Crane's definition touches on most of the common assumptions about the avant-garde that will be interrogated in this chapter:

> The term 'avant-garde' implies a cohesive group of artists who have a strong commitment to iconoclastic aesthetic values and who reject both popular culture and middle-class life-style. According to the prototype, these artists differ from artists who produce popular art in the content of their works, the social backgrounds of the audience that appreciates them, and the nature of the organizations in which these works are displayed and sold.[9]

Drawing on Crane's definition, it is important to ask whether a true avant-garde might be said to exist in the world of contemporary European comic book production, and, if it does exist, how that production has shaped the conception of the comic book in recent years. Indeed, I would argue that the specific example of comic book production problematizes a number of key issues in debates about cultural legitimacy and the relationship between modernist and postmodernist aesthetics.

Interestingly, the question of the existence of a comic book avant-garde arises in the 1990s precisely at a point where the continuing existence of an avant-garde in more consecrated fields such as painting was being questioned. As early as 1968, John Ashberry argued that the avant-garde had disappeared from the world of painting. Ashberry suggested in 'The Invisible Avant-Garde' that since the time of Jackson Pollock's appearance in *Life* magazine the media's fascination with avant-garde art practices had turned marginal artistic practices into a norm: 'in any case the result is that the avant-garde can now barely exist because of the immense amounts of attention and money that are focused on it, and that the only artists who have any privacy are the handful of decrepit stragglers behind the big booming avant-garde juggernaut.'[10] Ashberry's notion of stragglers could easily be applied to artists working in the comic book form, who were, of course, rarely at the centre of legitimated culture in any artistic context. Yet more than a mere sense of 'privacy,' the comic book form seems to offer some opportunity for the revival of a traditional sense of the avant-garde simply through its long neglect. Bridget Fowler argues that the energies of the traditional avant-garde have dissipated not through overexposure by the media but because modernism lost its vigour when the juxtaposition of old and new worlds became less tense. Fowler argues that

> The avant-garde was linked no longer to a substantive rationality but rather

to a demand for new shocks dominated solely by the 'tyranny of the calendar.' Modernism was now shown up as an empty category – by which Anderson means that it began to adapt to the calculative rationality or exchange-value which it once spurned.[11]

She concludes, therefore, that the avant-garde can exist in the present only at the global periphery, such as in Latin America, where artists still contrast tradition and modernity. I would contend, however, that peripheries are not defined exclusively by social geography. Indeed, artists working in genres and media long at the periphery of serious consideration have available to them the type of contrast that Fowler foregrounds in her argument. The distinction between tradition and modernity within the European comic book form is, as I have noted throughout this text, still entirely present in the works of contemporary comic book artists. By conceptualizing the relationship between neglected and consecrated cultural forms as akin to the relationship between modernity and tradition, Fowler's observation is easily extended into the field of contemporary European comic book production.

This reading would be similar to Thomas Crow's argument that the artistic avant-garde is a liaison between resistant subcultures and popular culture industries, as the avant-garde revitalizes art by drawing on the meanings that marginal subcultures attach to artifacts of popular culture. Crow suggests that 'the avant-garde serves as a kind of research and development arm of the culture industry: it searches out areas of social practice not yet completely available to efficient manipulation and makes them discrete and visible.'[12] Crow's argument that the avant-garde and popular culture are closely linked would seem to find full expression in comic book production because the field itself has been so long characterized as an expression of the popular par excellence. Indeed, Crow's contention of a close association between these poles is a clear rejection of many of the long-standing tenets of classical modernism, in particular the work of Clement Greenberg.

For an art critic like Clement Greenberg, the avant-garde was the last, best hope for a culture increasingly under siege from modernization, massification, commercialism, and, in the arts, academicism. The avant-garde, Greenberg suggested, was a form of art that depended on the existence of secure class hierarchies, as its audience was 'the rich and the cultivated.'[13] The possibility of a comic book avant-garde would be, from his perspective, impossible. The idea of a comic book avant-garde signals at least two significant differences from Greenberg's articulation of the movement in his classic 1939 essay 'The Avant-Garde and Kitsch.' First, comic books are not sold exclusively or even primarily to an elite audience. The price of comic books – even the most rare examples detailed in the preceding chapter – are still generally far lower than the price of even the least expensive paintings. This means, as Crane has noted about literature, that the social class level of the audience for the former is considerably broader than the audience for the latter.[14] Second, Greenberg characterized the avant-garde as a form of cultural production at war with commercialized mass-produced culture such as comic books. Indeed, Greenberg's definition of rear-guard kitsch includes comics alongside tap dancing, Tin Pan Alley music, and magazine cover illustrations as self-evidently valueless cultural refuse.[15] For many critics, this condemnation seemed to carry the day, and comic books were forever relegated to the dustbin of cultural history. Nonetheless, Greenberg's fuller elaboration of kitsch suggests precisely what the problem with the comics was:

> Kitsch, using for raw material the debased and academicized simulacra of genuine culture, welcomes and cultivates this insensibility. It is the source of its profits. Kitsch is mechanical and operates by formulas. Kitsch is vicarious experience and faked sensations. Kitsch changes according to style, but remains always the same. Kitsch is the epitome of all that is spurious in the life of our times. Kitsch pretends to demand nothing of its customers except their money –not even their time.[16]

Writing in 1939, he, of course, could not have predicted the changes that would occur within the field of comic book production long after his death, although many questions now arise. According to Greenberg, can a comic book that does not operate by formulas, does not change according to style, and that demands something of its audience rise beyond the level of kitsch? Or is the very fact of its mechanical reproduction enough to retain it beneath consideration, not to mention contempt? Put more simply, is it the comic book form that is kitsch or is it individual comic books? My suspicion is that Greenberg would fault the form itself and deny that a comic book avant-garde could be anything other than 'the debased and academicized simulacra of genuine culture.' Nonetheless, more contemporary critics sensing the decline in traditional modernist modes have thrown Greenberg's sharp distinctions into question.

Postmodernist claims to a break with the type of high modernism represented by Greenberg rest on three major assumptions or crises. First, there is the belief that, due to the crisis of representation, artists can no longer reveal the real world but can only play with simulacra or stereotypes. Second, due to the crisis in originality, the artist is limited to pastiche or the recapitulation of earlier patterns of representation. Third, postmodernism lacks the logical use of language that pervaded Enlightenment culture with its emphasis on rationality.[17] From the perspective of my investigation, the central presumption becomes the relationship between consecrated and non-consecrated forms of culture, between what Greenberg termed avant-garde and kitsch. Specifically, the question is whether a traditionally maligned form can generate an avant-garde.

Postmodernism would seek to vacate this question, arguing – as Jean Baudrillard and François Lyotard do – that the distinction between so-called high and low forms that characterized modernism has been abandoned. However, a specific examination of the field of comic book production demonstrates that this argument is at least premature, if not entirely fallacious. The fact that comic books remain considerably less consecrated than, for example, painting, illustrates the fact that distinctions between cultural genres are still pervasive. While these distinctions may – or may not – be receding in force, it is nonetheless clear that they continue to structure social understandings about the relative importance of the arts. If comic books continue to exist as kitsch even in these postmodern times, any attempts to mobilize the form in an avant-garde manner would necessarily seek to collapse the hierarchy in a postmodern fashion. From the perspective that comic books are inherently a part of low culture, therefore, avant-garde comics production would have to be inherently postmodern. Yet from a different starting point – namely that comic books are not self-evidently kitsch but are a cultural form with as much value as painting or prose – then a comic book avant-garde is no longer a postmodern intersection of high and low, but an attempt to create works in a modernist framework. Indeed, it is difficult to fully comprehend how comic books could move into postmodern culture without having paused first in modernism. For many of the artists working in what I would term the European comic book avant-garde the question is self-evident, and they explicitly reject the postmodern label. Operating long after the death of modernism has been pronounced in other cultural fields, these artists see themselves as among the first cultural practitioners to attempt to bring the lessons of modernism to the comic book form, and their approaches are as varied as those who proceeded them in other genres and at other times.

In returning to modernism, however, European comic book artists ask to be judged by the likes of Greenberg and other proponents of the modernist aesthetic. Greenberg's essay 'Modernist Painting' succinctly summarized the thrust of the modernist art project:

> Modernism used art to call attention to art. The limitations that constitute the medium of painting – the flat surface, the shape of the support, the properties of pigment – were treated by the Old Masters as negative factors that could be acknowledged only implicitly or indirectly. Modernist painting has come to regard these same limitations as positive factors that are to be acknowledged openly.[18]

Greenberg championed a painting style that foregrounded flatness and two-dimensionality because those were the conditions that, he argued, painting shared with no other art. Consequently, modernist painting oriented itself to flatness as it did to nothing else. For artists working in the comics medium, however, the formal element that renders it unique is most often assumed to be sequentiality. It is the sequential placement of images to define a narrative space that most clearly defines comics.[19] Thus, for the modernist project of comics to become fully engaged, artists must turn to comics that explore the formal limits of sequentiality. This is a project that has been most clearly articulated by OuBaPo.

OuBaPo (L'Ouvroir de bande dessinée potentielle) was founded by artists involved with L'Association (most notably Jean-Christophe Menu and Lewis Trondheim) and the comics critic Thierry Groensteen at a meeting in Cérisy-la-Salle, France, in 1987, where a workshop on 'bande dessinée oulipienne' was proposed. OuBaPo, of course, takes its name from OuLiPo, the Ouvroir de littérature potentielle founded by Raymound Queneau and François Le Lionnais in 1960. The goal of OuLiPo was the construction of literature within certain self-imposed constraints. For example, Georges Perec's *La Disparition* is a three-hundred-page mystery novel in which the letter 'e' (the most common letter in the French language) does not appear. OuBaPo oriented itself towards similar goals. Following the publication of Menu and Trondheim's *Moins d'un quart de second pour vivre* (L'Association, 1991), Noël Arnaud officially registered OuBaPo as part of Ou-X-Po on 28 October 1992. Since that time a number of OuBaPo members have sought to find new forms of narrativity by interrogating the limits of the comics form. The results of these efforts have been published in a number of books from L'Association and other publishers, including four volumes to date of the *OuPus* anthology, which collects short works and essays by the group.

Perhaps the most public elaboration of the OuBaPo ideas was the publication of 'Les Vacances de l'OuBaPo' by the Parisian newspaper *Libération* in July and August 2000. Over the course of thirty-six days, *Libération* printed one daily strip by each of six artists (François Ayroles, Jochen Gerner, Killoffer, Étienne Lécroart, Jean-Christophe Menu (figure 5), and Lewis Trondheim) working through one of six specific OuBaPienne constraints. Each of these constraints in some way addressed the core modernist question of sequentiality. The *pliage* was a strip that could be folded to create entirely new panels out of parts of the traditional panel grid. The *strips croisés* were comics that could be read meaningfully from left to right and from top to bottom, as in the text in a crossword puzzle. The *palindrome* was a strip whose panels were repeated in an ABCBA pattern. The *itérations* were strips that duplicated a common visual element in each panel while changing other elements. The *morlaque* was a strip with no beginning and no ending, reading in a never-ending circle. Finally, the *upside-down* was a strip – based on Gustave Verbeek's *The Upside-Downs of Little Lady Lovekins and Old Man Muffaroo* strips that were published in American newspapers between 1903 and 1905 – that could be read in a traditional manner and then flipped upside down to be read a second time. Each of these strips, which were collected into the third volume of *OuPus* (L'Association, 2000), stressed to varying degrees the unique element of the comic strip form, and in so doing made a case for the importance of comics within more consecrated domains of the arts.

These explicitly experimental short works provided, as the name implies, a genuine workshop in which modernist ideas about the comics form might be tested before being elaborated in more sustained works. Subsequently, a number of significant longer works from the OuBaPo artists have sought to build upon these short works in order to push the boundaries even further. These works include Lécroart's *Le Cercle vicieux* (L'Association, 2000), which is a palindromic comic book of thirty pages and eighty-nine repeated panels in length. Works such as these, though less acclaimed than works like Perec's, bring the field of comic book production into close proximity with the experimental modernist literary tradition in France and therefore constitute something of an avant-garde cultural practice. At the same time, however, it is difficult to characterize the OuBaPo movement as exclusively modernist.

Since its beginnings, OuBaPo has been interested in the revitalization

5 Read the strip and then turn the book upside down to read it again. From *Les Vacances d'OuBaPo*, by Jean-Christophe Menu.

of the comics form through the selective – perhaps even postmodern – rearticulation of elements found in older comics. The strategy of reappropriation can be found most notably in the work of Ayroles, who has hybridized a number of elements both high and low, including inserting the dialogues of Plato into a *Placid and Muzo* children's comic by Nicolaou.[20] The most sustained efforts in this direction suggest, however, a more thoroughly postmodern sensibility than a modern one. Jochen Gerner's *TNT en Amérique* (L'Ampoule, 2002), for example, is a sixty-two-page book that appropriates Hergé's 1931 book *Tintin en Amérique*. Gerner's book is a page-by-page recreation of the Hergé book in which only a small number of words and iconic elements (redrawn by Gerner) have been retained. The rest of the book, including the panel borders, has been obliterated by black ink. The result is sixty-two pages of black field populated by brightly coloured and seemingly randomly placed visual icons. Thus, unlike most of the other OuBaPo works that focus primarily on questions of sequentiality, *TNT en Amérique* reinscribes the textual as a particularly visual element of the book. It seems, therefore, that the moment of textual and sequential experimentation represented by OuBaPo played itself out extremely quickly.

Writing in *Lire*, Pascal Ory described the book this way: 'Think of a cave-dwelling Miró that would be nothing other than decorative if it did not ooze a kind of well-adjusted modern anguish.'[21] Ory's association of Gerner with Hergé and Joan Miró places the artist at the crossroads of the consecrated modernist Spanish painter and the beloved Belgian cartoonist. The effect of this evaluation is to suggest that in some way Gerner's comic book, which Ory describes as 'a bit perverse,' has equivalency with modernist painting. At the same time, however, the appropriation of Hergé clearly signals the text's intention to be read according to the principles of postmodernist pastiche and bricolage. On this front Gerner is explicit:

> This night is an American night: a filter on an image to give the day the illusion of night. Because with a second degree of reading the memory of another reading intervenes: *Tintin en Amérique* by Hergé. Beginning with this book, used as support material, I chose words that seemed significant to me, and zones of colours in which to place new forms illustrating the previously selected sequence of words. Then, I coloured the rest of the comic book page black.
>
> With this type of graphic intervention, I speak about America by using the comics of Hergé. But I also speak about Hergé's work by means of a work

based on the themes of America. These two universes, the clear line of Hergé and American society, can be interpreted in a similar fashion: two worlds that are rich, beautiful, and smooth in appearance, but troubled and violent in depth.[22]

Gerner, therefore, recaptures the popular and populist past of the comic book in order to rework the material and place it in a dialogue with itself. His work suggests that the contemporary European comic book avant-garde is, in fact, engaged in a postmodern project that seeks to consecrate the comic book form through a reinvention of its low-culture elements and association with consecrated aspects of modernism (the book, for example, opens with a quote from Georges Bataille). Yet this association with modernism is partial and tentative, with *TNT en Amérique* suggesting that OuBaPo moved through a modernist phase in the space of only a few years. At the same time, however, Gerner's work is the exception that proves the rule. While there are a number of avant-garde comics works that could be profitably understood through the lens of postmodern aesthetics, these are not the norm. Far more common are works that seek a place firmly within a modernist framework.

In his article 'Mass Culture as Woman: Modernism's Other,' Andreas Huyssen elaborates seven elements that constitute the 'ideal type notion of what the modernist art work has become.'[23] Huyssen's fundamentals include self-referential experimentality and the expression of a purely individual consciousness, both of which are criteria that – theoretically – comic book artists should have no more difficulty meeting than should artists working in more traditionally consecrated fields. Nonetheless, Huyssen also summarizes three distinct criteria that pose logical obstacles for the comic book artist. First, Huyssen notes that the modernist artwork is defined as 'totally separate from the realms of mass culture and everyday life.' He subsequently states that the work must avoid 'any contamination with mass culture and with the signifying systems of everyday life' in order to maintain a stance that is adversary to bourgeois culture. The difficulty here for artists working in the comic book form is that comic books have historically been an inextricable part of mass culture. Almost all of the comics that might usefully be termed serious or avant-garde have, at some level, a relationship to mass culture, if only through the process of mass production and circulation through the bookstore market.

Second, Huyssen, citing Flaubert's use of language and Manet's use of the frame, notes that the modernist artwork is defined by an elaboration of the medium itself. This is a less obvious problem for artists producing comic books, although the solutions are not entirely self-evident. The example of OuBaPo demonstrates the possibility of experimental works addressing the key issue of sequentiality, but comics also contain other common elements that make the persistent elaboration of the medium somewhat challenging.

Third, Huyssen argues that 'the major premise of modernist art work is the rejection of all classical systems of representation, the effacement of "content," the erasure of subjectivity and authorial voice, the repudiation of likeness and verisimilitude, the exorcism of any demand for realism of whatever kind.'[24] For comic book artists, working in a traditionally representational and narrative art form, this is an extremely difficult standard to meet. Of course, as even Huyssen himself notes, this list is an idealized type that is applied selectively according to the needs of various artistic forms (literature, painting, music, architecture, and so on), yet this summary also provides a starting point by which one can evaluate the relative status of avant-garde comics relative to the expectations imposed on other modernist works. It is worth taking each of these three obstacles in turn and examining them in relation to the most consistently avant-gardist European comic book producer, Frémok.

Frémok is a publishing co-operative that was established in June 2002 through the merger of two smaller artist-run publishing houses: the French publisher Amok and the Belgian Fréon group. Announcing their plan to combine their efforts, Frémok stated their principles in a manner that clearly recalls Bourdieu's dictum that the 'youngest' (least-consecrated) writers structurally 'reject what their most consecrated precursors are and do, everything which in their eyes defines the "old-fashioned" poetics or whatever (and which they sometimes *parody*).'[25] Frémok's announcement, or 'treaty,' creates both a new brand mark that mimics stock exchange abbreviations (FRMK) and a quasi-religious manifesto ('Le Frémok: Un dieu vivant').

Faced with globalization, Amok and Fréon side together and rediscover their primordial entity, le Frémok (FRMK).

In the South Seas and the North Seas, indigenous savages oppose them with the pedigreed dogs of the market. Against galloping mediocrity, they do more than resist: they propose. They erect totems, enlist themselves against laws and the good company. They invent their own language and make books.[26]

Frémok's initial press release, which rails against the demands of commerce, the effects of globalization, and the concerns of a bourgeois society, reads like a postmodern modernist manifesto. References to the necessity of assuring the 'eternal and always fragile victory of the direction over money and the uncultivated forces of KOMERF'[27] (the anti-Frémok, whose name is a near homonym for 'commerce') suggest how the press release knowingly parodies the 'old-fashioned' poetics of modernism, even as the productions of Frémok itself recall those very poetics. While it is never explicitly stated, it is nonetheless easy to presume that in this context the traditional large publishing houses of France and Belgium represent the forces of KOMERF.

Fréon's Thierry van Hasselt made the opposition between his group and the traditions of the comic book industry explicit when he noted in an interview that

> at the beginning of the 1980s behind the work of the large publishers there was really an ambition that was at least partly artistic. I especially think of *(À Suivre)*, this idea of a graphic novel. There was a thought behind that and I had the impression that that has completely disappeared. *Métal*, Les humanos were big publishing houses, they were big commercial enterprises, not what currently goes on in the independent scene, with the associations, it's something truly curious in fact.[28]

From this standpoint it is clear that, at least at the level of rhetoric, Frémok are seeking to position their work in opposition to the market, or in opposition to the heteronomous market for mass culture that has largely and historically characterized the cultural production of the largest Franco-Belgian comics publishing houses. This points to their desire to intersect with Huyssen's first major requirement for the modernist art object.

Amok, the first of the two halves that became Frémok in 2002, was founded in 1994 as the publishing arm of Dissidence Art Work (DAW), an association created in 1991 by two students of visual art, Yvan Alagbé and Olivier Marboeuf. Alagbé and Marboeuf, French-born children of immigrants from Bénin and the Antilles, created DAW as students. Their first project was a magazine entitled *L'Oeil carnivore,* but they became more concretely inscribed in the field of comic book production in 1994, when they launched the anthology comics magazine *Le Cheval sans tête*. With themed issues on the city of Marseille, the notion of heritage, and Georg Büchner's play *Woyzeck, Cheval sans tête* quickly became a venue for the exploration of many of the most urgent themes facing contemporary France: immigration, the quest for identity, the confrontation of cultures, and the *banlieue*. The magazine approached these subjects through a combination of comics, photography, illustration, and text essays that, Marboeuf explained, stemmed from the backgrounds of the editors:

> Yvan and I, we were always decentred, in everything that we did ... Because of our roots, already, and because neither one of us, we didn't come from a well-educated background. What we represent, in our work as well, is impurity. We're not purists, we don't work for a public of purists – what are the fans of the comics: 'the pure and the hard.' Us, we are always mixed up. We were always in the gap.[29]

This sense of mixture was, for Amok, an opposition to the traditions of the field of comics production in Europe, which functioned in a less open and heterogeneous manner. Alagbé explained: 'I like the possibilities that I see there, that interests me as a language. Up until now, comics have functioned as a closed circuit, as if they wanted to define a very restricted territory, to give itself a kind of identity, and refuse to venture to the outside.'[30]

Amok's efforts to break from this restricted territory took the form of a number of different comic book collections, each dedicated to a different task. The Collection Espèces included limited-edition artists' books that were produced in an artisanal manner. The Collection Feu! represented different aspects of contemporary comics through short works by young artists and established figures. Collection Octave was described as the 'reference book' for the best longer works of modern comics. The Collection Verité presented photographs and written textual testimony about the social realities confronting marginalized populations in France. Finally, the Collection Soprano was a separate line for works that function within the frameworks of existing genres, such as the crime novel, fantasy, or science fiction. The distinctions between these lines – new comics, classic comics, genre-based comics, artists' books, and photography-based illustrated prose – demonstrate both the heterogeneity of Amok's approach to creation and the possible frictions that arise when attempts are made to simply reduce their output under the label of modernism. The genre-based works in the Collection Soprano, for example, include works by Ben Katchor, Steven Weissman, and Igort

that stray from the strict expectations of mid-century modernist aesthetics. On the other hand, many of the books in the Collection Octave can
be most profitably understood in these terms. It seems safest to conclude
that Amok, despite their occasionally oppositional rhetoric, are no more
interested in modernist purity than they are in the purity of the comics
form.

Fréon, the Belgian half of Frémok, was created by a number of art
students studying engraving at the Institut Saint-Luc in Bruxelles. Thierry
van Hasselt, Olivier Poppe, Jean-Christophe Long, Vincent Fortemps,
Denis Deprez, and Olivier Deprez joined forces to create a comics
exhibition at the gallery Sans Titre in 1992 and to produce a silk-
screened anthology comic book entitled *Frigorevue*. In the following years
the group worked with editor Alain Corbel and his company Atoz to
produce subsequent issues of the magazine, which were printed by
Christian Humbert-Droz of Drozophile. From the beginning the group
was radically experimental. An unsigned editorial in *Frigorevue* #3 stated
the Fréon credo bluntly:

> Fréon is the search of an author for the tools that they use. You refer to the
> material means. Yes, which paper, which means of production, which work
> tools ... All that is experimental, with each time that you approach a new
> work, you put in place a new technique, whether it is etching, collage, or
> whichever other process. Yes, but this approach signifies something, experi-
> mentalism is not an end in itself. Of course not. You experiment because
> you're looking for openings.[31]

Fréon's explicit emphasis on experimentalism marked them as distinct from the rest of the Franco-Belgian comics scene in the early 1990s.
Further, the group marked itself as both experimental and theoretical
with the founding of its second anthology, *Frigobox*, which was created in
1994 following the failure of Atoz as a publishing house. *Frigobox* was
conceptualized as a workshop, appearing quarterly and serializing large-
scale projects by the group's core members and a few invited guests, as
well as densely theoretical articles on the history and current state of
comics as an art form. Thus, the second issue contained an essay by
Olivier Deprez on popular art and another essay on looking that was
inspired by the writings of Paul Virilio, while the ninth issue offered a
statement by Thierry van Hasselt on how theory had worn him down
('Comment la théorie m'a miné'). The combination of theory and
experimentalism marked a significant difference between Fréon and

their contemporaries in the European small-press comic book scene. Producing rigorously and unabashedly intellectualized works, the Fréon collective took the modernist rejection of mass culture further than anyone in comics had before in both rhetoric and production. While this stops short of a full-scale rejection of mass production – the Fréon books are produced with print runs in the thousands, perhaps not fully 'mass' objects, but also clearly not strictly artisanal either – it is nonetheless clear that the group has sought to mobilize an aesthetic of difficulty that is at odds with Greenberg's notion of kitsch. In joining efforts with Amok, furthermore, the two groups have become a single enterprise seeking to redefine the limits of the comics form in a variety of modernist ways: aesthetically, politically, and intellectually.

The aesthetic challenge posed by Frémok to the dominant conception of the European comic book is rooted in an examination of the traditional limitations of the comics form with an eye towards the expansion of possibilities. In the simplest terms, Frémok seeks to mine the territory that other publishers have abandoned. An editorial in *Frigobox* #5 put it directly: 'We are nomads in search of impossible territories.'[32] Much of this exploration takes place at the boundaries of the form, a space that Huyssen identifies as central to the modernist project. Where OuBaPo's works are primarily concerned with the formal requirements contained in sequences of images, the Frémok artists challenge the limited definition of the comics form by adopting visual strategies generally associated with the consecrated arts. To this end, much of the work published by Frémok has its visual roots in modernist painting, and the incorporation of this material serves to blur the boundary between these forms as it enunciates a different mode of address within the field of comics.

For Yvan Alagbé, the distinction between the two genres has dissolved in the publications of Frémok: 'When one talks about the type of books that we publish, it's always to say that it's better than comic books or not as good. Take, for example, *Berlin 1931,* by Raùl and Cava, where each panel is like a painting, it is to underestimate at the same time painting and comics.'[33] The comics produced by Frémok begin with the integration of painting and other non-traditional approaches to comics art within the comic book format. The use of engraving, monotype, acrylic paints, and watercolours more accurately recall, as Frédéric Paques observes, the work of artists such as Francis Bacon and Lucian Freud than those of cartoonists like André Franquin and Peyo.[34] If, as Huyssen notes, modernist fiction is a persistent exploration of language and modernist painting is an elaboration of paint, brushwork, and the frame, modernist comics – which are located at an intersection of literature and the visual arts – should exemplify a similar concern regarding the formal properties of the medium. For Thierry van Hasselt, the Frémok project is rooted precisely in the possibility that comics comprise their own unique language that integrates the visual aspects of narrativity:

> I think that a reflection on the story is predominant with us. The criticism that does not reflect badly on the independents is 'yes, but there's no story, it's drawing.' It's inconceivable, because the first reflection is on the story and for us comics are really a language, a vocabulary that is super, super rich, that interests us at the basic level, and I think that is necessary to bring these things back to the field of comics.[35]

Thus, for Van Hasselt the notion of the comic book is central to the conception of the work, even in those cases, such as in his own work, where the boundaries between artistic genres are most intensely interrogated.

To date, Thierry van Hasselt has published two books, *Gloria Lopez* (Fréon, 1999) and *Brutalis* (Frémok, 2002) (figure 6). The images in each were produced with monotype, and the illustrations within the books resemble paintings conceived with a total absence of colour. *Gloria Lopez*, a 200+ page story of sex and crime narrated by a doctor performing an autopsy, foregrounds the difficulty of narrative. Jan Baetens, who termed the book not an 'anti-comic book' but 'an other comic book,' suggests that the fiction is imminently reflexive insofar as the themes of the novel recall the material process of its construction: 'In the scalpel of the doctor-narrator one unproblematically recognizes one of the instruments of the artist Thierry Van Hasselt. And the searching police officers are hard to differentiate from the readers of the book, confronted as they are with more questions than answers.'[36] Baetens is correct to note the way in which the book foregrounds its own narrative construction, and one could go so far as to argue that the convoluted nature of the narrative itself serves as a means to refocus attention on the visual plane, just as the art serves as a commentary on the story.

A similar process is at work in *Brutalis,* a comic that may or may not contain a story at all. Produced in collaboration with dancer-choreographer Karine Pontiès, *Brutalis* is composed of several hundred wordless images. The book opens with a number of abstract images before changing into a series of landscapes. Subsequently a nude female figure appears in the landscape, and as she rises, the book is transformed into a

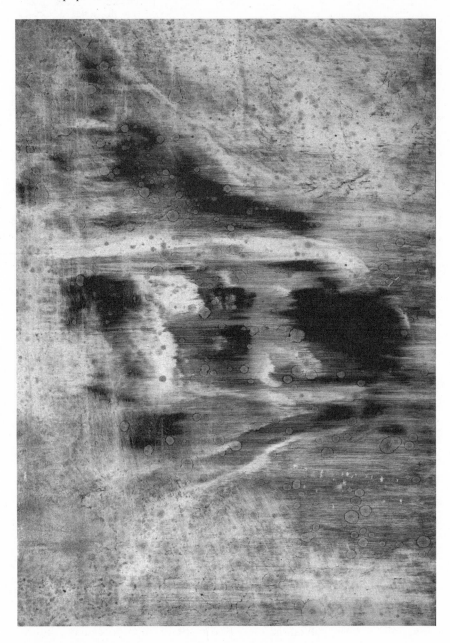

6 The end of the dance. From Thierry van Hasselt's *Brutalis*.

series of drawings by Van Hasselt based on the dance performance of Pontiès. The issue of narrative is foregrounded here by its absence, or by its possible absence. The question of whether the dance, as performed or as depicted, constitutes a story necessarily arises. Further, does the inclusion of framing material in the form of landscapes narrativize a non-narrative form? Or are attempts to read a story from this collection of successive images simply a case of the reader's baggage, seeking to concretize symbolic meanings where none are actually implied? Ultimately *Brutalis* cannot offer fixed responses to these queries but, rather, forestalls their resolution. Further, the book challenges the reader to explore the relationship between the fixed art object (the comic book) and the transitory nature of the performative (the dance). In an introduction to the work posted on the Frémok website, Van Hasselt hints at the various relationships that the book and the performance share (which was first staged at the Chapelle des Brigittines in Bruxelles, 12 December 2002):

> Only the book is read. It suffices in itself.
> The book is read as an extension of the performance.
> After having seen the performance, reading the book prolongs the intimacy with the body.
> The performance suffices in itself.
> The performance is regarded as an extension of the book.
> To attend the performance prolongs intimacy with the matter.[37]

Van Hasselt's work, therefore, can be seen to draw upon strategies alien to the traditions of the comic book in order to call into question accepted notions of what constitutes the narrative component of the comics work. His highly self-reflexive output is indicative of the general orientation of the Frémok group.

The comics of Fréon co-founder Vincent Fortemps raise similar issues. Fortemps's three books – *Cimes* (Fréon, 1997) (figure 7), *La Digue* (Amok, 2001), and *Chantier Musil* (Frémok, 2003) – are wordless novels that are visually unique within the field of comics production. Fortemps produces his images on transparent rhodoïd sheets upon which he draws with a heavy black lithographic crayon. He further refines the images by scratching away the crayon with a knife. This approach allows the artist to draw on both sides of an image before it is photographed for publication. This unique approach to the visual component of the work – which Fortemps describes as more akin to sculpture than to drawing[38] – is

7 Vincent Fortemps's grease pencil on acetate images from *Cimes*.

anchored by the narrative aspect of the works. *Cimes* is a story set in a remote mountain village, while *La Digue* takes place at sea and in harbour. Both are tales of tremendous sadness, and the artist's visual approach – which amounts to gradually eroding the solidity of his images – lends an air of decay to the work that brings the meanings fully to the fore. It is clear throughout the work that the primary influences here are not to be found in the world of comic book illustration. Indeed, Fortemps cites among his influences modernist icons such as Paul Cézanne, Samuel Beckett, and Carl Dreyer.[39] Further, he has – like Van Hasselt – pushed the boundaries of the comics form towards the performative, having created art for *Chantier-Musil (Coulisse)* live on stage during a multimedia performance by Compagnie François Verret in Rennes (2003). Inspired by Robert Musil's essay 'L'Homme sans qualités,' *Coulisse* foregrounds historical trajectories in a series of increasingly alienating vignettes. Fortemps's images move between isolated individuals and crowds, and between animals at rest and at war. Throughout the work, the notion of a murder exists as a subtext, although the complete lack of text and the inability to identify any individual as a singular character, mitigate against the generic sense that one might expect from a thriller. Indeed, this is a narrative virtually without text or characters, a dramatic and despairing slide into the abject elements of human history. The book itself follows the live performances, where Fortemps created art on stage that was projected onto a screen as he worked, an unusual form of visualization in the field of comics.

Like Fortemps, Italian artist Stefano Ricci, who has published two comic books with the Frémok group – *Tufo* (Amok, 1996) (figure 8) and *Anita* (Fréon, 1999) – as well as four collections of drawings and illustrations (*Dépôt noir* [Fréon, 2000, 2002, 2004, 2005]), produces comics that bring the traditions of sculpture into what had long been considered a primarily literary field. *Tufo*, written by Philippe de Pierpont, is the story of a young opera diva returning to her small town following an undisclosed scandal. The action of the book is set in a rock quarry, from which the book derives its name, and revolves around the diva's interaction with a local naïf sculptor. Ricci's visual approach, which involves sculpting images out of heavy oil pastels, rubber erasers, and ground graphite, is a complement to the story insofar as its physicality graphically recalls the very earth upon which the characters exert their will. This high degree of integration between story and métier is exceedingly rare in the field of comics.

The logic is reversed in *Anita* (written by Gabriella Giandelli), a

8 A disjointed portrait from *Tufo,* by Stefano Ricci and Philippe de Pierpont.

diaristic story of a young waitress that was originally serialized in the Italian fashion magazine *Glamour.* In this book Ricci moves from grey-scale images to full colour, utilizing a wide variety of exceedingly vibrant shades as the book unfolds. The highly intense chromatic scale on display here seems somewhat at odds with the story in which little of narrative consequence occurs. Indeed, the story is about a woman in a dead-end job who also has something of a dead-end life, but the choice of visual techniques signals a secret world much richer than that. Because the images so overwhelm the narrative construction of the novel, the reader is obliged to consider the apparent disparity and to reflect upon what constitutes a life without momentum. Ricci's images suggest that a great beauty surrounds Anita's choices in life, although this is not reflected in the text. From this standpoint the thrust of the meaning of the book is carried almost exclusively through image composition, with the textual elements serving as a structuring counterpoint. Critics who privilege a more closely shared interaction between images and text often condemn this approach to the comics form, which overloads the visual plane.[40] Ricci's work, however, can be best understood as a particular intervention into both the traditional techniques of comic book rendering and the privileging of a logocentric vision of the proper constitution of the comic book form. Indeed, his work forces a more active form of reading that borders on the performative and that seeks to counteract the logics of the narrative.

Dominique Goblet's two books for Fréon – *Portraits crachés* (1997) and *Souvenir d'une journée parfaite* (2001) (figure 9) – further complicate the traditional visual aesthetics of the comic book form. *Portraits crachés* is a collection of short works that originally appeared in *Frigorevue, Lapin,* and *Strapazin,* and at festivals in Angoulême and Luzern. Goblet approaches the page in a manner that is unusual in the field of comics, integrating words and images more directly than most cartoonists and rejecting traditional panel distinctions for the most part. Her drawings, which use watercolour washes, pencil, and ballpoint pen among other techniques, defy the conventions of the form with their rejection of perspective and their scratchy, sketchy tones. Goblet couples this visual approach with a narrative thematic that focuses largely on familial issues. She describes her approach to fiction as being rooted in her own personal history, but not entirely a part of that history: 'Yes, once more in my personal approach, the story tried to distance itself from an autobiographical connection, which has in fact brought it closer.'[41]

Souvenir d'une journée parfaite stresses the interaction between autobi-

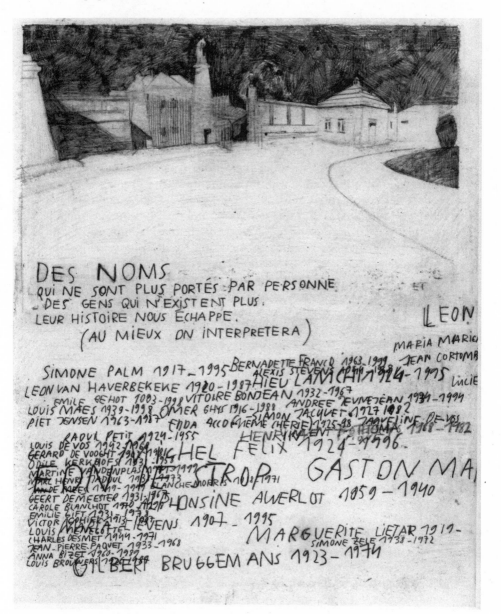

9 Dominique Goblet records the names of the dead. From *Souvenir d'un journée parfaite*.

ography and fiction to an even greater degree than do her short works. The book, created as part of Fréon's *Récits de ville* project, begins in a Bruxelles cemetery in which the author struggles to find the memorial to her father and moves into a fiction of familial dissolution. Goblet's images for the book, composed entirely in pencil on large sheets of yellow-coloured paper, hint at the fragility of memory. The faded colour of the paper, and the easily erased lines that the artist has placed upon it, suggest the transient nature of life – particularly in relation to Goblet's concern about her father's grave marker, a supposedly fixed artifact that may no longer be so. More to the point, however, is the challenge that the book offers to the dominant conventions of comic book storytelling. The long sections of wordless and figureless images, the unusual integration of text into the images, and the transitions between intensely rendered and casually sketched images all serve to challenge presuppositions about what a comic book looks like. All of these elements contribute to what Huyssen terms 'a persistent elaboration of the medium itself.'[42]

Other examples of this tendency in the work of the Frémok artists could be introduced here as well to further bolster this observation. M.S. Bastian's *Baluba* (Amok, 1995) introduces a riot of aggressively drawn images culled from popular culture. Atak's *Alice embrasse la lune avant qu'elle ne s'endorme* (Amok, 2000) details a highly individualized aesthetic rooted in a reconceptualization of quasi-folk imagery. Alex Barbier's two volumes of *Lettre au maire du V.* (Fréon, 1998, 2000) work through the psychodynamic erotics of horror fiction in a highly charged, lurid, watercolour aesthetic. Indeed, what seems to unite the Frémok artists is the sense that each individual contributor to the project is engaged with an entirely different set of aesthetic interests, but that none of them is particularly derived from the traditional aesthetics of comic books. From one perspective it could be argued that the Frémok project is a kind of renewal of the comics form and that by bringing to comic books pictorial models derived from outside itself a sense of rebirth is occurring. While this is undoubtedly true to some extent, it seems more important to note the precise nature of the change that Frémok is offering at the level of visual aesthetics. Specifically, there is an attempt to 'catch comics up' to the more consecrated forms of artistic expression. That is to say that Frémok is in the process of inserting comic book production fully into the aesthetic canons of modernism, more than a half-century after the fact and despite challenges to its dominance. This is accomplished through the rejection of the dictates of mass culture and through the celebration of the innovative graphic aspects of comic book storytelling. Where the group runs most afoul of Huyssen's ideal modernist form, however, is in the question of content and authorial voice.

Crucial to the intervention of many of the Frémok artists is the sense of a need to use the comic book form in order to engage with the important social questions of the day. The 1996–7 Amok catalogue made this involvement explicitly clear:

> During its century of existence, the comic strip has secreted a savage aca-demicism, constructed of a universe of dreams and adventures.
>
> The profound childhood nostalgia that still largely occupies the produc-tion of comic books condemns its efficiency vis-à-vis the current world and confines it to the periphery of contemporary issues.
>
> Amok's approach well understands, for its part, that it is situated at the heart of a creative confrontation with reality ...
>
> While choosing to publish comic books, Amok chooses to defend within this art a strong and ambitious creation, which combines the expression of a personal vision anchored in social, historical or cultural realities.[43]

Amok's active engagement with the social, historic, and cultural realities of the world in which they reside marks them as distinct from the classical conception of modernism described by Huyssen. Indeed, the distance between the art object and an engagement with social realities is a constant refrain in writings about modernism. Harold Rosenberg, for example, suggested, 'The big moment came when it was decided to paint ... Just TO PAINT. The gesture on the canvas was a gesture of liberation from Value – political, aesthetic, moral.'[44] According to Rich-ard Murphy, modernism's conservative relationship to autonomy stems from wariness about ideological commitments because such commit-ments are seen to tend towards limiting ambiguity:

> For modernism political solutions appear merely to be part of the problem rather than part of the cure. Instead, it clings to various autotelic forms of aesthetic autonomy and hermeticism in order to resist any kind of co-optation which would limit the work's meaning. As a result it frequently becomes a bastion of high-culture; elitist, arcane and inaccessible.[45]

Within the field of European comic book production there can be no doubt that the works published by Frémok constitute a form of high culture, or at least the highest culture that the form has attained to date.

Nonetheless, it is not entirely clear that the works are 'elitist, arcane and inaccessible.' If they are not, then it logically follows that the works have indeed broken from the modernism that the Frémok project sought to bring to the comics field. Indeed, in the end it is evident that Frémok's dedication to the social, historic, and cultural is stronger than their commitment to the outmoded tenets of high modernism.

The work of Yvan Alagbé, one of the co-founders of Amok, is indicative of both the type of works and the cultural politics that the publisher privileges. Alagbé's first book for his publishing house, *Nègres jaunes*, tells the story of a former *harki* officer who participates in the *ratonnade* of 17 October 1961 in order to carry out a pathetic sexual blackmail of an African family living in France without papers. By making the villain of a story an Algerian who had fought on the side of General De Gaulle, Alagbé upsets stereotypical notions of hero and villain in both the comic book plot and contemporary social discussions. Alagbé notes, 'It is for me, in fact, an act of showing how marginalized people, instead of helping each other, finally oppress each other.'[46] This is a more difficult conception of politics than a simple didacticism would allow, insofar as it does not reduce social relations to simplistic formulas. At the same time, Alagbé's visual approach, which highlights social alienation through a reduction of background detail and the elision of visual cues associated with the images of his protagonists, highlights his rejection of easy answers. He suggests in an interview, 'I don't want to reduce what we do to sociocultural questions. Recently, someone said to us on this subject: "Ah, well it's good what you do." No! That's not doing good. This "socialist" side irritates me.'[47] For Alagbé, therefore, the refusal to reduce the work simply to the level of its cultural significance is central to the definition of the Frémok project, which more accurately fuses a sociocultural agenda with a particular aesthetic of graphic and narrative innovation within the comics form. Alagbé described the policy of Amok as attempting to 'retranscribe the interrogations rather than to deliver a message.'[48] This policy, clearly, could be equally applied to the cultural arguments advanced by the artists as well as to their approach to form, which similarly calls for new understandings of the possibilities of the medium.

A similar effort to retranscribe the normative understanding of a particular social crisis can be found in Olivier Bramanti's books on the conflict in the former Yugoslavia, *Le Pont de l'ange* (Amok, 1999) and *Le Chemin des Merles* (Amok, 2001). The latter particularly challenges the received wisdom about the political situation. Set during the battle of

Kosovo in 1389, at which the Turks defeated the Serbs, the book is an attempt to come to terms with a legacy of resentment and nationalism without in any way vindicating the contemporary actions of the Serbs. Nonetheless, in presenting a book in which the historical victimization of the Serbs is depicted, *Le Chemin des Merles* serves as a rejection of the simple Manichean presentation of the Yugoslavian conflict found on the nightly television news. Bramanti's book addresses itself directly to the battle which is most emblematic in the sense of Serbian self-identity and nationalism in order to determine how this sense of defeat was transformed into an ideology of hatred against a third party, the Albanians. The author suggests that the contemporary war was a displacement of nationalist resentment based on the shared religion of the perceived enemies and brought about by the manipulations of those in power. The deeper question, however, is the one that the artist poses to himself with regard to the story that he has told: 'I wanted to know, if I had been Serb, if I could have been manipulated by all these poems and all the literature which gave rise to this history.'[49] Further, *Le Chemin des Merles* pushes the concept of the political comic book further than the artist's previous work insofar as it expands our notion of both the politics and the form. *Le Pont de l'ange* has, despite its non-traditional visual aesthetic, a narration that is very much in keeping with the comic book tradition, particularly as each page is composed of five or six panels. *Le Chemin des Merles*, on the other hand, with only one or two images per page, and long sequences without text, works through a different logic, pushing the boundaries of the comic book form to a greater degree. Here again it is evident that it is impossible to conceptualize the political intervention of the Frémok artists apart from the intervention that they wish to make into the traditions of the medium in which they are operating.

This tension between the political and the aesthetic is similarly strongly felt in the work of writer Felipe H. Cava. Cava, who has had a number of his Spanish books translated by Frémok, is a critic and editor primarily associated with the Spanish comics new wave of the 1980s, when he was the editor of magazines like *Madriz* and *Medios revueltos*. The works that have been translated by Frémok, done in collaboration with artists Raùl and Federico del Barrio, highlight two approaches to the creation of politically engaged comic books. Three of the four Spanish volumes of *Les Mémoires d'Amoros* have been published by Amok (2000, 2001, 2004) to date. These books, created in an extremely traditional comic book aesthetic of three-tiered panel layouts with line art and ink washes, concern the adventures of anarchist Spanish newspaper reporter Angel Amoros in the 1920s and 1930s. Narrated in flashback, the books are set against the real historical backdrop of Spanish history and politics, and they are set within the confines of marginalized ethnic communities within Spain. In short, these are classical genre tales brought to life through a combination of keen observation of historical detail and a clear adherence to the conventions of genre writing. These books are engaged at a political level but not at the level of aesthetic innovation.[50]

The same cannot be said, however, about Cava's work with the artist Raùl. *Fenêtres sur l'occident* (Amok, 1995) is based on the travels of the artist to Russia in the early 1990s. It begins as a straightforward depiction of four people gathering for an evening to drink vodka, but as each tells the others a story Raùl radically alters the visual aesthetic of the book. Each story is told using a significantly different visual aesthetic – highly detailed line art, scratchboard, photocopied iconography, and large, abstract non-figurative images. The divergent aesthetic strategies on display in the text help to visualize the polyvocality of the Glasnost era, and the heterogeneity of the approach challenges the more simplistic model offered by the *Mémoires d'Amoros* books.

A sort of hybrid approach is found in *Berlin 1931* (Amok, 1998), which was originally published in Spanish in the newspaper *El Pais* in 1988. This story, set against the backdrop of the rise of Nazism, follows a traditional comic book page breakdown but is innovative in terms of its visual approach. Raùl has painted all of the images in the book in a high modernist mode that recalls the works of German expressionist painters such as George Grosz and Ernst Kirchner, particularly in the dramatic tonal shifts in the colours. Using this technique Raùl recreates on the page a sense of the 'degenerate' art against which the Nazis campaigned. Indeed, the first words spoken in the book call attention to the idea of a degenerate art, within the confines of a cultural form that has similarly been regarded as degraded and degrading. Here Cava and Raùl mesh politics and aesthetics in such a way that each becomes a commentary upon the other.

The politics of Fréon, the Belgian half of Frémok, have been at once both more didactic and more elusive. On the one hand, they published in 2001 a re-edition of the biography of Che Guevara created by Hector Oesterheld, Alberto, and Enrique Breccia. This book, with its explicitly anti-capitalist intentions and controversial publishing history (Oesterheld was tortured and killed by the Argentine military in 1977) is the most blatantly didactic book yet published by Frémok. On the other hand, however, Fréon's *Récits de ville* project, five volumes of which have been created to date, offers a perspective on social realism that is highly abstract. The *Récits de ville* project was undertaken in collaboration with funding from Bruxelles 2000. It was a project in which a small number of artists were brought to Bruxelles, where they worked in an atelier for a short period of time and created a comic book story based on their experiences in the city. Of the five volumes published, three were stand-alone books: Eric Lambé's *Ophélie et les directeurs des ressources humaines* (Fréon, 2000), Dominique Goblet's *Souvenir d'une journée parfaite*, and Frédéric Coché's *Hortus sanitatis* (Fréon, 2000), a series of etchings visually recalling the work of Ensor, Brueghel, and Marcel Broodthaers.[51] The remaining two volumes were anthologies featuring the work of Gabriella Giandelli, Martin tom Dieck, Jan Lens, Olivier Poppe, Merkeke and Christian Coppin, Alain Corbel, Sylvain Victor, Jean-Christophe Long, Olivier Quéméré, Olivier Deprez, and Nathalie Lambert. The approach to the project was outlined in an editorial to the second volume:

> It is this myth of the new for the new that we need to free ourselves of. Like the pole of modernity that is always being redefined, let us choose the pole of the forms and of their tireless capacity for combinations, hyperconstruction lives! Therefore, let us militate not for an innovation in appearance but for a quality in arrangement. The comic book, the comic books that we must write, has (have) certainly a corner, albeit modest, to defend in a history of the relationship between art and the cities, or the opposite.[52]

Fréon's call for a link between the city and the comic book constitutes something less than a fully critical engagement with the processes of urbanization. Indeed, many of the stories collected in the *Récits de ville* series attempt to say very little in terms of politics, but rather take an opportunity to meditate generally on social relations. From this stand-point, it is possible to argue that Fréon was seeking an aesthetic not so much of political engagement (which might be evidenced in their publication of *Ché*) but of intellectual engagement. That is to say that the *Récits de ville* series addresses urbanity more as an intellectual and aes-thetic challenge to be met rather than as a political struggle to be won. It is possible, therefore, to conceptualize the Frémok project more as an intellectualization of the field of comics than a politicization of that field.

Certainly there is plenty of evidence to support this notion. The first book in the *Récits de ville* series, for example, is Eric Lambé's graphic novel *Ophélie et les directeurs des ressources humaines.* Lambé's almost wordless text tells a story based on the relationship of Portuguese writer Fernando Pessoa and his lover Ophelia. Lambé filters this relationship equally through Pessoa's letters as well as through the logic of urbanization and corporate structure. The narrative highs and lows are equated visually, as Lambé's images draw connections between, for example, the mystery of a message in a bottle and the banality of a recycling project. Throughout the book the myth and legacy of modernist romance haunt a thoroughly bureaucratized contemporary existence.

A somewhat similar effect is created by Lambé's next project, a collaboration with writer Philippe de Pierpont entitled *Alberto G.* (2003) (figure 10), co-published by Frémok and the large French literary press Seuil. *Alberto G.* tells a story about the life and death of sculptor Alberto Giacometti, particularly focusing on key moments in his youth and subsequent late career work. The novel is structured as a series of vignettes – the artist as a youth, the artist with Caroline (the prostitute-model whom he frequently sculpted), the artist in his atelier – that conceptualize the relationship of artist and work organically. Centrally, the book's actions and themes are examined most closely through the story of a late-career naturalist sculpture that the artist hopes to bring to life and that is in fact animated when it is discovered buried in a field by a group of small children. Giacometti's relationship with surrealism and, later, with Sartre's existentialism are not addressed in the book. Instead, the tensions between naturalism and abstraction are equated throughout the text with the tension between romance and existential anxiety, establishing a series of binaries that are resolved through the transformative power of youth. These two books, and to a much lesser extent Lambé's *Les Jours ouvrables* (Amok, 1997), signal an intention to re-read the history of modernism through the comics form. Moreover, in the conscious utilization of other forms of modernism – including poetry and sculpture – in a referential manner, rather than the use of the forms of comics in a self-referential fashion, some slippage ensues. Indeed, it is possible to regard Lambé's work as beginning a distinct move of Frémok towards postmodern aesthetics.

Books such as *Mr Burroughs,* by the Portuguese duo of writer David Soares and artist Pedro Nora, reinforce this tendency. *Mr Burroughs* is a surrealist, nightmarish reconceptualization of certain moments in the life of American writer William S. Burroughs, with a particular focus on examples of his non-literary artistic creations (painting, musical collabo-

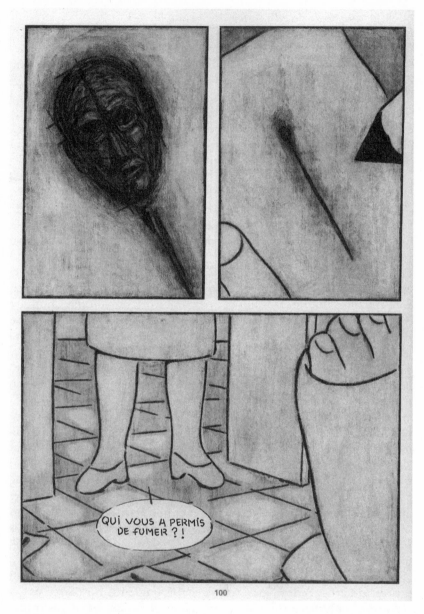

10 Alberto Giacometti draws a burnt match. From *Alberto G.* by Eric Lambé and
Philippe de Pierpont.

rations). In locating the importance of Burroughs's cultural creativity outside of the literary, the book suggests that genuine creativity is located in interdisciplinary undertakings, an argument that is flattering to the comics form, seen as it is by many as a cross between literature and the visual. Pedro Nora states this argument explicitly when he remarks 'I think that it is necessary to soak oneself in a maximum of disciplines. I believe that this is a postmodern approach to the comic book.'[53] According to Nora, this type of interdisciplinarity is a natural extension of the drive towards personal expression in the fields of both comic books and painting: 'I have no problem with the comic book artists who exhibit in the galleries and the painters who use the comic strip, and moreover I appreciate the benefit of such reasoning. Look at Raymond Pettibon, Mark Beyer, or David Schrigley.'[54] Nonetheless, Nora's work itself is far removed from the traditions of painting. When asked about the relation of the two disciplines, he responds bluntly, 'I am not a painter.'[55] *Mr Burroughs* is a book composed primarily of scratchily minimalist line drawings that reduce or totally exclude non-essential details (such as references to social spaces). Thus, Nora's comments can be understood to function generally as an endorsement of the excavation of the paintings/comic books distinction, even though his work does not particularly take part in doing that work itself. Instead, Soares and Nora suggest a general argument about the disintegration of artistic boundaries through the appropriation of the image of an author whose career pointed towards this kind of decay.

Where the works of Lambé and Nora suggest a sense of intellectual engagement at the level of artistic practice, an increasing number of Frémok books have pushed the boundaries even further by bringing philosophy into the pages of comic books. German artist Markus Huber, for example, created a short graphic novel, *Promenade à Saturnia* (Amok, 2000) (figure 11), that features a character named Walter, the entirety of whose dialogue is composed of quotes from philosopher Walter Benjamin's *Sens unique*. The story, which revolves around a number of jet setters gathered for a weekend party, touches briefly on themes of sexual and physical danger among a broader sense of social ennui. From this perspective the book bears a similarity to Michelangelo Antonioni's 1960 film *L'Avventura*. At the same time, however, the book possesses a stronger sense of the fantastic than does Antonioni's film. While most of the characters are drawn in Huber's form of stylized realism, Walter, the theoretical backbone of the work, is depicted as a legless torso with a skull-head and hat who magically roams the hills on a board with four

11 A visit to the Giardino Dei Tarocchi with a legless Walter Benjamin. From *Promenade à Saturnia* by Markus Huber.

wheels. Walter is half of a Mexican Day of the Dead figure come to life spouting German modernist philosophy at a high-end retreat in Tuscany. Narratively, of course, this makes little sense. The other characters engage with Walter as if he were a child when he gets lost on a visit to the Niki de Saint Phalle–designed Giardino dei Tarocchi, yet no one remarks on his bizarre appearance. While it is clear that Walter is at once both inside and outside the narrative, this makes sense only insofar as much of his commentary relates to notions of fantasy. Indeed, the book's epigraph – by Benjamin – reads: 'Incomparable language of the skull: it links the total absence of expression (black of the eye sockets) with the most wild expression (grimace of the teeth).'[56] This epigraph summarizes the themes of the book, in which Benjamin acts as a quasi-real character in order to symbolize the quasi-real philosophy emblematized by Saint Phalle's sculpture garden, and lends it a visual motif that reifies an ironic sense of play between the real and the fantastic.

Arguably, the fullest sense of an intellectualized comics sphere can be found in the work of another German artist frequently published by Frémok, Martin tom Dieck. Dieck's works, including *Der Unschuldige Passagier* (Alsfeld, 1993) and *Hundert Ansichten der Speicherstadt* (Arrache Coeur, 1997), have proved him to be one of the most distinctive voices in the 1990s European comic book scene. His books combine, as Aarnoud Rommens has pointed out, influences as diverse as Hergé, Otto Dix, Franz Kafka, and Buster Keaton.[57] Yet his work with Frémok – which includes frequent contributions to *Cheval sans tête*, participation in the *Récits de ville* project, and the publication of two graphic novels by Fréon – is the fullest elaboration of what I would like to term an intellectualized comics production. Two of Dieck's contributions to *Cheval sans tête*, in particular, signal his interests in using the comics form to interrogate the history of modernism and modernist assumptions in an innovative manner. 'Fragments fugitifs,' in volume 2, number 2, is a ten-page story recounting the exploits of German Dadaist writer Walter Mehring's exile in Marseille during the Second World War. 'Dada,' in the fourth issue of the second volume, is a five-page piece focusing primarily on Richard Heulsenbeck, Georg Grosz, and Mehring. In both of these works Dieck brings a highly expressionistic rendering style to the comics page in order to highlight the preoccupations of Dada within the comics form. The works do not so much recount the history of these surrealist moments as they reconstruct them visually through the innovative integration of image and original Dadaist manifestoes. In this way, the works have something to offer both the field of comics and the legacy of surrealist cultural practice. The connection between the forms is reinforced in the penultimate panel of 'Dada,' wherein Grosz is visited by the police. Asked if he is the painter Georg Grosz, Grosz is shown to reply 'Nope! Je pas connaître! I am a cartoonist.'[58] Grosz's escape from danger through the assumption of the mantle of low culture implies the relationship between consecrated artists working in legitimated forms and the non-consecrated cartoonist whose work draws upon that legacy. Grosz's uncharacteristically upbeat response to the authorities – note the two exclamation points in the text – hints at the joyous possibilities that are represented in reclaiming an artist like Grosz for the history of comics.

In his books for Fréon, written by Jens Balzer, Dieck goes even further, recasting French post-structuralist philosopher Gilles Deleuze as a comic book adventure hero. The first of these books, *Salut, Deleuze!*, originated as a short story in *Lapin* #15. In that story, Charon transports Gilles Deleuze to the afterlife, where they have a conversation about gardening, and where he meets Roland Barthes, Jacques Lacan, and Michel Foucault. The book-length version of the work opens with this story, and then the story repeats itself. The art is duplicated – with the exception of some very minor changes – but the text is subtly transformed. By the end of the book the same story has unfolded five times, and Charon and Deleuze have had a thorough discussion of some of the ideas put forward in Deleuze's *Différance et répétition* (1968). Indeed, these ideas structure the entirety of the narrative, based as it is on endless repetitions with nearly imperceptible differences creeping into the work with each subsequent iteration. For Dieck, the comics form is perfectly suited for this sort of experimental play:

> This repetitive structure enables me to present a complex problem in an accessible form. Thanks to the drawings, the reader no longer needs additional explanations. It's that which is significant for me. I hope that people who will buy the two books on Deleuze will buy them because they like the comics and not because they know Deleuze.[59]

The sequel to *Salut, Deleuze!*, *Les Nouvelles Aventures de l'incroyable Orphée* (Fréon, 2002) (figure 12), takes up where the previous volume left off, but in a completely different form. Originally serialized in the pages of *Frankfurter Algemeine Zeitung*, the book adopts the language and structure of a 1920s adventure comic strip in order to present its argument. This postmodern collision of the high – French philosophy – and the low –

12 Ignatz the Mouse meets Jacques Lacan, Michel Foucault, Roland Barthes and Gilles Deleuze. From *Les Nouvelles Aventures de l'incroyable Orphée*, by Martin tom Dieck and Jens Balzer.

adventure comic strips – is amplified by Balzer and Dieck's choice of references throughout. One lead character is the blindfolded Orpheus of Greek myth, struggling to rescue Eurydice from the Underworld without looking at her. Another common element is the cast of George Herriman's newspaper comic strip *Krazy Kat* and the Rube Goldbergesque contraptions that Deleuze builds to aid in his adventures. These combinations, coupled with the fact that the book is structured as a series of three-panel comic strips – many of them gags – has a tendency to throw the entire conception of a hierarchy of consecrated forms out the window. While Dieck maintains that he hopes 'the classic comic strip form renders the philosophy accessible,'[60] the book operates on a playful logic that is equally welcoming and frustrating. All of Orpheus's considerable dialogue, for example, is written in Greek and is only passingly understood by Deleuze, and not at all by the other characters (not to mention the vast majority of the readers). This tends to thwart the idea of rendering philosophy accessible, although *Libération* termed it 'a precise interpretation of the philosopher's oeuvre.'[61] Yet, at the same time, the incomprehensibility of the language establishes a large number of jokes. Indeed, the book's unwillingness to take Deleuze or his fellow philosophers seriously, using them as icons in a slapstick *feuilleton*, confirms a fundamentally ironic disposition that is characteristic of postmodernism.

The distinctions that are drawn between modernism, avant-gardism, and postmodernism have been the subject of considerable debate, but the example of contemporary comics production in Europe demonstrates that the terms are slippery and, ultimately, not entirely satisfying. Because of its diversity, the Frémok project is difficult to precisely pin down. A number of descriptors have been suggested in this chapter, each with certain strengths and weaknesses. While it is clear that some cartoonists associated with the movement can profitably be seen as working through a postmodern aesthetics, others are not. Moreover, Fréon, at the very least, has outright rejected this model. Writing in *Frigobox* #5, Jan Baetens draws a sharp distinction between the comics produced by Fréon and Amok on the one hand and postmodernism on the other and celebrates the return of modernism that I have discussed here.[62]

Nonetheless, it is clear that the works of Frémok cannot be completely understood through the modernist lens either. While Frémok has established a repudiation of the logics of mass culture in creating a self-consciously experimental body of work, it nonetheless strays in many instances from the modernist ideal in order to incorporate issues relating to the social and political realities of contemporary Europe. From this vantage, Frémok is neither modernist nor postmodernist, but both at the same time – and also, of course, perhaps neither. It is possible to determine the definitional question under a broader rubric of the avant-garde, for clearly within the particular field of European comic book production the works of the Frémok artists constitute one of the few examples of avant-garde production.

At the same time, however, this is something of a problematic term. Peter Bürger, for example, has argued, 'The intention of the historical avant-garde movements was defined as the destruction of art as an institution set off from the praxis of life.'[63] If this is the intention of the avant-garde, it is not one that has been met by Frémok. Bourdieu resolves this dilemma by taking a less programmatic view of the avant-garde, which may apply here. Bourdieu notes that avant-garde positions bring together artists from diverse backgrounds that unite in opposition to the dominant positions before splintering apart.[64] He further draws attention to the fact that avant-gardes, however they are defined, are always fleeting, partial, and ad hoc. The difficulties facing the avant-garde in a field such as comics, where the work is doubly marginalized by being cast outside the heteronomous market of the mass culture industry while simultaneously refused entry by the more autonomous market for consecrated arts such as painting, are particularly acute.

Ultimately, Frémok is a small coterie of comic book producers located throughout western Europe who collaborate on books and exhibitions and contribute to shared anthologies. One could suggest, for example, that the Frémok artists – having sought to bring the comics form fully under the influence of the modernist aesthetic in the 1990s – had, by the turn of the millennium, brought comics into the auspices of postmodernism. This, however, is a needlessly reductive argument. A more satisfying perspective suggests that the heterogeneity of the contemporary European comic book avant-garde is represented within the entirety of the Frémok catalogue. Again, Bourdieu's notion of a temporary group brought together primarily by a shared negative disposition to the dominant traditions seems to hit the nail squarely on the head here. What the Frémok books seem to share – if they share anything – is not a commitment to the precepts of modernism, postmodernism, or avant-gardism, but an opposition to the dominant traditions of the fields that is rooted in a rationalist refutation of affect.

From this perspective, the difference between L'Association and Frémok is enormous and crucial, despite their many affinities, overlapping projects, and common artists. The contemporary comic book modernism represented by L'Association's OuBaPo remains very different from the manner in which Frémok artists mobilize the visual element in comics to produce them as an artistic space more akin to painting than to literature. If L'Association stretches the limits of the comic book field by extending its roots, Frémok touches on the possibility that its own practitioners might rupture the field itself. Yvan Alagbé identified this tension when he indicated, 'When we made the magazine *Cheval sans tête*, in the early days of Amok, we opened it up to people who had never made comics – "Well, they still haven't done it," is what certain people must think.'[65]

Chapter 4

From Global to Local and Back Again

In July 2003, at the San Diego Comic-Con, the largest comic book convention in the United States, the annual Eisner Awards were presented. Named for legendary American cartoonist Will Eisner, the awards are voted on by industry professionals and are one of two significant comics prizes handed out in the United States each year. Since 1988, the Eisners have been inducting cartoonists into their Hall of Fame. One of 2003's inductees was *Tintin* creator Hergé, the first European cartoonist to be so honoured in the history of the awards. Accepting the prize on his behalf were the French cartooning tandem of Philippe Dupuy and Charles Berberian, international guests of honour at that year's convention, and cartoonists whose professional careers began around the time of Hergé's death. If the irony of being invited to accept a prize on behalf of an artist whom they had never met were not enough, the artists subtly mocked the absurdity of asking two French cartoonists to accept an award on behalf of the world's most famous Belgian cartoonist. For most of the audience, however, the irony was lost, as most attendees, if they were familiar with Hergé's work at all, likely regarded it as French, by language if not by nationality.

This confusion speaks to the way in which different comics cultures construct a notion of the 'other.' In practice, the world of comics is divided into three general regimes or markets: the United States, which includes English-speaking nations such as Canada and Great Britain; Japan, which includes all of Asia; and France, which incorporates not only Belgium, but all of western Europe and some parts of South America. For most of the audience at the Eisner Awards there was no fundamental disconnect between Hergé and Dupuy and Berberian; they were all simply European cartoonists.

In the European comics market since the 1990s, American and Japanese comics have taken on different significations. The Japanese manga market has, since the mid-1990s, been the single most important economic force in European comics. Indeed, while this book focuses exclusively on the aesthetic and social impact of the contemporary European small press, their economic effect is minuscule relative to the importance of manga, whose significance would require another volume of this size to properly explicate. The publisher Glénat introduced manga to the European market in 1989, when they translated Katsuhiro Otomo's *Akira*. The publisher followed this success in 1991 with *Dragon Ball*, a bestseller for young readers. In 1993, the company moved seriously into the translation industry. Glénat saw in manga a possible replacement for hardcover albums, whose sales had been in an unprecedented slump in the early 1990s. The success of manga has been incredible, bolstered by a number of social and technological factors, including the widespread availability of Japanese animation (animé) on television and DVD, the popularity of Japanese card games (Pokémon, Yu-Gi-Oh) among European children, and an increasing general awareness of Asian culture that has recreated Japan as an exotic other. In 2002, 377 Japanese comics were released in France, with that number rising above 500 in 2003 to reach more than 50 books per month in 2004. Sales for the most popular titles, such as *Kenshin, Captain Tsubasa,* and *Yu-Gi-Oh,* passed the million mark in 2004.[1] Although Gilles Ratier could complain about the 'agony of the press' in the 1990s, it was clear that this pain did not expand to specialists in manga, such as Kana, Tonkam, and Pika, who recorded spectacular profits through the importation of enormous back catalogues of Asian comics throughout Europe.

So great was the impact of manga on the European comics field in the 1990s that even the small press engaged in the process of recruiting manga superstars to their catalogues. Eschewing the teen romance and science fiction comics of mainstream manga, publishers like Casterman and Seuil produced Jiro Taniguchi as an important star of literary manga, with the publication of books like *L'Homme qui marche* (Casterman, 1995) and *Au Temps du Botchan* (Seuil, 2003). Similarly, Ego Comme X, a small publisher that specializes in autobiographical comics, translated the work of Yoshiharu Tsuge (*L'Homme sans talent,* 2003) and Kazuichi Hanawa (*Dans la Prison,* 2003), expanding the parameters of their own specialization across geographic and cultural boundaries. Thus, Japanese artists with particularly 'European' or 'global' sensibilities were championed by the small presses as a counter to the hegemony of Japanese genre material. Profiled in *Beaux Arts Magazine,* Tsuge and Taniguchi became the Japanese faces of the European small-press comics revolution.

The example of American comics in Europe is more mixed. The translation of American comics has a long history in Europe, dating back to the importation of American daily newspaper strips in the 1920s. While translations of the bestselling American comic books, superhero comics, have long been a staple of several European nations, these works tended to exist on the periphery of the comics market, popular among fans with a specialized interest. Further, the creators of superhero comics were generally not accommodated by the European small-press publishers and creators, who saw those works as crassly commercial products of mass culture, and an Americanized form of mass culture at that. At the same time, however, creators working within the American example of the small-press comics movement were regarded as kindred spirits or important trailblazers. Certainly, the artists associated with the American underground and post-underground comics movements, from Robert Crumb to Art Spiegelman, are seen as central figures in the European small-press comics renaissance. Similarly, dozens of more contemporary artists (Julie Doucet, Seth, Chester Brown, Joe Matt, Chris Ware, Adrian Tomine, Dan Clowes, Peter Bagge, Debbie Drechsler, Charles Burns, Joe Sacco, Jim Woodring, James Kochalka, Dylan Horrocks, among many others) have had their work translated by the publishers associated with the small-press comics explosion since the 1990s.

Because of the close aesthetic relationship these artists have with European comics circles, the United States is seen in some ways as simply another European comics nation, with works moving back and forth in a form of international exchange. This interchange has been bolstered in recent years by international co-publications which serve to reduce the production costs of a book (particularly full-colour books) by printing it simultaneously in a number of languages for a variety of publishers in different nations. By gang-printing books and altering only the final black plate (which includes the lettering), small-press publishers are able to achieve an economy of scale that they would not otherwise approach. One impact of this process is a wider availability of inexpensive editions of work in a number of countries, particularly as the reduced printing costs will often convince a publisher to take a risk on a potentially marginal work. A second is the increasing cultural cross-pollination that occurs when publishers are obliged to seek international partnerships and thus expose each other to works that they might not otherwise consider.

Nonetheless, it is clear that significant differences between the comics communities of the United States and Europe persist. Because it grows out of a tradition in which comics were published as monthly magazine pamphlets, the American comic book market has been more resistant to the idea of comics as books, with publishers such as NBM often opting to pre-serialize works that were published as stand-alone books in Europe. Further, while fanzine comics were quite widespread in the United States in the 1980s and 1990s, the type of innovative artisanal publications produced by Drozophile or BüLB are much more rare, appearing only in the 2000s (the Jordan Crane–edited *Non,* the Sammy Harkham–edited *Kramer's Ergot*), following on the heels of European challenges to the notion of the comics 'book.' The other significant difference, however, resides at the level of cultural impact. Historically, the American comics market has been reluctant to embrace non-superhero comics. This reluctance has extended to all corners of the market, with even ultra-popular European comics such as *Astérix* and *Tintin* struggling in the American market (significantly, André Franquin, one of the best-selling European cartoonists of all time, has had only one book translated into English).

In the American small-press or alternative comics market the situation is less pronounced, but still evident. Aside from Marjane Satrapi, few European cartoonists of the small-press movement have fared as well in the United States as they have in their own country, and some have been visible failures in the American market. Thus, the United States exists for many cartoonists as a potential publishing space not yet open to them, often despite successes in a variety of European nations and languages. From this standpoint, it is possible to imagine that the field of European comics production is more open and fluid. Yet the reality is that a large number of barriers exist within Europe as well. The most visible of these continues to be linguistic, with barriers to communication structuring the way comics are received in various national contexts. It is through the challenge of translation and the linguistic difficulty of language that the effect of the literary contribution to the comics form can be seen most clearly. Interestingly, a large number of cartoonists have begun the process of thinking past translation through an increased focus on visual techniques, which mitigate international cultural differences by allowing comics to circulate as visual art rather than as literature.

A comic book like *Bardín Baila con la más fea* (Medio Muerto, 2000) can only be understood as a product of the increasing globalization of the small-press comic book renaissance of the 1990s. The book tells the story of a danse macabre dreamt by the comic book character, Bardín el Superrealista. Written and partially drawn by the Spanish cartoonist Max, and based upon the character whose adventures he began publishing in 1999, the book is co-authored by seventy-seven additional artists from thirteen countries, including the likes of Jessica Abel, Hendrik Dorgathen, Matti Hagelberg, Batia Kolton, Gunnar Lundkvist, Peter Pontiac, and Charles Burns. Each of these collaborating artists contributes a single image in their own distinct style, and each image follows upon the one that precedes it. Narratively, this is a large-scale joint project that informs its surreal dream logic through the constant shifting of visual modes. Yet, more than this, the book functions as a sort of catalogue of small-press cartoonists working on the same subject matter and with the same visual referents. Given the diversity of visual approaches that characterizes the contemporary small-press comics scene, the book offers a rare opportunity to examine the works of various artists from around the world working in a similar fashion. Ideologically, however, the book functions to consecrate some notion of the internationalization of small-press aesthetics.

The question arises: What do these artists share in terms of aesthetic or ideological outlook that would attract them to participate in a project such as this one? The answer may be less abstract than at first imagined. Is it possible that these artists were compelled to contribute to this project for a simpler reason, such as the fact that they are friends of Max? Connections between artists based on personal relationships are, for the scholar, often difficult to examine and explain. Nonetheless, projects like *Bardín Baila con la más fea* point to the important ways in which the development of the field of comics production has taken shape in relation to personal affinities that have spawned complex transnational networks.

Any starting point for approaching these networks is arbitrary. It would be possible, for example, to begin with L'Association's David B., who scripted stories for a dozen different artists in *Lapin* #10. Moving outward from David B.'s collaborators, to the colleagues of those colleagues, and so on ever outward generates a complex map of the comics field that positions David B. as the nexus. Similar maps could be generated by starting with any of a hundred names, positing each as a new nexus of production. If one begins with an artist like Max, however, the focus can be productively transformed. Because Max exists in a liminal position, alternately on the margins and at the centre of these international developments, the nexus that has formed around him is particularly instructive.

Max began his career as a cartoonist in Spain in the early 1970s, publishing his first work in *El Rrollo enmascarado*. Working under various pseudonyms and in various styles, he published continuously in Spanish underground newspapers in the 1970s before debuting his character Gustavo in the first issue of *El Víbora* (1979), a commercial monthly Spanish-language comics magazine modelled on the French adult comics magazines of the same era. In 1983, his anarchistic character Peter Pank appeared for the first time in the French magazine *Métal hurlant*, and two years later he published two books in France under the name Alphamax (the pseudonym Max was already used by another French cartoonist). He abandoned comics for the more lucrative field of illustration in the late 1980s, ultimately returning to comics in 1993. Inflamed by the war in Bosnia, about which he created two widely translated short stories ('Nosotros somos los muertos,' 1993, and 'Bienvenidos al Infierno,' 1995 [figure 13]), and inspired by many of the artists of the small-press comics movement, Max self-published, with Pere Joan and Emilio Manzano, the fanzine *Nosotros somos los muertos* (1995). In 1995 the self-published fanzine changed to a slicker magazine format, with an increasingly international roster of artists beginning with the second issue. In 1997, he returned to *El Víbora* to produce *El Prolongado Sueño del Sr. T.*, which won a series of international awards.

Internationally, Max's work is known by many names: *Le Rêve prolongé de Mr T.* (L'Association, 1998), *The Extended Dream of Mr D.* (Drawn and Quarterly, 1999), *Der lange traum des Herrn T.* (Reprodukt, 1999), and *Il Lungo Sogno del Signor T.* (Mare Nero, 2000). Each new version of his work extends the international influence of Spanish cartooning, which itself is largely influenced by forces as diverse as the Franco-Belgian adventure tradition and the American undergrounds. At the same time, it is clear that Max's work is highly influenced by the opportunities and connections that are derived from the international nexus in which his career increasingly operates. Thus, for example, his biography in *Dreamspy* (La Cúpula, 2003), a collection of his illustration work, indicates that the turn in his work towards the frequent use of skeletons (evident in *Bardín Baila con la más fea*) stemmed from a 1993 commission for the Fumetto comics festival in Luzern, Switzerland, to decorate the replacement for the fire-destroyed Kappelbrücke. At that time he was exposed to the nearby Spreuerbrücke, and this exposure shaped the development of his work. Similarly, at an exhibition of his work at a comics festival in Porto, Portugal, in 1994, he met Julie Doucet, with whom he has frequently collaborated, and her Canadian publisher, Chris Oliveros, who would

13 Death comes to Sarajevo, in Max, 'Bienvenidos al Infierno.'

publish the English-language edition of *The Extended Dream of Mr D*. To note that any artist's work is shaped by various chance encounters and unpredictable exposures is, of course, to observe nothing new. Nonetheless, in the case of small-press comic book creation, the links established by different local, national, and transnational production contexts, whether in anthologies or comics festivals and art fairs, have served the specific purpose of defining an international movement that works as both an inclusionary and exclusionary force.

This distinction between the artist who is understood differently in a transnational context because his work is incorporated into a wider market for small-press comic books, and the artist whose influence is felt through a series of personal relationships that play out at festivals across Europe and around the world, draws on that made by Ulf Hannerz between the two frames that animate cultural flow: the market and 'form-of-life.'[2] For the comics artist, the market is most active when books enter the arena of commerce. For a figure like Max, this means participating in competing international markets simultaneously and differentially. For example, in Spain, Max is one of the most important contemporary comic book artists, if not the most important. La Cúpula has published eleven volumes in the *Todo Max* collection, a comprehensive reprinting of his oeuvre, and these books compete for shelf space with his own anthology *Nosotros somos los muertos,* collections of illustrations such as *Dreamspy,* and a number of illustrated books. On the other hand, in France, the largest comic book market on the continent, Max has only two books in print. Thus, in countries such as France, Germany, and Italy, where only a small percentage of his work is translated, he remains a more marginal figure who is better known among artists and comic book connoisseurs than by the public at large. In this way, working in a Spanish context permits Max the possibility of widescale recognition in his home country, but the vagaries of translation limit him in other national contexts. Howard Becker argues a similar point about literature:

> Music and visual art use languages that can, in some meaningful sense, be called international. But literature uses one of the world's languages, few of which are mutually intelligible. In practice, only a few Indo-European languages are known in enough countries that literature written in them has any chance of being considered in the global judgments which create international literary reputations. A novelist who writes in French or Spanish will be read more widely and have a better chance for an international

reputation than one who writes in Hindi, Tamil, or Swahili. The latter languages are read by millions of people, but not by the people who make international literary reputations ... If your linguistic community is small or unimportant, you cannot have a major reputation.[3]

In the field of comic book production, however, Spanish is not a primary language comparable to French, English, and, increasingly, Japanese. The choice for the individual artist, therefore, is between developing within a national context, working for the international market, or working to internationalize the local context.

An anthology like *Nosotros somos los muertos* represents this third option. Begun as a magazine in 1995, at a period in which the small-press comics renaissance was well underway in France and elsewhere, *Nosotros* was an effort to recreate some sense of the excitement of the contemporary comics movement in Spain at that time. The first issue, however, is largely local. Of the fifteen works, twelve are by Spanish artists, two are by Germans (Anke Feuchtenberger and Hendrik Dorgathen), and one is by the Italian duo of Lilia Ambrosi and Lorenzo Mattotti. Yet each additional issue contained increasing numbers of non-Spanish works, so that, for example, the fifth issue included comics by Stéphane Blanquet, Mattotti and Kramsky, Chris Ware, Max Andersson, Matti Hagelberg, Julie Doucet, Lewis Trondheim, and other non-Spanish cartoonists mixed among pages by Max, Pere Joan, Alex Fito, Laura, and Gallardo.

As with L'Association's *Lapin*, which *Nosotros*'s middle issues resembled in size, shape, and design, the focus was on non-genre works that expressed a unique point of view and demonstrated an unusual approach to the medium. An editorial in the fifth issue, for instance, suggested 'Our premises are clear: comics by authors, of a quality and difficulty that recall the capacity of other publications. The relationship to the market is not definitive. These are terms that make the rounds whose meaning we no longer know exactly: independent, alternative, and similar ideas.'[4] The participation of *Nosotros* within this difficult-to-define movement – independent, alternative, small-press – takes the form of replicating the successes of an anthology like *Lapin* in a new context, even going so far as to reprint works from that anthology. In this way, it is hoped, the enthusiasm of the French scene will be transported to Spain, with one of the few Spanish cartoonists to have crossed into that scene laying a foundation for others from that country.

This market-based possibility is, of course, activated in large measure by the personal relationships that exist between Max and similarly minded cartoonists across Europe. These relationships are particularly facilitated by comic book festivals, which serve, in the European context, to bring disparate publics together. On the one hand, these festivals, which generally feature large exhibitions of rarely seen original comic book art, permit comic book readers to meet with comic book creators. At the same time, however, and more significantly, festivals bring together artists from diverse contexts and place them in a social space where Hannerz's form-of-life, that is to say interpersonal, interactions take place. It is through this type of idea exchange that the small-press comic book scene has developed, with comic book translations and shared projects being only the market-oriented extension of the logic of transnational interchange. Comics festivals, therefore, are among the most important, yet least discussed, aspects of the field.

Hannerz has argued that 'world cities are places in themselves, and also nodes in networks; their cultural organization involves local as well as transnational relationships.'[5] When one thinks of the cultural organization of the comic book field, it is clear that spatially that world is organized into a series of festivals, which themselves become emblematic of core values associated with local comic book production. The ideological space of international comics production is framed by a network of festivals in cities like San Diego, Angoulême, Luzern, Haarlem, and Bethesda. The contemporary comic book festival is a site at which a particular artworld, to use Arthur Danto's term, coalesces for brief periods of time. The comic book festival is the only regular social space in which so many differing aspects of the artworld come together at one time, including writers, artists, editors, publishers, journalists, booksellers, and fans. These events serve to remind us that, romantic images of the garreted cartoonist heroically slaving over inky boards notwithstanding, the production of art is a thoroughly social process. Indeed, the image of the isolated artist is a dangerously misleading one, yet that image more than any other colours our understanding of the creative process and shapes our understanding of comic book production as a communicative form.

Generally speaking, comic book festivals in Europe have been modelled after the salons of nineteenth-century Paris. Indeed, Europe's largest comic book festival (in Angoulême) was once known as the Salon International de la Bande Dessinée until it changed its name in 1996, and the largest festival in Portugal is called Salão Lisboa. The salon is a place to come and see art, and indeed that is what is available at many festivals – a collection of gallery exhibitions focusing on both individual artists and publishing collectives, with a small retail space attached almost as an afterthought rather than as a central function of the event. The broadly social or educative function of the salon, which itself recalls Jurgen Habermas's notion of a rational public space wherein serious issues might be discussed and debated, is conveyed by the choice of names. The choice of the term carries with it associations about the powerful ability of national institutions to generate new forms of understanding. The American term 'convention,' on the other hand, which equally recalls the halcyon days of science fiction fandom and the capital logic of auto manufacturing, signals a congregation of devotees brought together to exchange information and, more importantly, capital.

Growing out of this opposition are two additional distinctions that I would like to make between an event like the San Diego Comic-Con and similar gatherings in Europe. The first of these centres around the relationship between the event and the city. An occasion like the San Diego Comic-Con, the largest comic book convention in the United States, benefits the city of San Diego, and in particular its tourism industry. At the same time, however, it is clear that the city itself has had little to do with the success of the convention over the years. The Comic-Con was started by a small group of dedicated fans and has grown over the course of decades without the direct involvement of the municipal government. This is not generally the case in Europe. Events like Salão Lisboa in Portugal and Fumetto in Luzern, Switzerland, rely heavily on state sponsorship. The success of these gatherings is completely reliant on the sense that comics are an important, albeit minor, aspect of the public sphere and that consequently they deserve access to traditional forms of arts funding.

In a town such as Angoulême civic support runs much deeper. The Festival International de la Bande Dessinée derives significant funding – in the millions of euros – from all levels of government. The Festival is a core part of Angoulême's promotional self-image. The town calls itself the city of festivals, has incorporated word balloons onto all of its street signs as distinctive markers, and in 2003 renamed the main commercial thoroughfare Rue Hergé, in honour of the Belgian creator of Tintin. It is clear that civic support for the ninth art places European comics production in a different social space than American comics. While comics communities exist as counter-publics in both locales, in many places in Europe comics are more closely integrated into the dominant public sphere.

The other significant difference between comic book conventions and comic book festivals revolves around the relationship of art and commerce. At a typical European festival the visitor is confronted with a wide variety of exhibitions, from as few as a half-dozen to more than twenty. Typically at American comics conventions, whether San Diego Comic-Con, Chicago's Wizard World, or Bethesda, Maryland's Small Press Expo, there are few or no art exhibitions. At the same time, European festivals tend to play down the role of commerce, which is more central at American conventions. Lisbon and Luzern each have small areas set aside for a single retailer to sell books, somewhat akin to a museum bookstore. Angoulême, the largest of the European festivals and the one most often derided for its crass commercialism, splits its available space roughly equally between exhibitions and publisher booths, with a very small area available to second-hand booksellers on the final two days of the event. San Diego, by contrast, offers little to see in the way of original art and dedicates the vast majority of its space to second-hand booksellers and publisher booths. The distinction between the two modes was suggested by Olivier Jalabert of the Angoulême Festival, discussing his trip to San Diego in 2005: 'It seems to me that Angoulême is much more anchored in artistic creation and culture. At the San Diego Comic-Con the smell of all that business is very clear, perfectly assumed by all of the participants, including the general public. Marketing, after all, completely forms part of the basic culture of the Americans.'[6]

As Jalabert notes, these distinctions help structure the orientation of the artworld, which is largely reflected by the elements of social organization that it chooses to minimize and those it chooses to promote. Moreover, the European festival model, with its focus on art exhibitions, has transformed the field in a way that American conventions have not. Specifically, the exhibition model calls for a celebration of artists whose work can be presented in a visually dynamic fashion to large crowds. This has had the effect of elevating small-press and avant-garde cartoonists, whose works are most akin to the traditions of painting, sculpture, and other consecrated visual arts, to a status above that which is accorded them by the market. The desire of festival organizers to produce a visually engaging exhibition experience goes hand in hand with the turn towards visuality in the small-press comics movement of the 1990s.

The specific example of Fumetto in Luzern draws attention to the specific ways in which comics are mobilized in a secondary European market. Switzerland generally occupies a marginal space in European comics. As a mixed-language nation, Switzerland's comics production has largely been bifurcated. On the one hand, many French-speaking cartoonists, including Daniel Ceppi, Cosey, Derib, and Zep, have had strong careers working for the traditional Franco-Belgian publishing houses, and these cartoonists are easily subsumed into the larger francophone market in which regionalism is not a particular concern. Additionally, in the unique political system of French-speaking Geneva, in which there is frequent voting, the parties of the political left have long relied upon young illustrators to create innovative and eye-catching campaign posters that stand out on city walls. This has created a social space in which young artists can find well-paid work, thus providing a milieu for cutting-edge publishers such as BüLB, Drozophile, and Atrabile.

On the other hand, German-speaking Swiss cartoonists are not as easily integrated into that market, and few of them are widely published by the large editors. The small press, with its focus on internationalism as an ideal, changed the situation significantly by publishing German-speaking Swiss cartoonists, such as Thomas Ott and Anna Sommer, across Europe, and by facilitating the creation of new indigenous small-press publishers in Geneva, such as Drozophile and BüLB. As an event around which the Swiss comics scene, particularly the Swiss-German scene, is mobilized, Fumetto performs an important role in shaping a sense of national or regional identity in comics.

Fumetto began in 1992 as a small event. Founded in a youth centre, the first festival featured an art competition, an exhibition of Swiss comic art, a speech, a film, and a concert.[7] Beginning with a local orientation, the festival added venues and sponsors over the years, eventually developing a full-time staff to deal with its expansion. By 2003 the name had changed from Luzern Comix Festival to something which more accurately reflected the new size and scope of the undertaking – Internationales Comix-Festival Luzern, which describes itself as 'one of Europe's most artistically ambitious festivals.'[8] Running over a period of two weeks each spring, the festival stages dozens of art exhibits at spaces around the downtown core of the city and also holds lectures, book signings, concerts, and films. According to the festival's website, the event is organized annually around four principles:

- Fumetto is the most important comic event in Switzerland and a trendsetter in Europe.
- Fumetto encourages young comic art and gives the impulse for modern comic works.
- Fumetto is a forum on the fine line of all comic related forms of expression.

- Fumetto is a meeting place to discover and experience both national and international comic trends.[9]

Of particular interest in this context is the festival's focus on national and international trends within a framework of 'modern comic works.' In practice, for example, Fumetto pays attention to Swiss cartooning in a number of ways. Exhibitions of the work of Swiss comic book publishers have been a mainstay of the festival, including retrospectives of the work of BüLB (Nicolas Robel, Frederik Peeters, Ibn al Rabin, Andreas Kündig, and others) in 1999, Drozophile in 2000, and a twenty-year retrospective of the Zurich-based German-language publisher Edition Moderne in 2001. Alternately, a significant number of Swiss cartoonists have also been the subject of solo exhibitions at the festival, including Anna Sommer (1999), M.S. Bastian (2001), and Thomas Ott (2002). At the same time, the festival has presented several group shows related to Swiss comics, including a focus on young cartoonists in 2002 (including Grrr, Fix, and Mickey Drei) and female cartoonists in 2001 (including Isabelle Pralong, Nadia Raviscioni, Nadine Spengler, and Anna Sommer). These and other exhibitions have defined a particular Swiss comics identity at the festival and, moreover, have helped to place that identity in dialogue with a large number of similar movements that exist internationally.

Despite the diversity of the exhibitions staged at Fumetto each year, it is nonetheless clear that certain selection principles activate the choices. The mixture of international solo and group exhibitions tends to break participants into two broad camps: star artists and artists who belong to larger comics movements. Beginning with the latter, Fumetto tends to privilege artists from the small-press comics movement to which it is partly a response. Thus, for example, the festival has presented exhibitions of noteworthy small-press publishers, including France's Le Dernier Cri (1999 and 2005), Hong Kong's Cockroach (2000), and Canada's Drawn and Quarterly (2001).

Similarly, large-scale comic-book-related undertakings have been the subject of retrospective presentations intended to highlight the specificities of certain books. In 2000, for instance, L'Association's *Comix 2000* was the subject of an exhibition, and in 2003 the festival presented an OuBaPo exhibition, with work by Jean-Christophe Menu, François Ayroles, Killoffer, Jochen Gerner, and other artists connected with the publisher's experimental comics workshop. In 2001, the festival exhibited pages from the anthology *Letter to a Dead Friend* (Colomba Urbana, 2001), which itself was the specific result of personal interactions between four artists who had participated at the 2000 edition of the festival. In 2000, Markus Huber and Katja Tukiainen were both exhibited as part of the Independent show, focusing on independent comics production. Lily Lau Lee Lee participated in the exhibition of works from Hong Kong published by Cockroach, and Tobi Gaberthuel took part in an exhibition of young Swiss cartoonists Der wicht. Together, these four artists agreed to create a series of short works as comic book letters to friends who had passed away. The collected results were published by a small Zurich-based press and distributed by the established German-language comic book publisher Edition Moderne, with the book's original art displayed at the subsequent festival. A project such as this forcefully demonstrates Hannerz's conception of transnational cultural production existing at the level of face-to-face interaction and, subsequently, in the space of the market for cultural goods. Moreover, it highlights the way comics festivals are productive social spaces in which cartoonists from around the world are given the opportunity to network and exchange ideas and working possibilities.

While Fumetto has consistently highlighted local comics production and group undertakings, the festival is also well known for presenting international guests of a privileged stature. Over the years, the guests of honour at the festival have included José Muñoz, Edmond Baudoin, David Mazzuchelli, Miguelanxo Prado, Chris Ware, Baru, Atak, Charles Burns, Dupuy and Berberian, Max, and David B. Other solo exhibitions have included the work of Bernd Pfarr, Lewis Trondheim, Anke Feuchtenberger, David Sandlin, Joe Sacco, Jason, Jim Avignon, Nicolas Mahler, Gary Panter, Marjane Satrapi, and Willem. Collectively, these artists are considered the superstars of the small-press comics explosion of the past decade. While some of these artists – Panter, Burns, Willem, Baru, Muñoz – despite their ongoing productivity, represent a previous generation that was inspirational to the small-press movement of the 1990s, collectively the group resembles a collection of some of the biggest stars in the author-driven comics movement. When Fumetto speaks of 'modern comic works,' these artists are synonymous with the modernizing movement that has shaped the development of the field over the course of nearly two decades. Stripped, by the necessities of the solo exhibition, from national contexts, these artists – whose works have been widely translated across Europe and around the world – come to occupy a position beyond the local as transnational comic book super-stars. Interestingly, almost every artist who has been the subject of a solo exhibition at this German-language festival is widely published in French,

English, or both, and often not particularly widely in German. Of the list above, only Feuchtenberger, Atak, Mahler, and Pfarr are native German speakers, and of these only Pfarr remains significantly better known in German-speaking Europe than in France. Thus, it is clear that even in the German-speaking parts of Switzerland, stardom requires a degree of external validation in a larger international comics market.

Of course, there is also a mediating level between the 'young comic art' that Fumetto explicitly champions and the international guest star. The national star, a position occupied at Fumetto by figures like Ott, Sommer, and Bastian, is, in fact, an international star in the making. If we recall Becker's argument about writing in minor languages, it is easy to see that because of France's hegemonic status within the European comics field, French comics artists are best positioned to emerge as international stars – first, by being recognized as innovative and important within the French context and, second, through exportation to less well-established comics cultures. For artists from smaller comic book industries – such as Denmark's, Greece's, or Austria's – the difficulty of earning international recognition is significantly pronounced, often requiring success at the local level, then in France, then internationally. The Norwegian cartoonist Jason is an example of a cartoonist whose books became significantly better appreciated only after they were translated into French (by Atrabile) and English (by Fantagraphics) than when they appeared in Norwegian (from Jippi Forlag), even though much of the work is wordless.

One route around this dilemma, although it does not solve the problem entirely, is to highlight different national cartooning traditions. For Fumetto, this tendency has been realized in exhibitions dedicated to cartoonists from, for example, Portugal (2003) and South Africa (2004). Further, the festival collaborates with *Strapazin,* the long-running Swiss-German comics anthology, to produce special issues based on the comics of these nations, which act as an introduction of sorts for cartoonists working on the margins of the field. For example, the March 2003 issue of *Strapazin* is dedicated to Portuguese comics and features the works of Pedro Burgos, Alain Corbel and Pedro Rosa Mendes, André Carrilho, Filipe Abranches, Isabel Carvalho, João Fazenda, Rui Ricardo and Paulo Patrício, and Pedro Nora, few of which had previously been translated into German but most of which were exhibited at that year's Fumetto festival.

Portugal has one of the least internationalized comics cultures in Europe. Despite a lengthy history in the medium, the work of Portuguese artists remains relatively little known outside of that country. Clearly, the fact that Portuguese is not a widely spoken language across Europe has contributed to this sense of isolation. Further, Portugal – like Spain, Italy, and Germany – does not have the large network of comic book specialty shops that are requisite for the development of a large fan and collector culture that supports innovative or new works. Portugal does, however, have a significant support system that exists in the form of comic book festivals in Lisbon, Porto, and Amadora, as well as a national comics library in Lisbon, the Bedeteca, that is funded in part by the local government.

Lisbon's biannual comics festival, Salão Lisboa, is, of the three events discussed here, the one that places the greatest emphasis on the small-press comics movement as it exists both within Portugal and around the world. Like Fumetto, Salão Lisboa offers a mixture of exhibitions of local and international cartoonists, grouped around themes. In 2003, for example, an exhibition on military conflicts in comics featured the work of America's Joe Sacco, France's Emmanuel Guibert, and Serbia's Aleksandar Zograf, among others. At the same festival, Slovenia's Stripcore was the featured publisher, exhibiting works from their fanzine *Stripburger*, and Germany was the guest nation. Among the German cartoonists on exhibition were Atak, Anke Feuchtenberger, CX Huth, Martin tom Dieck, and Hennig Wagenbreth. That two of these artists were also the subjects of major retrospectives at Fumetto demonstrates how the concept of artists as international stars is widely shared in different cultural contexts. The 2000 festival, which included the *Comix 2000* exhibition and focused explicitly on what it termed 'the independent revolution' in comics, included works by a large number of stars from the French-language small press, including Edmond Baudoin, Alex Barbier, Yvan Alagbé, Thierry van Hasselt, and Fabrice Neaud. The same festival also included solo exhibitions of the work of Max and Dupuy and Berberian, placing them in the realm of the international comics stars alongside Charles Schulz, who was celebrated for fifty years of the American newspaper strip *Peanuts*.

At the same time, Salão Lisboa, like Fumetto, provides extensive exposure for local cartoonists who are not yet well known internationally. The 2001 festival, for instance, included Portuguese artists Miguel Rocha and Ana Cortesão alongside international artists like Dave McKean, Ben Katchor, and Loustal in an exhibit focusing on music in comics. Similarly, the festival featured works by Filipe Abranches, João Fazenda and Marté, Pedro Nora, and Pedro Brito. By placing these artists in the same spaces as better-known international artists, the curators seek to define Portuguese comic book creation in sympathy with other national traditions. By defining Portuguese comics as akin to those that are more celebrated elsewhere, Salão Lisboa presents an argument for the importance of local production, even though this festival is seen primarily by Portuguese visitors. Thus, Portugal's internationalization takes place almost entirely within a resolutely local space.

A similar internationalizing tendency can be found in many secondary comics markets across Europe in the production of comic book anthologies. The success of anthologies like *Lapin* inspired many artists to develop like-minded efforts aimed at galvanizing local production. As Benedict Anderson has pointed out, it was in large part the commoditization of the printed word that made it possible for growing numbers of people to recognize that there were others like themselves beyond their immediate community. Following this line of thinking, it is possible to suggest that the creators and consumers of comics constitute a shared community, or what Anderson terms 'a deep, horizontal comradeship.'[10] In the field of comics, this comradeship defines a shared, transnational, aesthetic disposition rather than a nation-state. Thus, in response to anthologies like *Lapin*, cartoonists, editors, and publishers working in a variety of contexts have sought to create magazines and anthologies that respond in some way to the call for renewal issued by L'Association.

In Portugal, the Bedeteca in Lisbon, which published a thick, square, bound anthology comic entitled *Quadrado*, undertook this call for renewal. Tied in part, like *Strapazin*, to the comics festival, *Quadrado* regularly published works by artists exhibited at Salão Lisboa, including Max, David B., Alain Corbel, and Jean-Christophe Menu. Typically, *Quadrado* features a mixture of well-known international comics alongside Portuguese cartoonists, whose work draws upon similar avant-gardist traditions and independent tendencies. A typical issue, such as the third issue in volume three, consists of more than two hundred pages of comics and essays, and features work by almost two dozen international artists (including Gabriella Giandelli, Anke Feuchtenberger, Laura, Phoebe Gloeckner, Debbie Drechsler, Ariel Bordeaux, Renée French, Ellen Forney, Max, Christophe Poot, and Xavier Lowenthal) alongside contributions by a dozen Portuguese artists. This ratio, which dramatically privileges translations of international works, marks *Quadrado* as an anthology primarily concerned with publishing significant works from the small-press comics movement for a Portuguese audience without necessarily including local works that might be perceived to exist at a less lofty aesthetic plane.

Other Portuguese anthologies, however, represent different ambitions. *Satélite internacional,* for example, is an innovative small-press anthology that changes formats with each issue, one printed oversize, another printed on bright pink paper. Publishing comics and essays in both English and Portuguese, the anthology's 'alingual' stance leads, ironically, to a greater percentage of Portuguese authors. While the first three issues feature works by Atak, Martin tom Dieck, Ron Regé, Megan Kelso, and Olivier Deprez, they also publish significantly more work by Portuguese artists. Similarly, an anthology like *Para Além dos Olivais* (2000), published by the Bedeteca in association with the city of Lisbon, offers a slickly produced indigenous collection of works by Portuguese artists, many in full colour. The book, which focuses on the Lisbon neighbourhood in which the Bedeteca is located, points to the possibility of producing highly focused works for local constituencies that are nonetheless rooted in a particularly regional vision of an increasingly transnational creative movement. These three anthologies, which offer differing levels of integration between Portuguese and international artists, suggest the various possibilities open to magazine publishers in light of the changing field of comic book production across Europe today. That Portugal is able to support two small-press comics anthologies with high-end production values, as well as a large number of fanzine publications of varying quality, indicates that the small-press comics revolution has created possibilities for young cartoonists both within their home countries and, increasingly, abroad.

Similarly, many cartoonists in northern Europe – an area where linguistic difference and geography have created a separate cartooning climate – have seized upon the opportunities presented by the small-press movement in order to expand their influence in the field. In 1997, NordiComics, in association with the Nordic Council, published an anthology (in both English and French editions) entitled *Gare du nord,* a title whose nod to the Paris train station acknowledges the dominance of France within the contemporary comics field. The anthology features the work of thirty-six cartoonists from Finland, Norway, Sweden, Denmark, and Iceland, most of whom were little known in southern Europe at the time of its publication. While not all of the artists in the anthology shared the small-press aesthetic, it is clear nonetheless that many did. Writing in the introduction, Rolf Classon suggested that there was nothing intrinsically Nordic about the contributions to the book:

We found nothing specifically Nordic, and our only criterion became that of high quality.

If one is to generalize anyway, it can be said in broad terms that the Danish contributions were semi-pornographic action comics, the Norwegian, humorous and philosophical benders, the Finnish, inscrutable, madcap anarchist adventures, and the Swedish, absurd satires in a vein of folksy humor.

No, there is no specific trend in contemporary Nordic comics, but there does exist a very vital and original generation of creators.[11]

Nonetheless, the book does tend to provide some degree of national specificity to each nation's comic book scene, defined broadly within a northern framework. Moreover, it is clear that while some comics scenes in the north have become increasingly influential, a transnational outlook continues to predominate. This tension can be particularly witnessed in reference to cartoonists working in Finland.

A number of Finnish cartoonists have made names for themselves on the international comics scene in recent years, often overcoming the fact that their work is produced in a language that is almost completely unspoken outside of their home country. Finland, which has hosted a national comics festival in Helsinki since the early 1980s, produces a wide array of small-press comics and fanzines, many of which share talent. This has led to a comics scene that is particularly integrated in comparison with other national comics communities. The tension that exists in Finnish comics anthologies is generally between the production of high-quality work for the local market and a desire to export that same work. By the late 1990s, for example, Finland was producing full-colour, glossy comics albums featuring entirely indigenous productions. The fourth issue of *Sarja Kuvastin* (Otava, 1998), for instance, includes stories by sixteen Finnish cartoonists, each of whom works through a small-press aesthetic. The range of productions that characterizes Finnish small-press comics production, from the naturalistic to the experimentally avant-garde, differs little from other European nations, except insofar as the Finnish comics scene is considerably more restricted than that of other countries. Thus, it is possible to map a high degree of overlap between small-press comics anthologies that otherwise might be regarded as distinct: *Sarja Kuvastin* features Kati Kovács, Pentti Otsamo, Johanna Rojola (Roju), and Katja Tukiainen. *Suuri Kurpitsa* includes the work of Otsamo, Kovács, Tukiainen, Kati Rapia, and Jenni Rope. *Napa*, which is edited by Rope and Jussi Karjalainen, has contributions from

Kovács, Rapia, Rojola, and Tukiainen. The high degree of circularity among these magazines underlines the image of Finnish comics as highly insular and ideologically aligned towards the same goals, despite the fact that significant differences appear between publishers in terms of design, focus, and overall quality.

Owing to the question of linguistic difference, Finnish comic book publishers have come to terms quickly with their place in the global comics field. As with the Portuguese publishers, Finnish comics editors have positioned local comics production on a global stage by incorporating the work of non-Finns in their anthologies to act as markers of ideological and aesthetic affinity. Thus, for example, *Suuri Kurpitsa* has translated the work of artists like Ulf K., Julie Doucet, Anna Sommer, José Parrondo, and Adrian Tomine, while *Napa* has included pieces by Killoffer, Anna Sommer, Martin tom Dieck, and Caroline Sury. Interestingly, while a magazine like *Quadrado* incorporates some notion of the canonical European small press in its offerings, and positions local comics producers alongside that material, an anthology like *Napa* makes much more selective use of this non-Finnish material. Further, the pieces selected by *Napa* have a much clearer association with Finland than the pieces in *Quadrado* do with Portugal. Killoffer's work, which appears in the second and third issues, consists of two short stories (originally published in *Lapin*) that detail time that he spent in Finland. Thus, it seems that the self-presentation of the Finnish comics field is considerably more nationally delimited than are many other marginal comic book scenes.

Nonetheless, Finnish publishers have made an important, and interesting, concession to globalizing market forces. Recognizing that few readers are likely to pick up Finnish as a second language, these publishers have increasingly made their material – even among the smallest presses and at the fanzine level – available to readers by the inclusion of English translations packaged within the anthology. *Napa*, for example, began by presenting comics in Finnish, but included a pull-out insert containing a complete translation of the issue in English so that the dialogue could be read by English-language readers by turning from the printed book to the translation guide. When this method proved less than ideal, *Napa* began, with the fourth issue (2000), to include the English text on the printed page in small type, not unlike subtitles in film. This same technique has been adopted by the anthology *Laikku*. By subtitling these works, the publishers signal a disposition that is particularly outward looking. Presumably, few comics readers in Finland require

English translations of the work, and thus the subtitles exist simply as a means of connecting Finnish cartooning to a larger international network in the hopes of creating Finnish cartooning stars on a global stage.

Finnish cartoonists are, of course, best known internationally in the north, where their work circulates as semi-local. The third issue of the Swedish anthology *Allt för Konsten* (Optimal, 2002), for example, includes the work of Matti Hagelberg, Otsamo, and Tukiainen, alongside cartoonists from Sweden, Norway, and Iceland. Of all Finnish cartoonists, these three are in many ways the best positioned for international stardom, as each has been widely translated and is representative of a significant trend in small-press cartooning generally. Otsamo, for example, has been translated into English by Drawn and Quarterly on several occasions, including the stand-alone graphic novel *The Fall of Homunculus* (1998). Otsamo's work, which is slowly paced and naturalistic, focuses on small moments in contemporary city life. Hagelberg, on the other hand, produces work that is radically non-traditional. Featuring large, blockish, and highly stylized figures amid non-representational settings, the work is often more illustratorly than narrative. Hagelberg has been translated into English by Fantagraphics in the anthology *Blab!* and is widely published in French by both Le Dernier Cri and L'Association. Tukiainen's work is more traditionally linear than Hagelberg's but is no less experimental in terms of visual form. Drawn in boldly colourful painting and non-traditional panels and lettering, her work stretches the traditional conception of comics by incorporating elements of both painting and children's book illustrations. Tukiainen's comics have been published in French by L'Association and Le Dernier Cri, and in English in the anthologies *Rosetta* and *New Thing*. In particular, Hagelberg and Tukiainen have contributed to the image of Finnish cartooning as a hotbed of non-traditional story structures and illustration styles that challenge the limits of the field. At the same time, however, it appears clear that it is not possible for cartoonists working in a comics culture as marginal as Finland's to achieve fame within the broader international context without the benefit of translation, no matter how innovative or important the work.

Existing closer to the international comics mainstream, Italy produced some of the most recognized cartoonists of the 1970s and 1980s generations. In particular, Milo Manara became well known throughout Europe and in the United States for his tightly rendered adventure and erotic comics, which were widely translated and celebrated for their 'adult' sensibilities. Lorenzo Mattotti, on the other hand, was a significant precursor of the new comics renaissance of the 1990s. Working in a variety of media and styles from ink to pastels, Mattotti created albums featuring strong mythic and symbolic elements free of many of the narrative and formal conventions of the comic book series that characterized the 1980s. As such, he was an important forerunner in the development of an explicitly visualist international comics movement. By the 1990s, Mattotti was creating long-form graphic novels akin to small-press productions for the French book publisher Seuil and published smaller books with the avant-gardist Amok.

Despite the successes of these artists, the indigenous Italian comic book scene was not particularly strong with regard to small-press or art comics. The Bonelli group, who produce comics in a particular style, dominates Italian comic book publishing. Released as a series of ninety-six-page black and white volumes (with colour covers), the Bonelli books are stand-alone adventure stories featuring the exploits of a single character. The series, which are always named for the lead, feature rotating artists, each producing one monthly volume in the series before beginning another. These mass-produced serials feature an array of characters and genres, from the western (*Tex*) to science fiction (*Nathan Never*) and horror (*Dylan Dog*) in potentially never-ending adventures. For instance, Tex, who was created in 1948 by writer Giovanni Luigi Bonelli and artist Aurelio Galleppini, has appeared in his own monthly adventure for more than a half-century, totalling more than 500 individual stand-alone books and more than 50,000 pages. The pre-eminence of the Bonelli style, coupled with the fact that many artists working outside this tradition have found their greatest success in France, meant that there was little opportunity for cartoonists hoping to explore other possibilities.

Nonetheless, the small-press comics explosion of the 1990s created a space in which Italian cartoonists could begin to create their own niche, largely in relation to the work that was taking place in France and elsewhere. In 2001, Igort, an Italian cartoonist who has been publishing comics since the late 1970s, launched *Black,* a new magazine inspired by both the American post-underground comics scene and the contemporary European small press. The first issue, subtitled 'underground: europa chiama america,' was a 240-page volume printed primarily in black and white but with some two-colour pages. The issue contained the works of many of the most prominent figures in the contemporary Italian smallpress comics scene (Stefano Ricci, Andrea Bruno, Francesca Ghermandi, and Leila Marzocchi) in addition to a number of notable international figures (David B., Seth, and David Mazzuchelli). Subsequent issues have added an array of international small-press comics superstars, including Charles Burns, Dan Clowes, Adrian Tomine, Baru, Emmanuel Guibert, Jason Lutes, Loustal, as well as lesser-known small-press authors such as François Ayroles and Matt Broersma. The combination of extremely well-known international cartoonists, many appearing in Italian for the first time, and the cutting edge of the Italian small press recalls the strategy undertaken by anthologies such as *Quadrado* and *Nosotros somos los muertos* of situating local comics production within a broader international context. This strategy, of incorporating elements of the comics metropole in order to subsume the cultural capital for the hinterlands, is taken to another level by Igort, whose Coconino Press has emerged as one of the most expansive of contemporary small-press publishers.

Featuring more than forty artists in their roster, Coconino Press stands as one of the quintessential international small-press comics operations. Publishing artists from the United States, Canada, Europe, and Japan, Coconino presents Italian editions of a large number of the most important and influential small-press comics works of the contemporary period. Among the artists whose books they have translated are French artists such as Jacques Tardi, David B., Joann Sfar, Frédéric Boilet, and Emmanuel Guibert; Japanese cartoonists like Suehiro Maruo, Kazumasa Takayama, Jiro Taniguchi, and Yoshihiro Tatsumi; and Americans James Sturm, Dan Clowes, Craig Thompson, and Charles Burns. The works of these artists cover the range of topics common to the small press – slice-of-life stories, autobiography, and historical work. At the same time, Coconino has published a series of sketchbooks of both established (Andrea Pazienza) and up-and-coming Italian artists. Indeed, the title of Alessandro Pessoli's sketchbook, *Tex Is Dead* (2003), acts as a sort of promise and threat in relation to the dominance of the Bonelli comics tradition in Italy.

All of this work serves as a context in which the production of Italian cartoonists can be better understood. Artists like Leila Marzocchi (*L'Enigma*, 2001), Gipi (*Esterno Notte*, 2003), and Igort himself are seen to exist within a publishing milieu that is akin to comics movements taking place across Europe, in the United States, and Japan simultaneously. Further, collecting these works together in a single volume minimizes national differences in favour of a conception of the small-press comics community that exists beyond linguistic barriers. Insofar as a Japanese, French, or Canadian cartoonist can be read as a part of Italy's comic book culture, it is presumed that these kinds of works exist as a global literature and the movement as worldwide. To this degree, the promise of a book like L'Association's *Comix 2000* is enacted, if only at the level of the most prominent international artists.

The notion of an international comic book community that is structured by an editorial vision like that of Coconino, is extended even further by an anthology such as *Mano*. Edited by Stefano Ricci and Giovanna Ansechi, *Mano* self-published five large annual volumes before entering the Coconino catalogue in 2001. Subtitled 'fumetti scritti designi,' *Mano* was an international anthology that placed equal emphasis on Italian and non-Italian cartoonists but which placed them within a context of aesthetic exploration long held to be the domain of the fine arts. For example, the second issue (1996) featured the work of a large contingent of Italian avant-garde cartoonists, including Igort, Gabriella Giandelli, Ricci, and Mattotti. In addition, the magazine contains contributions from Art Spiegelman, David Mazzuchelli, and Aleksandar Zograf. To this end, *Mano* #2 is not particularly different from other comics anthologies on the outskirts of the European small-press comics scene. What sets *Mano* apart, however, are contributions from non-cartoonists, whose work serves to illuminate the field of comics and place the independent movement within the framework of high modernism. Thus, this issue contains works by traditional fine artists like Louise Bourgeois and Alex Katz, writers like Peter Handke, and filmmakers Chris Marker and Gianluigi Toccafondo. Subsequent issues included contributions from artists such as Alberto Giacometti, Edward Hopper, Antonin Artaud, William Kentridge, Raymond Pettibon, and Rosmarie Trockel, as well as text pieces by writers like Jean-Luc Godard, Gilles Deleuze, Raymond Queneau, and William S. Burroughs. The inclusion of artists not traditionally associated with the comic book field in a magazine that is largely, but not exclusively, dedicated to the presentation of comic books, serves to dislocate cultural assumptions about the respective status of the various forms. *Mano* begins with the straightforward assumption that comics can be regarded as simply a combination of words and images. The logical result of this assumption is the incorporation of significant text and image pieces within the context of the comics field, but this is very rarely actualized in practice. By situating the international comics avant-garde (*Mano* has published, among others, Anke Feuchtenberger, David B., Frédéric Poincelet, Yvan Alagbé, Martin tom Dieck, and Max) within the larger fabric of twentieth-century modernism, *Mano* creates a space in which it is possible to conceptualize comics existing as a legitimate field that functions like the more traditional fine arts. This is accomplished not only by extending the comics field beyond local contingencies to the transnational, but by incorporating a more encompassing sense of the place of comics within the general field of culture. This possibility is engendered, I would suggest, by the restructuring of the comic book field in the 1990s, which has created models for local production that facilitate the intersection of national tendencies on an increasingly international stage.

The tension between national comic book traditions and the transnational cultural marketplace will continue to play out in the field of comic book production. Indeed, it is possible to point towards a large number of comic book publishers in countries with traditionally marginal comic book industries that are building catalogues of national and international artists to rival Coconino or L'Association (Sinse Ntido in Spain, Reprodukt in Germany). Discussing the internationalization of culture, Ulf Hannerz writes:

> There is now a world culture, but we had better make sure we understand what this means: not a replication of uniformity but an organization of diversity, an increasing interconnectedness of varied local cultures, as well as a development of cultures without a clear anchorage in any one territory. And to this interconnected diversity people can relate in different ways. For one thing, there are cosmopolitans, and there are locals.[12]

The widely translated comic book superstars of the current renaissance, from David B. to Anke Feuchtenberger, are the cosmopolitans. Their work circulates in a variety of contexts, and they travel widely to festivals and exhibitions, where their fame is augmented. Their successes are held to be exemplary of what can be accomplished within the comics field, but at the same time they are potentially cautionary tales, insofar as the small press might be read as a space in which a different international aesthetic orthodoxy has merely supplanted the possibility of local outlooks. Depending on one's perspective, the fact that books from La Pastèque, a Montreal-based, French-language, small-press comics publisher, are more widely available in France's big box media stores than they are in English Canada is either a nationalist nightmare or an internationalist dream.

One effect of the transnational global marketplace has been to break down the barriers that have long structured the comics industry. In the twenty-first century, Japanese manga have begun to occupy an increasingly large space within a number of non-Japanese comics cultures, including those of the United States and France/Belgium. The traditional formulation of three comics culture solitudes – the United States, France/Belgium, and Japan – divided by vast oceans and linguistic differences has increasingly begun to break down, as Japanese manga and animé have begun to restructure comic book publishing traditions around the world. Hannerz's suggestion that culture has come unmoored from the specificities of local production and entered an arena of cultural diversity is a vision that provides a compelling hope for the comics field in an era increasingly marked by the exploration of the small-press aesthetic.

Chapter 5

Autobiography as Authenticity

Je dessine les gens pour vivre psychiquement un peu plus à leur côté.
C'est l'inverse du fantasme.

Fabrice Neaud[1]

A three-page short story by Lewis Trondheim published in *Lapin* #26 outlines the stakes at play in contemporary autobiographical comics. Trondheim's autobiographical essay, 'Journal du journal du journal' (figure 14) is a peculiar mise-en-abyme. Trondheim begins by depicting himself reading page 241 of Fabrice Neaud's autobiographical novel *Journal (III)* (Ego Comme X, 1999). On that page, Neaud depicts himself reading Dupuy and Berberian's autobiographical novel *Journal d'un album* (L'Association, 1994), specifically pages 57 through 59. At that point in *Journal d'un album*, Philippe Dupuy depicts a momentous intersection in his personal and professional life. Having chosen, with his partner Charles Berberian, to undertake an autobiographical comic book detailing the creation of the third book in their *M. Jean* series, Dupuy shows a number of early pages to his colleagues in L'Association. Their assessment of the work is rather tough, noting that the work seems to have lost its rhythm and that it could be done more concisely. Returning home, he falls into a despairing dream before being awakened by a phone call from his father informing him that his mother has passed away. The following page encapsulates his mother's life in just six images, recalling the advice that Trondheim offers in the story: 'You could do it in one page.'[2]

Reading this passage in *Journal (III)*, Neaud is impressed by Dupuy's work, but finds himself enraged by the comments offered by the mem-

14 Lewis Trondheim reads Fabrice Neaud reading Philippe Dupuy. From
Lapin #26.

bers of L'Association. He suggests that their inappropriate remarks may be a displacement of their inability to be interested in the lives of other people. Visually, through the use of a non-diegetic intercut, he associates the intemperate observations of the L'Association artists with the dismissive commentaries on his own work that are levelled at him by his close friend and love interest, Dominique, thereby casting aspersions on their motives.

Trondheim's essay is an exact replica of Neaud's page, drawn in Trondheim's style. Visually, the page's seven-panel grid is recreated, and the figures are placed in identical positions. Further, Trondheim duplicates the narration, shifting the details slightly from Neaud's commentary on Dupuy and L'Association, to Trondheim's commentary on Neaud's commentary on Dupuy and L'Association. Where Neaud was shocked at the opinions offered by L'Association on Dupuy's work, Trondheim is shocked that Neaud would make such basic judgments about their roles as editors and publishers. On the second page of Trondheim's essay, which again visually reiterates Neaud's page, he rereads his own first page and finds himself shocked that he would make such a rash judgment of Neaud's work. The work potentially recedes to infinity as Trondheim comments on his own commentary regarding Neaud's commentary on L'Association's comments about Dupuy's self-reflexive work. The game is in play; the text is never finished but always ripe for reinterpretation.

Clearly, Trondheim approaches the question of the autobiographical essay in a satiric and toying manner, playing with the similarities between the titles of the books and the closeness of the content initiated by Neaud. At the same time, however, his work contains a few barbs that suggest it is something more than mere whimsy. Where Neaud depicts Dominique dismissing all autobiographical writing with the phrase '*The Diary of Anne Frank*, that pisses me off. I find it badly written,'[3] Trondheim reacts to L'Association president Jean-Christophe Menu's dismissal of the mainstream genre comics of Jean Van Hamme this way: '*XIII*, that pisses me off. I find it badly written.'[4] This transition re-centres the discussion away from the concerns of autobiography to those of the small press. This is an entirely apt displacement. Since the beginning of the 1990s, autobiography has become an increasingly prominent genre within the small-press and independent comics scene, with strengths in a number of European nations. Indeed, autobiography has become the genre that most distinctly defines the small-press comics production of

Europe in its current revitalization. Specifically, a number of cartoonists have made the narrativization of comic book production a central signifier of authenticity in the contemporary European small-press scene.

Central to the study of autobiography has been the project of defining it as a genre distinct from biography and fiction. Philippe Lejeune's often-cited definition of the genre is widely regarded as normative: 'Retrospective prose narrative written by a real person concerning his own existence, where the focus is his individual life, in particular the story of his personality.'[5] Lejeune's definition has, of course, opened up a number of challenges, and the policing of the boundaries of autobiography in relation to other literary forms has become a major undertaking. Indeed, it is fair to say that the study of autobiography is dominated by inquiries into the particular traits of autobiography and comparisons between autobiography and other literary forms.[6] Paul de Man, writing in 1979, indicated how these assumptions had driven the study of autobiography down a dead end:

> The theory of autobiography is plagued by a recurrent series of questions and approaches that are not simply false, in the sense that they take for granted assumptions about autobiographical discourse that are in fact highly problematic. They keep therefore being stymied, with predictable monotony, by sets of problems that are inherent in their own use. One of these problems is the attempt to define and to treat autobiography as if it were a literary genre among others.[7]

For de Man and others, theories of psychoanalysis, post-structuralism, and feminism have called into question the self-evident nature of the subject and knowledge. Post-structuralism in particular had deposed the unified subject of autobiography by positing discourse as preceding and exceeding the subject, calling the very basis of the genre's distinctiveness into question.[8] Nonetheless, the study of autobiography continues to dwell upon the questions that de Man sought to vacate, often complicating notions of 'truth' and 'self' in light of current theorizing, but proceeding with that work of definition all the same.

Two ideas predominate in the study of autobiography: the relation of the text to historical truth and the relation of the text to the conventions of biography. Timothy Dow Adams, for example, argues, 'a promise to tell the truth is one of autobiography's earliest premises.'[9] He suggests that autobiography is an attempt to reconcile one's life with one's self and that therefore the core of autobiography is not historical accuracy but metaphorical truth. Philippe Lejeune identifies the 'referential pact' as central to the process of autobiography:

> As opposed to all forms of fiction, biography and autobiography are *referential* texts: exactly like scientific or historical discourse, they claim to provide information about a 'reality' exterior to the text, and so to submit to a test of verification. Their aim is not simple verisimilitude, but resemblance to the truth. Not 'the effect of the real,' but the image of the real. All referential texts thus entail what I will call a 'referential pact,' implicit or explicit, in which are included a definition of the field of the real that is involved and a statement of the modes and the degree of resemblance to which the text lays claim.[10]

This focus on the issue of truth – whether metaphorical or historical, simple verisimilitude or 'resemblance to the truth' – fundamentally deadens the instrumentality of autobiography study. As critics have narrowed the debate to the precise definition of genre, it has become trapped in merely formal questions.

The creation of autobiographical works, particularly in terms of how the form has been understood and mobilized by contemporary European comic book producers, is better thought of as a social process. Autobiography, with its implicit claims to replicate the 'real world,' stands in stark contrast to a European comic book heritage that has celebrated adventurous boy reporters, wisecracking Gaulish adventurers, cowboys, astronauts, and other heroes of escapist literature. Indeed, the central issue relating to the use of autobiography in contemporary comics is not whether it can be demonstrated that L'Association actually criticized Dupuy's comics or that Neaud reacted violently to reading these critiques, but rather how various authors have adopted autobiographical work as a distinctive device that sets them apart from the normative elements of the comics market.

The importance of autobiography in the field of contemporary comic book production stems at least in part from the renewed importance of the genre in the field of French literature in the 1970s and 1980s. Indeed, autobiographical comics derive much of their importance from their insertion of modes of visuality into an increasingly legitimated literary genre. Writing about autobiographical tendencies in contemporary French painting, Monique Yaari suggests that the turning point for autobiography – which had been devalorized by modernism – occurred in 1975 with the publication of *Roland Barthes par Roland Barthes,* Georges Perec's *W,* and Philippe Lejeune's *Pacte autobiographique.* Subsequent years saw the release of Michel Beaujour's *Miroirs d'encre* (1980) and autobiographies from noted French intellectuals Marguerite Duras and Alain Robbe-Grillet. Similarly, in the field of painting a number of shows focusing on the self-portrait also helped to revitalize the genre in the 1970s.[11] Thierry Groensteen has argued that French autobiographical cartoonists drew inspiration from this revitalization of the self-portrait and the autobiography, as well as from innovative forms of autobiographical cinema, such as those by Jean-Luc Godard, Nanni Moretti, and Cyril Collard.[12] If autobiography was in the air – and, more importantly, in the art schools – in the early 1990s, what did the new generation of cartoonists hope to achieve by adopting its form? Of all the neglected literary forms, why autobiography?

In the first instance, autobiography is the genre that offers the most explicit promise of legitimizing cartoonists as authors. The death of the author pronounced by Roland Barthes in the 1960s was confirmed in the decades that followed, as Janet Staiger has pointed out, by the prevalence of post-structuralist criticism and the ubiquity of a mass-mediated marketplace of ideas.[13] According to Michel Foucault, the author-function continued to exist to the extent that the concept upheld bourgeois sensibilities about art.[14] For cartoonists, this assertion functioned as a promise. If cartoonists could assert their own identities as authors by conforming to these sensibilities and meet the expectations placed on artists in other fields, their social position could be improved. For cartoonists an important precursor in this regard was cinema, a medium in which the development of an auteur theory had created the social conditions under which film could come to be regarded as a legitimated art form.

At the same time, however, cartoonists were arriving late to the party, and the possibility existed that these doors had already closed. From this standpoint, cartoonists occupied an aesthetically marginal space in much the same way that certain social groups were – and are – marginalized politically. As Nancy Hartsock has noted, 'Why is it that just at the moment when so many of us who have been silenced begin to demand the right to name ourselves, to act as subject rather than objects of history, that just then the concept of subjecthood becomes problematic?'[15] Similarly, Julia Swindells points to the way in which autobiography itself has served as a liberating space for oppressed peoples:

Autobiography now has the potential to be the text of the oppressed and the culturally displaced, forging a right to speak both for and beyond the individual. People in a position of powerlessness – women, black people, working-class people – have more than begun to insert themselves into the culture via autobiography, via the assertion of 'personal' voice, which speaks beyond itself.[16]

Swindell's notion of the culturally displaced inserting themselves into culture might seem particularly appealing to comic book artists of the 1990s seeking to have their work valorized as serious or important. I do not intend to claim that cartoonists belong in the same category as those who are socially and politically marginalized based on race, class, or gender. However, in terms of artistic production and the processes of legitimation, and because their chosen métier has so long been regarded as a devalued subculture intended for children, the adoption of an autobiographical tone can be seen as empowering.

Autobiography, therefore, becomes a mode which foregrounds both realism (as opposed to the traditions of fantasy) and the sense of the author as an artist demanding legitimacy (in contrast to the view of the cartoonist as a cultural hack slaving away to turn out mass-mediated product). In the field of contemporary comic book production, autobiography holds a promise to elevate the legitimacy of both the medium and the artist. Far from propounding the death of the author, as de Man would have it, autobiography in comics holds the possibility of giving the author birth for the first time.

Arguably the most important forerunners of the recent surge in European cartooning come from the American underground comics movement of the 1960s and 1970s. Harvey Pekar is probably the most representative figure, although the importance of Robert Crumb and Justin Green as innovators should not be minimized. Pekar's *American Splendor* series began in the 1970s and is often regarded as a major departure point for realist comics production, although Pekar is not particularly widely translated in Europe. The best-known – and best-regarded – autobiographical comic in Europe to have come out of the American underground comics movement was Art Spiegelman's *Maus*. Part autobiography, part biography of his parents, Spiegelman's work dealt with the personal legacy of the Holocaust, and in particular with his parents' experiences of Auschwitz. Combining cartooning and the Holocaust allowed Spiegelman to develop a 'personal voice' within the comics idiom, and his book is widely regarded as the most important 'serious' comic book ever published, earning a Pulitzer Prize in 1992. The success of translated editions of *Maus* in Europe in the 1980s and 1990s was suggestive of the possibilities afforded to both autobiographical and non-conventional comic books. What the American underground demonstrated to European cartoonists was the possibility of creating comics that were primarily addressed to questions of personal subjectivity. The American underground movement was at once both a liberatory, personalizing visual aesthetic as well as a working model of authorial independence that favoured personal expression above all else. The insertion of the self into the aesthetic and business practices of the underground movement suggested new possibilities for the promotion of the field of comics as an art movement, possibilities that played out in Europe in a different manner.

In the 1970s a number of cartoonists – such as Marcel Gotlib and Moebius – had begun to place their self-images into their work, often in an ironic fashion. Gotlib, for instance, frequently portrayed himself in *Rubrique-à-brac* (Dargaud, 1970) as a megalomaniacal, beret-wearing 'artiste' character. Other than such satirical efforts, however, straightforward autobiographical comics were rare in the 1980s. Readers could speculate about the relationship between the life histories of artists like Baru and Yves Chaland and the protagonists of seemingly autobiographical fiction such as *Quéquette blues* (Dargaud, 1984) and *Le Jeune Albert* (Humanoïdes Associés, 1985), but neither of these books explicitly signalled an 'autobiographical pact.' Their work pointed towards the viability of an autobiographical approach within the traditional full-colour album format, but it did not mark the type of fundamental shift in perspective that is represented by the current generation. The precursor of that transition was Edmond Baudoin.

Baudoin helped to launch the field of autobiographical comics with his work in the 1980s for Futuropolis. *Passe le temps* (1982) and *Couma Aco* (1991) were central to the reputation of Futuropolis for publishing serious-minded, non-genre, and artist-driven works. In terms of delving into real situations and people rather than fantasies and adventure, Baudoin signified a growing sense of maturity in French cartooning, both in terms of audience expectations and personal aesthetics. With the death of Futuropolis as a publishing house in 1994, Baudoin moved much of his artistic output to L'Association, where he continued to produce autobiographical works like *Éloge de la poussière* (1995) and *Terrains vagues* (1996). His autobiographical output largely frames the possibilities inherent in the genre for a number of European cartoonists. It is important that Baudoin is not merely chronicling the passage of his life. His works are framed within poetic narratives complemented by a very loose rendering style. As such, Baudoin primarily offers meditations on his life and his personal relationships, often with women, rather than straightforward accounts of his activities and reminiscences. His books contain roughly equal parts eroticism and philosophy.

In 2002 Baudoin began a new project that is typical of his interests in autobiography. *Le Chemin de Saint-Jean* is an oversized (27 × 37cm) black-and-white book that tells of Baudoin's connection to a mountain near his childhood home in Nice. The book is structured as a series of sketches of the mountain drawn at various points in Baudoin's life. There is no narrative as such, simply a series of notes regarding the feelings and memories that the metaphorical road of the title evokes in the artist. Further, the book – like so much of Baudoin's autobiographical work – is not fixed. Because Baudoin anticipates returning to this material throughout the rest of his career, the book is described as being in 'permanent elaboration.'[17] The first edition of the book was given a relatively small print run of two thousand copies. Each subsequent reprinting of the book will contain new material as Baudoin develops it, allowing the text to mutate over time in much the same way that memories themselves develop and recede. Indeed, the second edition of the book (2004) was expanded in page count, but reduced to the more traditional size of the French album in L'Association's Collection Éperluette. Baudoin's poetic approach to the representation of his own memories and relationships marked a decidedly different approach to autobiographical cartooning than could be found in the work of previous European cartoonists, throwing open the door to contemporary autobiographical comics in Europe.

While Baudoin represents the most important precursor of European autobiographical comics, Marjane Satrapi better represents the critical and financial importance of autobiographical comics as a movement in Europe. Satrapi, termed the 'Persian comics star' by the French daily *Libération*,[18] is among the most commercially successful of the new generation of European small-press cartoonists. Her four-volume autobiographical comic book, *Persepolis,* has been translated into numerous European languages, and an English-language edition was published by Pantheon – the publishers of *Maus* – in two volumes (2003, 2004). The French editions of her book, published by L'Association, have sold more than 100,000 copies.[19] Moreover, the third volume of the series was pre-published in the pages of *Libération* in the summer of 2002, giving the work the same kind of national media exposure that a famous novelist or essayist might expect.

Persepolis is the strictly chronological story of Satrapi's life from childhood to young adulthood. Born in Tehran to middle-class parents, Satrapi evokes the hardships that her family suffered under the Islamic revolution that swept through Iran when she was ten years old. The series recalls her efforts to circumvent the strict religious teachings in Iran, the devastation wrought by the Iran–Iraq war of the 1980s, her schooling in Vienna, and her return to art school and a brief marriage in Iran. Satrapi's books, which are presented with a spare, stripped-down visual aesthetic, define for many the contemporary autobiographical comics movement. The wide exposure of her work, and its warm reception beyond the confines of the traditional comics reading public, has served to reinforce the association between serious subjects in contemporary comics and autobiography. Indeed, by dealing with her youth in an autobiographical manner rather than through fictionalization, Satrapi's work draws upon common assumptions about autobiography and truthfulness for much of its power.

While Satrapi has achieved the greatest commercial success in the autobiographical genre, her work is by no means normative. The visual aspects of autobiographical approaches within contemporary European comics are remarkably heterogeneous and plural despite evidence of considerable overlap within the thematics of the movement. Moreover, because the narrative content of so many autobiographical comics is roughly analogous, it is primarily through the processes of rendering and visualization that these works differ from each other. In 1996, for example, Thierry Groensteen identified a number of traits common to the narrative component of autobiographical comics. The two most prevalent of these were recollections of childhood and a recounting of intimate or sexual encounters.[20] These categories clearly encompass the work of Baudoin and Satrapi but also incorporate a large number of practitioners working in different contexts. Jean-Christophe Menu, whose own *Livret de phamille* (L'Association, 1995) is a central early text in the autobiographical comics movement, foregrounds his familial relationships – particularly to his wife and children – in his work. Swedish cartoonist Åsa Grennvall details her relationship with an extremely demanding and insensitive mother in *Det känns som hundra år* (Optimal Press, 1999), as well as her relationship with an emotionally and physically abusive boyfriend in *Sjunde våningen* (Optimal Press, 2002). Maaike Hartjes portrays her quotidian life and her personal fears in *Maaikes Grot Dagboekje* (Oog & Blik, 2002). The 381-page Finnish anthology *Sarjakuvapäivät* (Suuri Kurpitsa, 2001) features twelve artists – including

Kati Rapia, Katja Tukianinen, and Johanna Rojola – recording their diaries for a month apiece in comics form. Each of their pieces foregrounds the intimate in a very direct and highly personal manner. Frederik Peeters's 2001 book *Pilules bleues* (Atrabile) addresses his romantic involvement with an HIV-positive woman and her young HIV-positive son. While each of these artists utilizes a different visual approach – Menu's loose cartooning, Hartjes's minimalist quasi-stick figures, Peeters's highly symbolic figures within a traditional page design – the intent behind their projects bears a considerable degree of overlap. Indeed, the social and narrative concerns of contemporary European autobiographical cartooning have been codified, even across national borders.

The most notable of all autobiographical comics publishers is France's Ego Comme X. Begun as an anthology publisher in 1994, Ego Comme X was started by students from the Atelier Bande Dessinée at the École Régionale des Beaux-Arts d'Angoulême. Their stated desire was to highlight the importance of 'the real' in contradistinction to the dominant comics aesthetic of escapist fantasy. While various other publishers had pushed autobiography to the forefront of the new comics scene in the 1990s – particularly L'Association and Cornélius – Ego Comme X was the first to make autobiographical comics something of an imperative. Writing in the first issue, Thierry Groensteen argued: 'Still, at one time, the full-colour adventures of irreproachable heroes were rolled out on glazed paper. They neglected reality, preferring to turn to any elsewhere, provided that it was synonymous with escape, and the promise of entertainment. But all that is finished! The comic book has changed.'[21] The artists published by Ego Comme X – Aristophane, Xavier Mussat, Fabrice Neaud, Frédéric Poincelet, Frédéric Boilet, Matthieu Blanchin, Pauline Martin, among numerous others – share a common concern with detailing their intimate personal relationships, and often recollections of their childhoods, in the comics form.

Loïc Nehou and Poincelet take this tendency to the extreme in *Essai de sentimentalisme* (Ego Comme X, 2001) in which Poincelet illustrates explicit stories of Nehou's sex life. The doubled disclosure that this effort entails – Nehou's openness to Poincelet, the artist's frankness with the reader – is unusual in the field and pushes the portrayal of the intimate to its logical extreme. Poincelet's visual approach is perhaps the least conventional in the field of autobiographical comics. Coming from a fine arts and painting background, Poincelet uses no traditional panels, and his pages are mostly composed of white space. Indeed, his work is an obvious bridge between the autobiographical comics movement and the avant-garde tendencies of Frémok (he published a book, *Livre de prières,* with Amok in 1998).

If Poincelet's work is proof that, as Groensteen suggested, the comics had changed as a result of these formal and, more accurately, thematic shifts, it is also evidence of an increasing concretization of opposition to the heteronomous comics market. Autobiography, as a largely untapped genre offering the opportunity to speak directly for one's self as an author, represented to the new generation of creators a credible alternative to the fantasies that comprised the majority of European comics production. The diverse approaches that autobiography accorded the comics form served as a reinforcement of the idea, as another editorial in *Ego Comme X* #1 indicated, that 'a comics that reflects, wonders about its means, realized by authors conscious of being able to express themselves differently with a great deal of accuracy, becomes a language of its own.'[22] At the same time, however, autobiography risked calcifying into a genre that was as formalized and structured as those that it sought to reject, becoming the small-press genre par excellence. The tension between the heteronomous regimes of fantasy comics publishing in Europe and the more autonomous sector of artist-driven autobiography is highlighted in a number of books published by Ego Comme X and L'Association. Specifically, the work of David B., Dupuy and Berberian, and Fabrice Neaud offers concrete assessments, within an autobiographical form, of the shaping of an independent or alternative European comics culture rooted in personal psychodynamics.

In outlining the common tropes in autobiographical comics, Thierry Groensteen suggests that a distinctively French aspect of the movement is a focus on 'the chronicle of the professional life, the *mise-en-scène* of the author's trade in comics.'[23] In the case of David B.'s six-volume *L'Ascension du Haut Mal* (L'Association, 1996, 1997, 1998, 1999, 2000, 2003) (figure 15), the author combines his childhood recollections, the history of his family, and his own growth as a cartoonist in order to place his life story in dialogue with his other comics work, genre-based fantasy comics. In an interview, David B. defined his particular approach to autobiography, which extends far beyond recollections of his own life:

Often, people in autobiographical comics tell their life. Period ... Me, I try to tell another thing, I tell what has happened to my family, I also tell memories of my grandparents, of the things which I heard told, a kind of family mythology, memories of grandparents, great-grandparents. For ex-

15 David B. discusses his work with his father. From *L'Ascension du Haut Mal* volume 4.

ample, the war of 14 in the case of my grandfather, or the colonization of Indo-China in the case of my great-grandfather, things like that. And then, I try to tell, parallel to that, the construction of my imagination and the influence that all that I lived could have on this imagination.[24]

Indeed, the strong family element in David B.'s autobiographical comics is suggested when he says, 'of course, it is not a work that I undertook all alone, egotistically. It is a work that I make for my sister as well, for my parents and my brother.'[25] The sense of producing comics not only for one's self, but for an entire family, is highlighted by the content of the books themselves.

L'Ascension du Haut Mal tells the story of the Beauchard family's attempts to deal with the severe epilepsy of their eldest son, Jean-Christophe. Failed by medical science, the family turns to a variety of alternative options in France during the 1970s, including macrobiotics, acupuncture, spiritualism, magnetism, and alchemy. Jean-Christophe's illness structures the entire social life of the family, forcing them to move and entirely redesign their lives in an effort to find a cure. David B. details this as a series of traumas that the family is forced to confront, crises that ultimately shape and structure his own approach to the world in which he lives. As the child of art teachers, David deals with the difficulties that his family faces by retreating into comic books and his own imagination. He finds refuge in his art, where he is most fond of drawing large-scale battle scenes featuring the likes of Genghis Khan, images that recall a traditional stereotype of juvenile interest in escapist adventure comics. The artist's visual aesthetic, which is dominated by highly symbolic and non-representational images, is shown to be derived from the twinning of his interest in fantasy and the occult (brought on by his parents' search for a spiritualist answer to the problems of Jean-Christophe) and the social world in which he was immersed as a boy. In the second volume, for example, David learns that he can turn the adult disapproval of his violent drawings of battle scenes by simply changing the images to those of samurai, which, as products of a Japanese iconography, are endorsed by his macrobiotic community.[26] Indeed, David B. explicitly relates his brother's epilepsy with his desire to create violent battle imagery in the first volume of the series: 'I'm not any one person. I'm a group, an army. I have enough rage in me for one hundred thousand warriors. I relate my brother's seizures to this rage.'[27] *L'Ascension du Haut Mal*, therefore, can be largely read as the story of a young man who learns to cope with a severe and chronic familial crisis through the cultivation of his own artistic and creative impulses, and the book even retains examples of the comics that he created as a young boy.

A significant subtext in this book series is David's increasing professionalization as an artist, a point that is particularly highlighted in the final volume, when he moves to Paris to attend school. David chooses to enroll in an art school where the cartoonist Georges Pichard is an instructor. Pichard, best known for his erotic adult comics material from magazines like *Charlie Mensuel*, takes an interest in David's career as a cartoonist and becomes his mentor. David B.'s attempts to break into the mainstream of the European comics market in the 1980s met with limited success – he published one album with Glénat and a number of short works in magazines such as *(À Suivre)*, *Circus*, and *Okapi*. It wasn't until the creation of L'Association in 1990 that he found his real calling as an artist. He describes the establishment of L'Association, saying, 'That was an opening for me. There, I really had the impression of filling a vacuum.'[28] At the same time, however, he deals with the formation of this influential group in a single panel of the 300+ page autobiography, noting only that the creation of the organization saved him from the despair that had been brought on by his inability with his partner to have a child.[29]

Given the centrality of L'Association to the small-press comics movement, particularly by 2003 when the sixth volume was published, and of the therapeutic power of art within the books, it is somewhat surprising to find these events dealt with so casually. Indeed, it is clear that while David B. is happy to discuss his professionalization as a background to the larger question of his own psychological development as a person, he does not privilege his work for L'Association beyond the work that he has subsequently undertaken for larger publishing firms like Dargaud and Dupuis. He notes that '[Jean-Christophe] Menu very often says: We do not make the same things as these people there. On the contrary. I think we do exactly the same thing. But we do not do it in the same manner.'[30]

For David B., who notes that he is a voracious reader of all sorts of comics, the ideology of independence is not central to the work of cultural production, nor is it integral to the story of how he became the person he is. *L'Ascension du Haut Mal* is not a break from genre work for the large publishers but an extension of that work that enables him to frame it within a distinctly personal context. Yet, crucially, such a commentary on the relations of readers to genre comics can only be published outside of the system of genre comics itself. The ideology and social organization of alternative comics in contemporary Europe situates autobiography outside of the dominant sphere of the market, placing David B. in a liminal state. He can only work for the large publishing houses once he has worked out his relationship to them at an independent press.

This idea is one that is explicitly endorsed by David B. in a number of interviews. He has said, for example, regarding his fiction, '*L'Ascension du Haut Mal* gives keys to the reader that are not in the other books.'[31] It is clear in reading the artist's autobiographical comics that there exists a deep interconnection between his interests as a child, his personal aesthetic as an adult, and the fantasy work that he produces for the large publishing houses. He explained in an interview:

> For me the autobiography is not an end in itself. Now, I want to tell important things, which, in my opinion, can be of interest to the readers. Because what happened to us does not happen every day and because it is at the same time a testimony over time, of people etc. More, it is a slightly expanded autobiography since I speak about my grandparents, of my great grandparents, people that I don't know. I do not speak solely about me; I try speaking about the family circle. It's true that I intend afterward to write fiction.[32]

He directly ties *L'Ascension du Haut Mal* into one of his first books, *Le Cheval blême* (L'Association, 1992), insofar as material is virtually reiterated from one to the other. *Le Cheval blême* is a collection of comics based upon the artist's dreams. Similar dreams appear sporadically throughout *L'Ascension du Haut Mal,* and with more particular frequency in the final volume, depicting events around the time that *Le Cheval blême* was initially published. From this standpoint, the autobiographical work extends retroactively to incorporate a small-press publication that preceded it, placing both in the same psychological orbit.

Other books are also hinted at throughout the autobiographical text. The author's penchant for drawing samurais in battle as a young man is a clear link to *Le Tengû Carré* (Dargaud, 1997), a book that recounts traditional Japanese legends. Indeed, the link between the author's dreams, fantasies, and personal psychic symbology is rendered explicit throughout the text. 'Rêver, raconter,' he tells himself in the final volume.[33] By the end of the series, David B. has included literally dozens of references to his work in other books. Jean-Christophe, for example, is described in the final volume as living in a 'universe that has become hostile,'[34] with an image of menacing physical effects ranging from books to alarm clocks. This image recalls the central narrative of *La Révolte d'Hop-Frog* (Dargaud, 1997), a western that David B. wrote for artist Christophe Blain in which a gang of man-made objects led by a teapot attacks the inhabitants of a small town. Whether this is a retroactive acknowledgment of that earlier genre work or whether the mental image inspired by the artist's brother was the spur for the Dargaud album, is unclear. What is evident, however, is the fact that David B. has used *L'Ascension du Haut Mal* as a sort of explanatory text that provides insight into the mind that has created some of the most offbeat genre comics in recent publishing history. From this standpoint the distinction between autobiographical and fictional work in contemporary European comics production is revealed as more fluid than defenders of the genre might otherwise claim. It is clear, in fact, that autobiography is simply one strand of a complex web of possibilities that constitute the contemporary field of European comics production, albeit a strand for which particular ideological claims have been regularly made.

While David B.'s autobiographical work provides a sort of roundabout insight into his more conventional genre work, a much more explicit relationship is enacted in *Journal d'un album* by Philippe Dupuy and Charles Berberian. Dupuy and Berberian are a Paris cartooning and illustration duo who have been working together since the 1980s. Together they have created two successful book series – *Henriette*, about a young girl, and *M. Jean*, about a middle-aged author in Paris. Their relationship is unique in the world of comics insofar as they co-author their scripts and each contributes to the drawing process, often with one pencilling the figures and the other inking – although other combinations also arise. While each artist has done some small amount of work alone or with other collaborators, the vast majority of their creative output over the course of two decades has been done in tandem. Their autobiographical book is at once a break from that tendency and a reinforcement of it.

Journal d'un album chronicles the making of the third *M. Jean* book, *Monsieur Jean, les femmes et les enfants d'abord* (Humanoïdes Associés, 1994). It is a 115-page black-and-white comic book about the creation of a 46-page full-colour hardcover album. Moreover, it is the only instance in which each of the artists has published work that is solely his own under the Dupuy and Berberian banner; Dupuy does not directly contribute to Berberian's work, and vice versa. As such, the book represents an effort to work singly, but because it is an autobiography in which two people contribute chapters, it is also another instance of working jointly.

In a letter to *9e Art* magazine, Berberian outlined something of the pair's approach to the project and the difference between this project and their more traditional work:

> I have a subject to treat. If I can develop it by using a character other than me, I do it. I transpose, for example, in M. Jean. I can say 'we,' because in this case, Dupuy and me, use M. Jean like a screen.
>
> But in the case of *Journal d'un album,* the subject (inter alia) was my rapport with comics. There, I needed to write in the first person. I then treated myself like a character. I caricatured myself, and from there, it was no problem to stroll through panels. In fact, I created a character that incarnated a certain idea of me.[35]

Key to the relationship between autobiographical practice and commercial album production in the case of Dupuy and Berberian, therefore, is the distinction between transposing life experiences into a fictional setting and transposing them within the autobiographical pact.

In many ways, *Journal d'un album* is a conventional autobiographical novel. Many of Dupuy's chapters, for example, delve into the territory of intimate confession. As I have already noted, in one chapter he recounts the death of his mother. Elsewhere, he addresses the fears that are brought about by his father's failing health. More centrally, he discusses in great depth his troubled relationship with his wife Tessa. Dupuy's depiction of his relationship is in stark contrast to the way he depicts the marriage of Berberian. While he shows Charles and his wife Anne as perpetually happily in love, his own marriage is seen to be falling apart. He frequently discusses the situation with friends and colleagues, and his marriage enters into a crisis phase while they are producing the *M. Jean* book, although it is resolved by the time they have completed it.

A lengthy sequence midway through the book makes the connection between Dupuy's despair and the darkness consuming the life of the fictional Jean explicit. Dupuy recreates an image of a despondent Jean, only to transform the image into a self-caricature in the next panel. From that point onward Dupuy moves through the fictive universe of M. Jean as his real life and fiction blur together in an expressionistic nightmare (figure 16). Later in the book, Tessa reads the pages that her husband has drawn about the near-dissolution of their marriage, agreeing to have this dark period in their relationship placed before the public for consumption. It is one of several moments in the book where the process of creating an autobiographical comic is explicitly addressed

16 Philippe Dupuy grieves. From *Journal d'un album*.

in a self-referential manner. This type of self-referentiality is one of the key markers that distinguishes the narrational mode and invokes the autobiographical pact. Tessa's commentary on the pages serves in a way to notarize the interpretation of events, to confirm that they have happened and that it is not simply a melodramatic invention, as Dupuy fears.

While the familial relationships are important to *Journal d'un album*, central to the book's narrative is the relationship of the authors to the field of comics: as consumers, as producers, as colleagues, and as authors. Berberian introduces this subject in the book's first chapter, travelling in a taxi with a driver who does not recognize cartooning as a valid profession. In the second chapter, he recounts a story about a lecture he gave at a vacation village in Quercy, where none of the attendees was in any way familiar with his work. In both instances, the profession of cartoonist is presented as something laughable and beneath contempt (interestingly, a more successful lecture following the first is dismissed in just two panels). Indeed, the cover of the album depicts the authors wearing eleven-armed alien costumes, saying, 'We are artists, we make comic books'[36] in an entirely unconvincing manner. Berberian depicts his relationship with comics as an entirely unhealthy one that stems from his childhood in Baghdad. Alone in Paris while his wife and daughter are out of town, he spends his time in bookstores buying books that he fondly recalls from his childhood. He tells Anne that he must keep these volumes because they are his only link to a youth spent in Baghdad, a city that has now been mostly destroyed. At the same time, however, he is forced to acknowledge to his younger self that he did not collect *Simpsons* figures as a child but that he does now. Further, he refuses to let his young daughter play with them. Later in the book he outlines in great detail his fixation on the American superhero character Batman.

Throughout *Journal d'un album* Berberian triangulates his life's work with his childhood interests (figure 17), seeing it as both an abject embarrassment and also a source of genuine joy, as when a new book is released and he races to the publisher to see the first copies. Where Dupuy is forthright about the influence of his personal and marital problems on his life and work (outlining a number of personal 'demons' at one point in the book), Berberian addresses the ongoing importance of his childhood obsessions on his life as an adult. If, as Groensteen suggests, the dominant tropes of autobiographical comics are childhood experience and intimate interpersonal relationships, it seems that the duo has both covered symbiotically.

17 A young Charles Berberian lectures his older self. From *Journal d'un album.*

At the same time, however, the book is also very much about the personal and creative relationship that exists between these two artists. In the book's second chapter, Berberian attempts to explain to an uncomprehending public the unique way in which the two collaborate on projects, but is largely unsuccessful. Later chapters illustrate the working relationship more clearly. For example, Dupuy recounts the chapter that most explicitly details the creation of the M. Jean book, particularly through an anecdote regarding M. Jean's hair. In one chapter of the *M. Jean* album, the character fantasizes about being a medieval king whose castle is assaulted by beautiful women hurling babies at the ramparts. Dupuy phones his partner to complain that Berberian has pencilled M. Jean without the medieval haircut that Dupuy had given him in the roughs. They dispute the character's hairstyle and fax each other images. Dupuy then spends a good deal of time inquiring among his colleagues as to which version they find more appropriate, before ultimately conceding the issue to Berberian. From Dupuy's perspective, therefore, the completion of this story requires the sublimation of his own professional instincts.

The accommodations that an artist makes in order to realize a work are also the subject of the final chapter, which details many of the obstacles that the pair had to overcome to get the finished book published. These include problems with the colourist, the rumoured bankruptcy of their publisher, the creation of a *M. Jean* agenda book without their knowledge or consent, and a fire at the offices of Humanoïdes Associés. The drama of each of these crises, which are presented as severe, is mitigated somewhat by the reader's knowledge that the third book in the series had, in fact, been published before the release of *Journal d'un album.* The book presents not an image of the pitfalls of commercial publishing, therefore, so much as an extended essay on the relationship between art and commerce. The challenges posed by the obstacles on the road to publishing the third *M. Jean* volume are characterized through a board game metaphor, with the authors running wildly about while dice crash around them. These, the reader is led to believe, are the common travails of working within a highly commercial publishing industry. Yet the rest of the book prods the edges of the commercial–independent split within the field of contemporary comic book production.

Throughout *Journal d'un album,* the relationship of Dupuy and Berberian to the independent comics scene in Paris is an issue. Dupuy shares an atelier with the artist Blutch and frequently depicts himself interacting with members of the so-called *nouvelle bande dessinée* move-ment. In a seven-panel parenthesis, Dupuy presents the tension between Humanoïdes Associés and L'Association that he perceived at that time. The decision to undertake an autobiographical comic was influenced by the work of many of L'Association's artists, who were engaged in autobi-ography. Further, Dupuy and Berberian share a common interest in the author-centric ideology of L'Association, and the duo was responsible for one of the company's first major books, *Les Héros ne meurent jamais* (1991). Fully intending to publish *Journal* with L'Association, the pair had informed Humanoïdes Associés, their primary publisher at that time, of their autobiographical comic as a courtesy, not anticipating that the large publishing house would be interested in a project of this type. However, Humanoïdes Associés insisted on publishing the book, arguing:

> I understand perfectly your passion for l'Association, we share in it! But Humanoïdes Associés also have the vocation of publishing atypical books (as long as we consider them interesting). Also think of what we can bring: distribution, impact when grouped with the M. Jean album.
>   And in the end, it is necessary to be logical: we cannot claim to have an author-driven policy and not want to put out this journal.[37]

Dupuy then spends three panels in a nightmare, worrying about the reaction of his more militant, independent colleagues who would call the duo opportunists, traitors, and 'arrivistes.' Ultimately, however, L'Association president Jean-Christophe Menu greets the news with quiet understanding, noting that he would do the same thing in the same situation.

Nonetheless, L'Association publishes the final book in the end, for reasons that the book never attempts to make clear. The final page finds Dupuy and Berberian discussing the decision and agreeing that it is best if Humanoïdes Associés were to publish the book, but the reader is fully aware that this is a product decidedly of the small press. The refusal of an explanation in the text naturalizes the distinction between the large publishing houses and the independents. Moreover, it shifts the moral weight of the contemporary publishing industry behind the indepen-dent presses, whose commitment to an author-driven policy is realized in the action of publishing the book, while the rhetoric of the Humanoïdes Associés executive is left, with no fuller elaboration, at the level of empty discourse. As such, a book like *Journal d'un album* draws upon the conventions of the autobiographical comic book extant at that time and expands upon them in order to present an argument that the authors should be regarded as legitimate artists, and that legitimate artists are those whose work is most akin to the current independent aesthetics and philosophy.

A similar argument is advanced in the work of Fabrice Neaud, particularly in his ongoing autobiographical series *Journal*. Neaud began publishing autobiographical comics in 1994, in the first issue of *Ego Comme X*. His work since that time has constituted the most ambitious autobiographical comics project yet published. Every second year since 1996, Neaud has released one volume of his autobiography. Ranging in length from 71 to 374 pages, these volumes have retraced the author's life from February 1992 to July 1996. The books place quotidian aspects of Neaud's life within a much larger philosophical framework that addresses issues of representation, self-identity, and creative work. Neaud's books are structured around several poles, the most notable of which is his position as a struggling artist and gay man living in small-town France. Two of the books – volumes one and three – place Neaud's homosexuality at centre stage, as each book focuses on the author's love for someone who does not reciprocate his feelings. Volumes two and four place much greater emphasis on Neaud's status as a cartoonist, his struggles at art school and on the professional market, and his colleagues in the visual arts.

Since publishing the first volume of his autobiography in 1996, Neaud has become, essentially, a professional autobiographer. While he has published a small number of non-autobiographical comics works – mostly essays – the act of telling his life story has become Neaud's primary career. Unlike David B. or Dupuy and Berberian, whose autobiographies help to shed light on a larger corpus of work, Fabrice Neaud's work consists almost exclusively of comics that are, at least in part, about his involvement in the field of comics. As such, Neaud's work offers a much more forcefully and dramatically enunciated argument about the way autobiography has the potential to consecrate the artist working within the field of comic book production.

I have already pointed to the way Neaud reveals his disappointment that the members of L'Association critique the autobiographical work of Philippe Dupuy. Neaud's comments on what he sees as an inappropriate critique of form are ironic given the fact that he clearly works harder on formal composition than most cartoonists. He argues that his autobiography is a specific type, a diary, and this is signalled by the work's title. Swindell's assertion that autobiography is a form in which the culturally displaced forge a right to speak for themselves has a great deal in common with this notion of the diary, which has often been character-ized as existing outside the mainstream of heroic and masculine autobi-ography. Linda Anderson argues 'the unchronological and unprogressive form of the diary could be viewed, therefore, as a reflection of women's different experience, or as a deliberate strategy, an escape into a poten-tial or protean form of subjectivity.'[38] In emphasizing the importance of subjectivity, Anderson's description highlights a central aspect of Neaud's work, which is the reconstruction of subjective personal experiences and emotional states of being. At the same time, however, Anderson's em-phasis on unprogressive and unchronological work is a challenge to Neaud's sense of his project as diaristic. By unchronological, Anderson means specifically those works intended for private, rather than public, consumption – works that address minor shifts in routine, for example.

Neaud's published diary evokes a more masculinist trajectory, seeking to elevate the diary within the traditions of autobiographical writing by minimizing quotidian and repetitive aspects of his life while emphasizing the least typical moments. Neaud speaks directly to this point in the fourth volume when he notes that he has dedicated six pages of his journal to a man he knew for less than an hour:

> The proportion of pages allotted to men in this journal is not representative of the presence of the latter in my life ... But it is completely of the place that they occupy for me. If I were more just, more objective, more mathematical, I should rather draw a vacuum. To try to represent their absence.[39]

Indeed, Neaud has repeatedly stressed that the chronology of events is strictly respected in his work, though clearly this chronology is filtered through the author's editorial process. Not all events are represented even in passing, and some events are given much greater weight than are others. The principle that guides the book's focus is, as Neaud indicates above, those experiences that continue to haunt his thinking and shape his sense of self-identity. In this way, Neaud's work is much more clearly a chronology of his psychosocial subjectivity than a strict recording of the events in his life.

This tension between objective and subjective recording of life experi-ences is, of course, at the very heart of autobiography. Neaud's work, which is produced retrospectively at a distance of several years, tends to highlight the subjective representation of sentiment within a highly realist framework. This formal structuring is a consequence of time.

Neaud's attempt to produce a more direct comics journal, created con-temporaneously with events, was published as 'Première Tentative de journal direct' in *Ego Comme X* #5. Neaud abandoned these efforts, sensing that this work was no more 'direct' than the comics that he produced at a greater distance in time: 'It is never more difficult, on the contrary, than to remove the distance, especially with a drawing like mine. One would need a minimal writing to manage to hold a journal that would claim the abolition of this distance, which would remain an illusion. There is always transposition.'[40]

Neaud's rejection of direct autobiography stems from his acknowledg-ment that the artist is always in the process of selecting and editing when creating. There is, therefore, no way to create autobiography in an unmediated manner. This forces the author to prioritize subjective, personal experiences. Yet, at the same time, Neaud is interested in distinguishing his work from fiction, a form with no necessary claims to external ideas of realism. To this end, Neaud's process of transposition stems from the reworking of written and drawn diaristic notes that he makes in the present, as well as extensive use of photo reference. In some cases, Neaud has been able to convince his friends to pose for him as he draws images of their past selves.[41] Thus, Neaud presents his work as distinct from fiction insofar as it is positioned as a form of subjectivity rooted in a sense of 'reality.' Realism thus becomes the central axis around which Neaud's comics revolve.

The techniques of photo reference, note-taking, and life drawing all highlight Neaud's elaboration of a realist aesthetic within the confines of the representation of highly subjective experiences. Neaud's emphasis on realism as a legitimating tendency for comics production may initially seem odd, given the general disdain with which other forms of strict realism are regarded in the arts. Writing on realist painting, for example, John L. Ward notes

> There is a widely held belief that realism, because it is normative, even conventional, is inherently antithetical to fundamental modernist prin-ciples concerning the primacy of personal experience, the necessity to overturn conventions and traditional ways of seeing and thinking, and the importance of using the medium to redefine its own nature and possibili-ties.[42]

Neaud's reliance on realism – which has become increasingly prob-lematized in each volume since the first – exists, as Sébastien Soleille notes, in opposition to certain tendencies found in the autobiographical work of Dupuy and Berberian, or Lewis Trondheim, whose stylized renderings resemble the fiction produced by those artists. Neaud evokes an aesthetic that is rarely used in comics in order to mark his distance from the traditions of the form. At the same time, however, his emphasis on subjective and emotional responses to events moves him away from realism.

In this manner, when he depicts his body increasingly covered by enormous spiders – as he does in *Journal (I)* – the departure from realism is used to heighten the symbolic effect of the image. Similarly, when he depicts his first extended conversation with Dominique – in *Journal (III)* – as an eighteen-page mute sequence filled with non-diegetic backgrounds, the sequence shifts the definition of realism away from objective representation and places it into subjective territory. This episode, which Neaud has described as a conscious effort to produce a sequence that is avant-garde or 'oubapienne,'[43] is perhaps the instance that most forcefully highlights the twinned oppositions that structure the *Journal* series: a realist aesthetic/a symbolic aesthetic; objective social reality/ subjective responses to that reality. It is in the working through of these oppositions that he is able to escape the trap suggested by Ward and use realism to redefine the comics medium in reference to its own possibilities through a particularly visual strategy of creation. Indeed, the ability of Neaud to utilize realist imagery, extended narrative sequences, and text points to the significant ways that realist comics differ from realist painting.

Writing about self-portraiture in painting, Philippe Lejeune has suggested that because there is no internal sign that allows a viewer to distinguish a self-portrait from a portrait, there may be no such thing as a first person in painting.[44] The same cannot be said for comics, however. The ability to move between representational and subjective modes – as Neaud, and all of the cartoonists considered here, do – distinguishes the comics form from the traditions of portrait painting and situates the play of reality and subjectivity as central to the autobiographical project.

A short sequence in *Journal (4)* serves as an attempt to place Fabrice Neaud, and his colleagues in Ego Comme X, within the larger field of small-press cartooning in Europe. In this section, which details a trip to Brussels to participate in the 1995 Autarcic Comix festival, with more pages dedicated to the drive from Angoulême to Brussels than to the actual festival itself, Neaud highlights the casual manner in which he positions his work within a larger context. He indicates that he was not unhappy to meet with a number of artists whom he highly regards, specifically noting Jean-Christophe Menu, Mattt Konture, and Yvan Alagbé. At the same time, however, he deals with the festival itself only fleetingly, preferring to dwell on other issues. It could be argued, therefore, that his autobiography – while it is concretely focused on the question of producing an autobiography – is more concerned with processes of reception and communication than it is with processes of production.

While cartoonists like David B. and Dupuy and Berberian bring up the question of how others read their autobiographical comics, Neaud pushes this tendency further, tying it to his particular definition of realism. At the same time, however, his emphasis on the reception of his work serves to highlight his tendency to undercut strict realism to emphasize the subjective experience of his personal reactions. In his *Journal* Neaud has given examples of reception and miscommunication that can be divided into two general categories: the reaction of his intimate friends to his work and the reaction of complete strangers.

To date, the reaction of intimates has been the most central of these relationships in the *Journal* series. Specifically, the third volume of the series, with its primary focus on Neaud's relationship with Dominique, addresses this issue most concretely. He depicts Dominique's reaction to his work on a number of occasions in this volume, and the relationship between the two men is often framed in relation to their different dispositions towards art and autobiography. One of the artist's first encounters with Dominique takes place at the 1994 Salon International de la Bande Dessinée in Angoulême, at which an exhibition of work from *Ego Comme X* #1 is presented. As the centrepiece of the exhibition, the artists moved Neaud's bed into the space in order to symbolize the dismantling of the distinction between the public and private realms, in much the same way that their comics do. Pushing this even further, a near naked Neaud occupies his bed on the Saturday of the festival, laying in a fetal position that recalls one of his story's panels.

As recounted in *Journal (III)*, he positions his relationship to the festival – and to the mainstream of French comics production – in terms of avant-gardist artistic practice as he is engaged in both non-traditional comics production and a minor form of performance art. He writes that occupying the bed for the day allowed him time to meditate on the artistic project undertaken by Ego Comme X, and, as he later details in the book, the exhibition allowed him to gain insight into the views of the man with whom he was in love at the time. However, Dominique's

interest in Neaud is mitigated by three important factors, which intersect
at various points in the book. First, Dominique is not gay. Second,
Dominique, as an art student, prefers painting to comics and sees almost
no value in Neaud's chosen medium. Third, Dominique does not value
autobiography. He dismisses the work of Anne Frank, for example, as
poorly written, arguing 'the greatest suffering does not excuse literary
mediocrity, if one does not have a talent. Of course, a comic book
autobiography ...'[45] The intersection of these factors, of Dominique's
disdain for Fabrice and for the work that he creates, is central to the
events of *Journal (III)*. Further, the denunciation of this work by Dominique serves as a negative basis against which the artist justifies his
aesthetic.

Neaud seeks to legitimize autobiographical comics against the disap-
probation of Dominique in a number of ways in *Journal (III)*, some
successful, some not. He recounts, for example, his creation of a mini-
comic entitled 'Le Doumé, vers un machisme cultivé' that he created to
mock the object of his affections. Needless to say, this volume, when
discovered by Dominique, does little to convince him of the merits of
the comics form or to win his heart. Indeed, he is never able to convince
Dominique of the value of his chosen mode of expression, instead
having to retroactively demonstrate his abilities through his reconstruction of events in the *Journal*.

Two conversations in particular fully establish the painful futility of the
relationship between Fabrice and Dominique. The first of these, recounted on pages 130 through 139, takes place in June 1994 as Fabrice
presents six pages to Dominique recounting an erotic dream that he had
concerning his friend. Throughout the scene Neaud shifts from strict
realism to highly subjective imagery. As he hands Dominique the pages,
for example, they take on the shape of a gun. He intercuts images of a
mute Dominique reading the pages with images of his friend Cyril
warning him not to show him the work. Finally, in a series of five
successive panels over three pages, he depicts a still Dominique engulfed
in an explosion that destroys his apartment, leaving the town in ruins
and bringing about, as Cyril warns in voice-over, the end of the world.
Sitting among the ruins of Fabrice's hopes and desires, Dominique can
find nothing to say about the work. His full response is delayed until
more than one hundred pages later in the book, when Fabrice again
visits him in his apartment. This eighteen-page sequence is composed
entirely of a monologue by Dominique – neither Neaud's image nor his
words appear in any of the panels, and the entire sequence is drawn as if

from the artist's point of view. Throughout the sequence Dominique harangues Fabrice, rejecting his offers of love and, in the end, of friendship. When Dominique tells Fabrice that he has no right to use his image in his work or in his fantasies, Neaud continues to draw him but with a black bar across his eyes, like a television station making a half-hearted attempt to conceal the identity of an informer. As the conversation continues, Neaud allows Dominique's image to fade away entirely, becoming a series of empty panels with word balloons in them, before finally culminating in back-to-back full-page images, the first a portrait of Dominique commanding 'forget me,' the second a blank page with the same behest.

Neaud's use of highly subjective techniques in these pages – whether the metaphorical destruction of his fantasies or the recreation of a sense of blacking out in a conversation gone horribly awry – is the artist's ultimate response to Dominique's dismissal of autobiography. Indeed, Neaud ably depicts a great deal of emotional suffering without resorting to the sort of 'literary mediocrity' that Dominique diagnosed in the work of Anne Frank. In retrospect, it seems, he is able to communicate to Dominique through his work in a way that he was not able to do in person.

Journal (4) moves the issue of communication away from Neaud's circle of friends and colleagues and brings it more directly to a question of audience. The fourth volume of the series recounts the time immediately following the release of the first volume of the series. This volume was tremendously well received by the critics, winning the Alph'Art Coup de Coeur at Angoulême in 1997. He has indicated in interviews that winning that prize changed his life and his work to a degree.[46] For the first time, Neaud had to interact with people who knew him first and foremost by the way he presented himself in his books rather than reading his work after knowing him for some time.

In a fourteen-page sequence in *Journal (4)* detailing the 1996 Salon International de la Bande Dessinée in Angoulême, he recounts three anecdotes that present different reactions to his work, as well as his own reaction to these reactions. The first of these is between Fabrice and a woman he accuses of having 'squatted' his book – that is, she sat in the back of the Ego Comme X booth and read the whole thing without buying it. This galls Fabrice, but what upsets him even more is her feeling that she is entitled to criticize the book without bothering to purchase it. The two end up screaming at each other and trading insults before Fabrice storms away.

The second conversation is more satisfying for the artist. Fabrice talks to a young woman for whom he is doing a *dédicace*, or a personalized drawing in the book. Because Neaud's comics are drawn entirely from his daily life rather than his imagination, the drawings that he does in books are of the people who have asked for the *dédicace*. This tendency leads to an engaged conversation between the two about the nature of his work, and particularly about the morality of Neaud's interjection into the public sphere. Is it appropriate, the woman wonders, for Neaud to involve his friends and acquaintances in his comics against their will? He responds with the spirited defence of his interpretation of the nature of privacy that he had failed to deliver to Dominique.

The final conversation is a radio interview done in conjunction with the festival. Fabrice is uncomfortably interrogated by a radio announcer about his publishing house, his book, and his so-called homosexual agenda. In the end he engages in a spirited attack on the interviewer's interpretation of the first volume of his autobiographical comics, arguing that because the work is drawn directly from his life, the man essentially has no right to his clichéd reading of the work. Indeed, Fabrice insists that the man's interpretation of an early part of the series has the effect of reducing reality to a simple trick of amateur fiction, thereby serving to delegitimate the work as both a form of realism and a form of legitimate culture.

These three conversations – arguments, really – allow Neaud to frame his own artistic career in relation to the dominant traditions of the comic book in France. He depicts himself in relation to his art and to the demands of the commercial aspect of that art. Significantly, he casts the commercial element of the Angoulême festival as foreign and alienating, losing his temper with a woman who doesn't buy his book and with a radio host who is helping him promote his book to potential buyers. Neither approach – helping him commercially or hindering his sales – seems to please Neaud, and indeed the book presents the commercialized aspect of comics production as an opposition to the true nature of art, rather than simply critiquing the specific behaviour of these individuals. Similarly, his argument with the woman for whom he drew a *dédicace*, which never turns heated but is always engaged at the level of philosophical exchange, is presented as one of the high points in the narrative. Neaud's amicable conclusion demonstrates how he offers up the intellectual give and take as the preferred reading of his work – it's not about the conclusions, but about the process of argumentation and discovery. This conclusion, which insists upon the communicative rather than the commercial aspect of comic book creation, is a straightforward affirmation of the autonomous principle of art in opposition to the heteronomous demands of the marketplace that he condemns.

From this standpoint, therefore, it is possible to regard the totality of Neaud's *Journal* project as an attempt to stake out a particularly legitimated space in the field of comics production that finds its origins in the intersection of reality and subjectivity within the specific sub-field of autobiographical work.

The sense that autobiographical comics represent an altogether new alternative to the traditions of the European comics market has been widely remarked upon. Indeed, the idea that autobiography and *la nouvelle bande dessinée* are virtual synonyms is hinted at in this anecdote from David B.: 'For example, [François] Boucq in a debate in which I was also participating said: "Yeah, L'Asso, they're the guys who tell us how they brush their teeth."'[47] David B. takes this attack from one of the most celebrated fantasy-adventure comics artists of the previous generation as a harmful reduction, insisting that he is moving on from autobiographical works to concentrate on his fiction. Dupuy and Berberian, of course, have focused primarily upon realist fiction for their entire careers, moving into autobiography for a single book that is intended, at least in large part, to shed light on their relationship to the larger comics community and to each other. Fabrice Neaud, on the other hand, has produced no fictional comics of note and is by far the most militant of the cartoonists discussed in this chapter with regard to the status of autobiography within the field of comics production. These varying dispositions towards autobiography indicate how it is a tool that is taken up by various cartoonists at various moments to signify something about their relationship to the dominant traditions – to shed insight into their work or to oppose the traditions.

Autobiography is not a set of static genre conventions but a tendency that has to be defined in relation to the dominant orthodoxies of the medium at any given historical juncture. Moreover, it is a tendency that can be defined in a variety of ways, depending on the orientation and disposition of the artist. Writing about Marjane Satrapi, *Libération* described *Persepolis* as a book that was filled with 'irony and tenderness, far from the didacticism and the sclerotic heroism that characterize the historical comics.'[48] This casual opposition – the superiority of an intelligent and engaged autobiographical form of comics set against a vulgarized and debased tradition of genre-fiction – serves to legitimate one tendency of contemporary European comics production at the expense of a longer tradition. While this is perhaps beneficial for some specific producers of certain forms of comics, it is nonetheless complicated insofar as a great deal of the energy of the new comics movements of the 1990s has been directed towards resurrecting certain genre conventions long perceived as moribund. If autobiography is the commonplace caricature of the art comics of the 1990s, heroic fantasy is increasingly the reality. The impact of the independent generation of European comics publishers on the established houses is the flip side of the aesthetic revolution ushered in by a focus on personal subjectivity.

Chapter 6

From the Small Press to *La Nouvelle Bande Dessinée*

Guy Vidal, là-dessus, disait que c'était 'L'Association avec du pognon.'

David B.[1]

The hardcover comic book album is so central to the history of European comic book production that for many critics and historians it is virtually impossible to think about that history except as a continuity of album production over time, with a few exceptions. For generations the primary aspiration of European comic book producers has been to create a successful comic book series that can be extended indefinitely in a continuity of forty-six-page volumes. The industrial logic of the largest Franco-Belgian publishing houses – which dominate the European market – has been rooted, as Thierry Groensteen has noted, in the eternal return of popular characters in identifiable and marketable comic book albums.[2]

The album format was introduced to French cartooning in the early 1900s with Joseph Pinchon's creation of *Bécassine* and Louis Forton's *Pieds-Nickelés*. The serial story, an outgrowth of the *feuilleton* tradition, quickly became the major mode for storytelling in comics. For publishers, series offered a high degree of regularity and predictability. A popular series often grew more successful over time as it broadened its audience and as new readers bought the perennially in-print back catalogue in order to keep up with current adventures. The example of René Goscinny and Albert Uderzo's *Astérix*, for instance, demonstrates the huge impact that a successful series could have. The first book, published in 1961, sold only 6,000 copies. Forty years later total sales of the series had reached 300 million.[3] Series featuring popular characters were so crucial to the ongoing financial health of the largest comics publishing houses that they were often continued by new artists and writers beyond the death of the original artists. Groensteen notes that the 1970s, with its focus on stand-alone stories and shorter works, promised an end to the series tradition by elevating comics fully into the realm of literature, but in fact the reverse proved true. Innovative French cartoonists in the 1970s ultimately developed their own popular series – for example, Jacques Tardi's *Adèle Blanc-Sec* and *Nestor Burma* books and Jean-Michel Charlier and Jean Giraud's *Blueberry* – and the 1980s actually witnessed an expansion of the importance of album series in the market. Groensteen notes that in 1983 63.5 per cent of all albums released were part of a series, but by 1992 that figure had risen to 73.5 per cent.[4] In 1997, sixty-seven of the seventy top-selling albums were part of a larger series, featuring ongoing characters, with the three non-series bestsellers attributable to canonical authors from the previous generation (Jacques Tardi, Milo Manara, and Wolinski).[5] The ability of series to construct a faithful audience – whose loyalties could often be expanded to include similar series from the same or different publishers – created a publishing institution rooted in nostalgia, an inbred culture in which projects are promoted based on their similarities to previous work.

Like all inbred cultures, the French comics industry of the early 1990s was remarkably unstable and was approaching a crisis. In 1991, 765 comic books were published in France, a record up to that point. The following years, however, witnessed declines in sales, profitability, and titles published. In 1995, when sales bottomed out, the industry produced 481 titles, with four companies (Dupuis, Dargaud/Lombard, Casterman, and Glénat) accounting for 70 per cent of the volume of titles released and 90 per cent of the sales.[6] By 1997, the industry had nearly rebounded to the levels of 1991, with 726 titles published over the course of the year and several bestsellers breaking the 100,000 sales mark, led by *XIII* (Jean van Hamme and William Vance [Dargaud]), with 490,000 copies sold, and *Joe Bar Team* (Stéphane Deteindre, Vent d'Ouest [Glénat]), at 340,000 copies.[7] By 1999, with the rising importance of translated Japanese manga (often published in monthly volumes), new titles totalled 1055, and sales continued to increase. The big four publishers continued to dominate the market, with Dupuis recording sales of 370 million francs, ahead of Dargaud/Lombard (272 million), Flammarion, which had purchased both Casterman and *Fluide Glacial* (187 million), and Glénat-Vents d'Ouest (180 million).[8]

A further indicator of the success of the traditional comics industry at this point was the fact that four comics placed among the top ten bestsellers for all forms of books in France during the year, although two were by artists who were already dead (a posthumous book by André Franquin and a re-edition from Hergé). By 2001, the industry recorded a seventh consecutive year of growth, and total publications rose beyond 1200, or approximately 25 new comics released each week. At the same time, however, the growth merely continued a consolidation logic within the industry, with traditional bestsellers (*Titeuf, XIII, Thorgal, Blake et Mortimer, Petit Spirou,* and the record-setting *Astérix,* with three million copies sold in less than a year) dominating the entirety of the market.[9] So pronounced was this tendency that in 2003 the left-leaning daily *Libération* simply tired of reporting the industrial statistics, replacing the report with a brief essay questioning the logic of the marketplace:

> Each Angoulême brings its batch of industrial statistics. But the trouble with surveys of this kind is that one doesn't know very well what is being talked about when weighing up '*la BD.*' Is a film by Cédric Kahn the same thing as a rubbishy Hollywood film? Does one, in the statistics on the sales of novels, also include the *Bibliothèque rose*? And the fact that *Star Ac'* sells more albums than Brigitte Fontaine, must that necessarily inspire flabbergasted commentary? We learn that the comic book bestsellers in 2002 resemble those of the past ten years, with its winners being *Titeuf, XIII, Largo Winch, Titeuf, Titeuf, Titeuf, Titeuf, Titeuf* and *Titeuf* (note that there are several volumes).[10]

At the same time, however, the paper also noted for the first time that artists of the independent generation were factoring into the lists of bestsellers: 'It's Marjane Satrapi who has broken the glass ceiling with 100 000 copies of the first three volumes of *Persepolis,* followed closely by Christophe Blain.'[11] The success of artists like Blain and Satrapi indicated that the small-press comics revolution was no longer entirely small and had entered into a new economic and cultural phase that meant that its separation from all those *Titeuf* volumes was no longer so cut and dried.

To come to terms with the significant ways in which the small-press comics explosion of the 1990s differed from – and later resembled – the album heritage of European comics production, it is necessary to consider some work that resides in the mainstream of contemporary comics production. Comic book writer Jean Van Hamme best represents this tendency. Known as 'Mr. 10%' because his books account for that percentage of all comics sold in a given year,[12] Van Hamme is, as journalist

Bruno Canard among others has pointed out, rejected out of hand by defenders of a 'bande dessinée de creation.'[13] Indeed, in Lewis Trondheim's strip about Fabrice Neaud's autobiography, he twice cites examples of Van Hamme's work as 'badly written.'[14] While it is not clear that Trondheim's comments should be taken entirely seriously in the context of that parodic strip, it is nonetheless noteworthy that he assumes that the *Lapin* audience will recognize a contempt for Van Hamme and his work as commonsensical.

Van Hamme's success in the 1990s can be seen as the confluence of several factors. First, Van Hamme himself is a prolific writer. He began working in comics in 1968 with Paul Cuvelier, before turning to gag writing for *Modeste et Pimpon* and *Gaston Lagaffe,* where he worked with André Franquin. In 1977 he created, with artist Grzegorz Rosinski, the Viking series *Thorgal* (Lombard). In 1984, with William Vance, he created the spy thriller series *XIII* (Dargaud). Six years later, with Philippe Francq, he launched a suspense series set in the world of international finance, entitled *Largo Winch* (Dupuis). Finally, in 1992 he created, with Francis Vallès, *Les Maîtres de l'orge* (Glénat, 1992–8), a series of historical novels tracing the rise of a Belgian family-owned brewery.

Working constantly with four different artists – and four different publishers – has meant that a steady flow of Van Hamme's work has appeared in comic book stores and also that each series is aggressively promoted by its publisher, with none falling to secondary status. Further, Van Hamme truly arrived as a writer in the 1980s as the previous generation of comic writing stars – such as Hergé, Goscinny, and Greg – retired from the field or passed away. Van Hamme arrived at precisely the right moment with a collection of works ready to fill a large number of holes. Finally, his work fell entirely within the classical model. He writes within the traditions of the album format and with artists whose work – highly skilled as it may be – does not challenge the conventions of the form. As Bourdieu notes, popular artists such as Van Hamme remain popular in a circular fashion precisely because they are the most readable, having successfully defined what is 'readable.'[15] In short, Van Hamme emerged in the 1990s as the ultimate comic book traditionalist. Indeed, Canard goes so far as to note that the neoliberal politics of his books – which are celebrations of masculine control and in which women are regarded as the tributaries of male power – are perfectly suited to the masculine subculture that is comic book reading.[16] Van Hamme, therefore, personifies virtually every attribute that the new European small press positions itself against. He is perceived as the ultimate middlebrow artist, writing books in order to maximize public demand rather than for other, more autonomous, goals.

As Lewis Trondheim's parody of Neaud demonstrates, Van Hamme's comics occupy the space that those associated with small-press comics define as self-evidently beneath contempt. For example, *XIII*, a series inspired by Robert Ludlum's novel *The Bourne Identity* and pre-published in *Spirou*, follows the adventures of an amnesiac secret agent whose identity has been stripped from him and who is known by the Roman numerals tattooed on his neck. As the series progresses XIII uncovers a variety of false identities that he had taken on in his previous life, ultimately coming to believe that he may be the assassin of the president of the United States. Central to *XIII* is a narrative of large-scale government and military corruption and an attempt to create a military dictatorship in the United States. The end of the fifth book in the series essentially resolves this coup plot, with subsequent volumes maintaining a number of the supporting characters and villains as XIII moves into new international adventures in a quest to discover the truth about his past. The books are presented in a classically realist visual mode that makes them resemble the aesthetics of the spy film or television series. They often have cliffhanger endings that encourage the purchase of the next volume, a tendency slightly at odds with the traditions of French album publishing, which generally sought to present a story that was complete in a single volume but which nonetheless featured ongoing and recurring characters. *XIII*, on the other hand, cannot be read as a set of single-volume stories, with the series moving forward as a succession of five interconnected novels followed by another series of three, another of two, and so on. *XIII*, therefore, can be defined as a potentially open-ended collection of spy novels told in a realist fashion with tremendous emphasis placed on continuity in order to build a faithful audience dedicated to reading about XIII's continuing action adventures.

The formula has proven extremely successful, with the first *XIII* book selling less than 20,000 copies in France and the twelfth – prepublished in *Libération* in 1997 – selling more than 400,000 copies in France in its first three months of availability. Clearly, then, *XIII* represents the antithesis of the contemporary European small press: a bestselling genre series published in the most traditional of formats and visual styles.

An extremely different image of Van Hamme's work can be found in *Les Maîtres de l'orge*, a closed series of eight novels. Each of these books takes place over a short period of time, although the series as a whole spans the years 1854 to 1997. As the novels follow the fortunes of a

Belgian beer-brewing family, there is a high degree of continuity in which characters introduced as children in one volume emerge as the central adults in the subsequent volumes. From this standpoint, the series is closely related to any number of generations-spanning series of historical novels, despite the fact that this has not traditionally been a central genre in the field of European comic book publishing. Indeed, *Les Maîtres de l'orge* began as a historical novel by Van Hamme.

Like *XIII, Les Maîtres de l'orge* is drawn in a classical realist mode that recalls the aesthetics of film and television, and the series became the inspiration for a television mini-series. The books are roughly self-contained. Each volume stands alone as a story, although it also has a greater role in the development of the overall narrative featuring the rise to prominence of the Steenfort family. In many ways, this series is more traditional than *XIII,* although the atypical subject, and the use of domestic melodrama genre conventions, has meant that it has found less success than Van Hamme's work in the classical comic book genres.

Marking a further departure from the work in *XIII* is the fact that the final volume of the saga, *Les Steenfort,* takes on a radically different form than the first seven. *Les Steenfort* is not entirely a comic book. Half of its pages comprise a series of comic strip short stories that serve to flesh out important back-story elements left out of the main narrative. The remaining pages, however, take the form of a fictional prose diary by a Belgian writer named Jean-Francis V..., a stand-in for Van Hamme, who recounts his meeting with the central character of the final volume of the series. Jean-Francis becomes the ghostwriter for François Fenton, the Steenfort heir unjustly convicted of a murder that he did not commit, and writes his autobiography, which is eventually turned into a television series, just as Van Hamme himself created a novel, a comic book series, and a television mini-series. The incorporation of a narrator stand-in for Van Hamme himself within his own fiction is a radical departure from the traditions of the Franco-Belgian comic book series and calls into question – to some degree – our ability to simply dismiss Van Hamme's work as straightforward classicism.

Van Hamme's relationship to the heritage of Franco-Belgian cartooning is further problematized by his high-profile 1996 book *L'Affaire Francis Blake* (Blake & Mortimer), created with artist Ted Benoit. This book was based on characters created by E.P. Jacobs which debuted in the pages of the first issue of *Tintin* in September 1946. Jacobs, who had once worked as an assistant to Hergé, created a series of books that are among the most popular and most celebrated in the history of the Franco-Belgian school. Revolving around the postwar adventures of British nuclear physicist Philip Mortimer and MI5 director Francis Blake, the twelve books in the series found the adventurers fighting dastardly villains around the globe in a distinctly pre–James Bondian British fashion. In the early 1990s the Jacobs estate authorized the production of new books based on the characters, turning to Ted Benoit – an artist whose work was highly influenced by that of Hergé and Jacobs – and to Van Hamme, the most popular of contemporary comic book writers.

L'Affaire Francis Blake was a tremendous commercial success, although the ethics of continuing the series without Jacobs – who had died in 1987 – was widely questioned. The book itself is marked by a rigorous fidelity to the spirit of the source material. The story is told very much like a Jacobs story, with a complicated but not convoluted plot that unfolds like a smartly written boy's own adventure book. In short, the text is an homage to one of the most beloved figures in the canon of Franco-Belgian cartooning, and a book that seeks to further consecrate that work through the loving recreation of its spirit. Whether this is a success or not is clearly a matter of personal preference. More importantly, however, the book signals Van Hamme's investment in placing himself within the heritage of Franco-Belgian cartoonists as an equal, rather than as a rebel. Indeed, despite the gestures towards self-reflexive modernism in *Les Steenfort*, Van Hamme's work is a model of neoclassicism in the comic book form, celebrating the conventions of established genres through the rigorous application of skills that are frequently dismissed as workmanlike. It is precisely this mobilization of classical compositional skills that problematizes Van Hamme's work for cartoonists involved with the challenge to the established traditions offered by the contemporary small press.

What Van Hamme's work signals most of all is the ongoing relevance of the Franco-Belgian album heritage in contemporary comic book production. While independent comic books may generate a large amount of the public's attention, it is still the stalwart album series that carry the bulk of sales. The aesthetic structures of the album may have come under fire from the small press since the beginning of the 1990s, but its centrality to the economics of the industry has hardly wavered. In 1999 Groensteen suggested that

the alternative editors that appeared in the 1990s (L'Association, Cornélius, Amok, Fréon, Ego Comme X ...), insensitive to the 'charms of the series,' reinvented *la bande dessinée d'auteur* while joining with the transitory conquests of the 1970s ... With twenty years' distance, it is not as though the same part is being replayed. Even through the conception of the printed form (characterized by a greater diversity of formats), the will displayed to organize young creation on an international scale, and certain tendencies of creation itself (illustrative, formalist, literary, social or autobiographical), there is a new approach to the medium that, gradually, continues.[17]

Yet I would point out that the opposite could be just as easily argued: that the new approach to the medium has, far from being affirmed, already been absorbed into the traditions of the Franco-Belgian school. The scope of this school – its sheer economic force and the nostalgic and ideological pull that it exerts on artists who were raised reading its output – cannot be underestimated. The sheer number of artists who began their careers with the small press but who have moved to the creation of traditional album series – as a part of their artistic practice or as the whole of it – is increasing as the small-press challenge to the market continues. It is clear, following Bourdieu, that the heteronomous market of large-scale production has begun the process of converting the new legitimacy of the small press by incorporating their productions into the traditional model. While this process is, at best, selective, it is nonetheless thorough and ongoing. Some of the largest publishers of comic books in Europe – the traditional Franco-Belgian publishing houses like Casterman, Dargaud, Dupuis, and Les Humanoïdes Associés – have met the challenge offered by the small press by hiring those artists to bring the 'small-press style' into the mainstream. In so doing, they have threatened not only the long-term viability of their fledgling rivals, the small-press publishers, but have resituated the criteria of legitimacy within the field of comics production. Just as avant-garde visual practices and artisanal productions had succeeded in establishing a new criteria of value outside the confines of mass production, the game has been shifted by those most closely affiliated with the heteronomous principle.

By bringing small-press cartoonists under their tent, the large publishing houses reassert their authority and their legacy. Once the gatekeepers of the most lucrative comic book traditions – whether represented by Hergé, Jacobs, Goscinny and Uderzo, Charlier and Giraud, Tardi, or any of dozens of other celebrated cartoonists – the large houses champion selective representatives of the small-press scene in order to suggest that continuity – rather than rupture – characterizes the development of cartooning since the 1990s. The small press, having raised the question of what constitutes an artist in the field of comic book production, risks losing the ability to define a response in the face of a mass migration of artists to the larger houses. The net result is artists working from both ends of the field.

The migration of cartoonists from the small presses to the established publishers raises the question of whether it is possible to maintain one's status as an author while working in the domain of large-scale cultural production. In other words, what does the field of large-scale production have to offer as a legitimating principle in light of the increasing autonomy of the field under the small press? Processes of mass production, the hallmark of the largest publishers, have long been suspect in the arts. The notion that the 'cultural industry' has a negative impact on the arts has been a constant since Adorno and Horkheimer first used the term in the 1940s to argue that cultural items were being produced in a manner analogous to how other industries manufactured general consumer goods. Adorno and Horkheimer decried the rise of mass production and the regularization of culture through genre. Despite the fact that the vast majority of cultural production at any given moment takes place within relatively stable 'genre worlds,'[18] genre has been frequently mobilized as a term of derision within various cultural fields. In the case of contemporary European comic books, for example, genres such as heroic fantasy and the spy thriller – styles at which writers like Jean Van Hamme excel – are often dismissed as self-evidently less serious than 'personal' works or books in more esteemed traditions such as autobiography. According to this logic, the distinction between the small and large publishing houses is articulated as a function of economics.

While it is possible to approach the question of genre in formal terms, I wish to minimize that approach by drawing on Steve Neale's concept of genres as sociological, 'not ... as forms of textual codifications, but as systems of orientations, expectations and conventions that circulate between industry, text and subject.'[19] Specifically, since the beginning of the 1990s, the notion of 'independent comics' has been formally codified by publishers into assumptions about markets that are then strategically manipulated by comic book publishers to achieve greater sales.

The perceived opposition between large cultural enterprises and artists derives, as Pierre Bourdieu notes, from a conception of artistic autonomy that was greatly accelerated by the Industrial Revolution and the Romantic reaction.[20] Writing about popular music, a field that shares with comics an attenuated degree of fan–artist affect and a heightened concern with the politics of authenticity, David Hesmondhalgh argues that this conception of autonomy has produced the widespread view that creativity can only flourish when it is removed as far as possible from the realm of commerce. This view is encoded into the myth of the artist unrecognized by commercial success in his own lifetime (Van Gogh) and the myth of the artist driven to despair by the superficiality of the commercial world that he inhabits (Kurt Cobain).[21] He further argues that the rise of so-called independent music, or popular music produced by bands and record labels beyond the reach of the largest record companies, was predicated upon the notion that it was superior to other genres because it was based on new relationships between creativity and commerce. Hesmondhalgh notes 'no music genre had ever before taken its name from the form of industrial organization behind it.'[22] Indie music did not rely exclusively on the idea that it represented a more relevant and authentic connection to youth culture, but this assumption was ideologically bound to the model of independent creation.

Keith Negus points out the way in which independent hip hop record labels derive an aesthetic of authenticity and credibility by positioning themselves as 'closer to the street' than the major labels in the field.[23] In this way, an economic position within the field is celebrated for its aesthetic potential. Writers like Charlie Gillett have suggested that the most important developments in the history of popular music – from rhythm and blues to rock 'n' roll – originated with independent record companies before being co-opted by the majors.[24] The suggestion of co-optation, of course, is central to common understandings of the development of popular culture, which has long been regarded as cheapening the advances made by avant-gardes in various fields of cultural production. The notion of the authenticity of the independents – exemplified in the field of contemporary comics production by atypical, non-genre comics made in an artisanal fashion – carries with it the constant threat of co-optation or, worse, 'selling out.' Since at least the era of 1970s punk, the idea of independence has been rigorously politicized to the point that professionalism of any kind risks accusations that an artist or publisher has abandoned his or her political or aesthetic commitments for financial gain.[25] The allegation of 'selling out' carries with it a particularly nasty ideological charge, rooted in a sense of betrayal. As Stephen Lee observes, the notion of independence in the cultural field is tied to the creation of a sense of community among cultural producers and their fans.[26] A shift away from independence can create an affective rupture between artists and fans that is experienced by fans as a betrayal of common assumptions and aspirations. In the specific case of contemporary European comic book production, charges of 'selling out' have been levelled at a large number of artists who are perceived – fairly or unfairly – to have moved beyond the narrow confines of independence and into the field of unabashed commercial production.

The inverse of the 'selling out' phenomenon is co-optation. Although they essentially describe the same process, the former defines a moral failure of the artist while the latter describes a business practice of commercial publishers generally held to be predatory and pernicious. Writing about the experience of rock 'n' roll music, Steve Chapple and Reebee Garofalo have suggested that it is the structure of the music industry that sets up the specific processes of co-optation. They argue that it is the system of selling records that commodifies the artists, reducing them to images consisting of selling points that are then circulated through advertising.[27] This line of argument, hearkening back to the writings of Adorno and Horkheimer, assumes that any participation in systems of economic exchange constitutes an act of co-optation of the artist. Yet at the same time it suggests one of the central ways in which markets for cultural goods are maintained. Negus reminds us that markets are not simply out there in the world but are carefully constructed entities requiring the investment of staff and systems for monitoring and researching purchase trends.[28] In the field of cultural production, small or independent companies are often seen to have one advantage over their largest competitors insofar as they are – due to their proximity to the 'street' – more capable of reacting to new trends and discovering new talent.

Lee suggests that independent record companies turn a market disadvantage (their inability to compete for a general audience) into an advantage by concentrating on new and innovative sounds targeted at niche audiences.[29] Clearly, a similar argument could be made about comic book publishers like L'Association, Frémok, BüLB, and others that have come to demarcate the 'indie' space in contemporary European comic book production. Lee suggests three possible outcomes of the subordinate relationship of the independent cultural producer in relation to the larger companies: first, the major buys the indie; second, the major forces the indie out of business; third, the major converts the indie to its own ideology of 'proper business practice,' thereby encouraging consolidation in order to eliminate competition.[30] From this perspective, the co-optation of the independent cultural producer – either through incorporation, elimination, or conversion – reduces the status of the 'independent' to a brand within the field of consumption representing a set of practices or attitudes rather than an aesthetic and institutional position.[31]

Bourdieu has noted how 'the professional ideology of producers-for-producers and their spokespeople establishes an opposition between creative liberty and the laws of the market, between works which create their public and works created by their public.'[32] Nonetheless, this opposition is unstable and constantly under assault. Indeed, participation of any kind in the operations of the market demonstrates how this opposition is little more than an ideological stance. The modes of production identified by Bourdieu – large-scale production oriented towards the conquest of the market and restricted production oriented towards the autonomous principle of consecration – cannot be established as fixed entities but are more clearly seen as relational positions within the field. While the category of large-scale production corresponds to the publishers of contemporary genre comics such as those created by Jean Van Hamme, the category of restricted production coincides with the concept of the independent press only in imprecise terms, for these publishers are not autonomous but simply present themselves as less heteronomous than their larger counterparts. Each type of publisher is, however, oriented towards its own economic survival, although each uses different approaches to achieve this goal. Moreover, the migration of artists from the independent presses to the larger publishing houses calls into question the possibility of claiming that the small press represents a substantially different model of cultural production.

For many commentators, the increasing interdependence of the large and small publishing houses in Belgium and France is a sign of the corporatization of the independent comics movement that began in the early 1990s. These critics see interdependence as a signal of failure, as the end of the possibility that the independents could offer a legitimate and totalizing alternative to the established presses. As Herman Gray has pointed out regarding the production of jazz recordings, however, 'the reality of the music industry is sufficiently complex that the activities of large majors cannot be equated only with the commodification of music (and the corruption of its meanings) and independents only with preserving its cultural significance.'[33] The simple ideological binary that privileges the products of independent producers is needlessly reductionist and fails to consider the important ways in which the field has been restructured by the confluence of an independent ideology and a professionalized market system.

Since at least the mid-1990s, French comic book publishers have sought to account for the challenges presented by the small presses. The contemporary market situation resembles what Negus has described in the music industry as a complex web of relationships between majors and minors.[34] The particularities of this web can be best understood through an examination of the way a number of artists traditionally associated with the independent movement of *la nouvelle bande dessinée* have collaborated in the production of genre works for well-established commercial publishers like Dargaud, Delcourt, and Dupuis.

The specific case of the French publisher Dargaud offers the greatest insight into the current relationship of the large and small presses in the contemporary francophone comics industry. Dargaud was founded by Georges Dargaud in 1936. The company began publishing comics in 1943 with *Allô les jeunes*. In 1948 it acquired the rights to produce the French edition of the popular Belgian magazine *Tintin*, published by Lombard. In the years that followed it also began distributing a number of Lombard titles in France, including *Blake et Mortimer, Alix, Ric Hochet, Michel Vaillant,* and many others. In 1960 the company bought *Pilote* magazine, which was facing financial difficulties at the time. Placing faith in that magazine's artists and editors led to a tremendous success, with cartoonists like René Goscinny, Jean-Michel Charlier, Uderzo, Jean Giraud, Fred, Philippe Druillet, and Enki Bilal passing through its pages. At the same time, it launched an extensive collection of its own albums, including *Astérix, Barbe-Rouge, Blueberry, Lucky Luke, Achille Talon,* and others. By 1984 its catalogue had swelled to more than 1500 titles, representing more than 40 per cent of the French-language comics market. In 1988 Georges Dargaud sold his interest in the company to Média-Participations, a larger media company that continued to run the company under his name.

Dargaud's intersection with the new comics movement of the 1990s came from editor Guy Vidal's desire to work with Lewis Trondheim, at that time published by Cornélius, L'Association, Rackham, Seuil, and several smaller presses. In 1995 Dargaud published *Blacktown,* Trondheim's first traditional full-colour hard-cover album, and in 1997 it published a completely redrawn version of his Alph'Art-winning, black-and-white, L'Association-published album *Slaloms,* this time in full colour. That same year it launched its own black-and-white album collection in a format that resembled L'Association's Collection Ciboulette. The earliest books in the Roman BD series included work from L'Association co-founder David B. (*Le Tengû Carré*), as well as from L'Association-published artists such as Joann Sfar (*Paris-Londres*). Having signed two of the six L'Association co-founders to publishing contracts, the publisher seemed poised to quickly capitalize on the success of that particular independent publisher.

Dargaud's efforts to expand its offerings based on the work of these – and other – independent artists hit a roadblock in September 1998, when the French court of appeals ruled in favour of Albert Uderzo that the publisher had deprived him of his authorship rights as the co-creator of the bestselling *Astérix* series. Dargaud had published the earliest adventures of Astérix in *Pilote* in the 1960s, and the magazine's success was largely due to the popularity of the character created by Uderzo with writer René Goscinny. Dargaud published the first twenty-four *Astérix* albums, but when Goscinny died in 1977 Uderzo began to self-publish the subsequent books through his own company, Éditions Albert-René. The lawsuit brought by Uderzo charged that Dargaud had deprived him by selling the rights for Spanish- and German-language editions of the books to its own subsidiaries rather than to the highest bidder. Because of these actions, the court ruled that Uderzo was free to move the original twenty-four volumes of his series to Éditions Albert-René and to renegotiate the foreign rights on his own, cutting his former publisher out of the loop entirely.

The effect of this decision on Dargaud's revenues was substantial. In close to four decades more than 250 million *Astérix* books had been sold. *Astérix* represented 1.5 million books sold by the company each year, or roughly 60,000 copies of each title annually. Those sales represented between 35 and 40 per cent of the company's revenues and approximately 80 per cent of its profit margin. The sudden loss of this title – in addition to compensation that the company owed to Uderzo – nearly caused the collapse of the firm. The company was completely restructured in the wake of the departure of its cornerstone publication, and editor Guy Vidal was among those charged with discovering new revenue streams. He turned towards L'Association.

In the wake of the relative success of Trondheim's *Lapinot* series, Vidal chose to create a new line at Dargaud entitled Poisson Pilote. With a name chosen to recall the magazine that had placed the company firmly at the vanguard of French comic book production in the 1960s, the Poisson Pilote line brought together the work of Trondheim and David B. with a number of other artists who shared a similar sensibility or aesthetic. Indeed, it is fair to say that Poisson Pilote represented an attempt to sell the idea of independence within the confines of a major traditional album-publishing house.

Among the artists who launched album series in the Poisson Pilote line were Joann Sfar (*Le Chat du rabbin, Le Minuscule Mousquetaire*),

Patrice and Manu Larcenet (*Les Entremondes*), Guy Delisle (*L'Inspecteur Moroni*), Christophe Blain (*Isaac le pirate*), Pierre and Franck Le Gall (*Les Petits Contes noirs*), and a host of series involving the participation of either David B. or Lewis Trondheim. These series were grouped together, according to Vidal, as a process of maximizing the investment of Dargaud in the small press: 'There is an indisputable air of family between them; we thought of joining them together under the same banner to better defend them commercially.'[35] Launched in 2000, the series won two Alph'Arts for 'Best Album' in its first four years (Christophe Blain's *Les Amériques* in 2002, and Manu Larcenet's *Le Combat ordinaire* in 2004), marking the line as an immediate critical success story.

At the time the line was created a number of critics called it a transparent effort to co-opt the vitality that was associated with L'Association. David B. responded to these criticisms by noting:

> The large publishers who solicited us, asked us to come and make at their place the same things that we had made at L'Association. Ultimately, the same thing, with the necessary concessions. Black and white was not inevitable; we made 46-page colour books or 54 pages in colour. There were obligatory passages. But apart from that, I was always absolutely free to do what I wanted at Dargaud, at Dupuis.[36]

David B.'s emphasis on freedom – however limited by the conventions of the 46- or 54-page colour album – was reinforced by the publisher's positioning of the artists as comic book rebels who – while working for Dargaud – were in revolt against the traditions of the marketplace that had been established by publishers like Dargaud. Vidal argued:

> But there is always a revolt against the established things. I cited Goscinny and Charlier ... they also revolted a bit in the 1960s against the existing comics magazines. In the same way, in the years 70–5, Mandryka, Bretécher, Gotlib ... they revolted against Goscinny who represented the old school ... In the same way, these young people who come from l'Association have revolted against the dominant paradigms of the 80s and 90s and created what they have created, and enlarged, to my eyes, the field of the comic book. The comic book is considerably enriched compared to when I started in the 60s. When I was a kid, comic books were for children ... Now, that is perhaps fortunate – I'm thinking of *Boule et Bill*, of *Titeuf* ... – but the field of investigation and exploration in comics has been considerably enriched and I find that wonderful.[37]

Nonetheless, this field of exploration did not extend beyond the confines of the traditional album and series format, which was retained by all of the artists at the company's insistence. Vidal, while insisting that Dargaud is the most generalist publisher of comics in Europe, drew attention to the fact that things are simply different when one moves from the small press to the larger houses:

> These authors have intelligently realized that Dargaud was not L'Association and that Dargaud was a relatively large machine in the publishing universe. We can't have the same operation as a structure like L'Association, which is a small organization and which allows things that Dargaud cannot allow.[38]

Thus, the question ultimately becomes: How central are those things that L'Association permits and Dargaud does not to the project of contemporary comics production in Europe? Are small-press comics simply bestsellers in waiting? Or is there a substantive formal difference between the work of Jean Van Hamme and the artists who publish in the Poisson Pilote line?

Two artists occupy the position between the small presses and the major publishers most clearly: Lewis Trondheim and Joann Sfar, who together are responsible for the mammoth Delcourt-published fantasy album series *Donjon* (Trondheim, and *Donjon,* will be discussed in the next chapter). If, as Chapple and Garofalo argue, popular musicians sow the seeds of their own co-optation through the commodifying process of selling records, reducing the artists to little more than images, it is easy to see this same process at work in the case of Joann Sfar. In July 2003, for example, Sfar appeared on the cover of the French music magazine *Les Inrockuptibles,* a visual space generally reserved for rock stars rather than cartoonists from the small press. At that time Sfar had published more than fifty books in the preceding six years, a breakneck pace vastly outstripping the production of more traditional mainstream stars like Van Hamme, who averaged about one book per year to Sfar's nine.

Sfar's production of two pages of finished art per day[39] marks his most notable difference from a figure like Van Hamme, although the distinction can be drawn in a number of other important respects. First, unlike a neoclassical figure like Van Hamme or the classical figures of the postwar Franco-Belgian comics industry, Sfar claims to have no idea where his stories are going.[40] Sfar maintains that his work is largely improvised from loose structures and that he responds to the voices that he hears in his head by developing his work with no set agenda. Similarly, his art is a departure from the norms of the classical Franco-Belgian school. While not as challenging to the established hierarchies as much of the work that constitutes the contemporary avant-garde of European comics, Sfar's sketchy art – praised as 'sensual and protean' by *Beaux Arts Magazine*[41] – little recalls the realism of the classical period.

Despite his differences from traditional representational norms in the comics field, Sfar shares only a passing resemblance to the comic book avant-gardes that posit comics in relation to painting. He argues that comics have lost the war with painting but that it can win a war against writing:

> I think that comics definitely lost the battle with the fine arts because a page hung on a wall always remains less impressive than a painting. And each time we try to make museums for the comic book, we only arrive at the ankle of the Louvre! On the other hand, the battle that comics must win is with literature. Because, undoubtedly, a comic book is a book, is an object that has literary and cultural content that is often more interesting than what is created in contemporary literature.[42]

Sfar's focus on the textual rather than visual potential of comics is the primary marker that he has 'betrayed' the small-press movement. By privileging the textual, Sfar breaks with the avant-gardist tendency that has championed the pursuit of legitimation from the visual arts. Sfar's recognition of comics' ability to fill the gaps in contemporary literature appears to be an offshoot of his own particular intervention into the field, which is in fact tied more concretely to the textual than to the visual.

In narrative terms, Sfar's comics often highlight questions of Jewish cultural identity. Correctly identifying Jewishness as a key absence in the history of European comics production,[43] Sfar draws on a large number of Jewish archetypes for characters and Jewish folklore for inspiration. Thus, a cartoonist like Sfar is distinguished from a writer like Van Hamme through his choice of subject matter, narrative trajectory, and volume of production. Yet, Sfar is still distinguished from more traditional writers insofar as the art on his books breaks from the classical aesthetics characterized by Van Hamme's collaborators. Thus, despite the fact that he has 'sold out' the small-press movement by distancing himself from one of its central tenets, his work remains equally distant from that of the mainstream. In short, Sfar represents the possibility of a third way forward, actualized by the intrusion of a small-press aesthetic into the domain of large-scale production.

Sfar's credentials in the small-press world of contemporary comics publishing are well established and deep. Despite the large number of projects that he has undertaken for publishers like Delcourt and Dargaud, his publishing origins are with Cornélius, L'Association, and Amok, and he continues to work for L'Association on two major undertakings. As one of the most prolific cartoonists of his generation, Sfar is responsible for a large number of series, many of which stem from his time in the small press. Sfar's earliest books – *Noyé le poisson* (L'Association, 1994), *Les Aventures d'Ossour Hyrsidoux* (Cornélius, 1994–5), *Le Borgne Gauchet au centre de la terre* (L'Association, 1995) – were largely irreverent small-press glosses on the type of adventure comics published by the large houses. During this time he introduced explicitly Jewish themes in his stories, as in *Le Petit Monde du Golem*, serialized in *Lapin* and *Cheval sans tête* from 1994 to 1996.

By 1996 he had begun to make the transition to full-colour albums, creating series such as *Pétrus Babygère* (Delcourt, 1996) with writer Pierre Dubois, and the award-winning *La Fille du professeur* (Dupuis, 1997) with artist Emmanuel Guibert. In 1998, with the release of the first volume of *Donjon*, his transition to the large publishing houses seemed complete, yet he maintained a connection to L'Association, publishing *Pascin* (in the pages of *Lapin* from the fifteenth issue onward, as well as developing a series of *carnets* for the publisher.

Sfar's two ongoing projects for L'Association serve as counterpoints for the work that he does at the larger publishers. *Beaux Arts Magazine* called *Pascin* 'the most personal part of his approach to comics,'[44] privileging the work against his more commercial production. *Pascin* (figure 18) is a biography of the Jewish modernist painter from Montparnasse, with a particular focus on his personal and erotic life, depicted in a decidedly non-erotic manner. Sfar, who wrote his university thesis on the relationship that Jewish painters have with the human body, with a particular emphasis on Chagall, Soutine, Kokoschka, and Pascin,[45] uses *Pascin* as a sort of laboratory in which new representational and storytelling modes are developed in an environment more hospitable to experimentation.

More recently, he has undertaken an even less traditional series of publications for L'Association, a series of autobiographical sketchbooks mostly named for musical instruments and household objects: *Harmonica, Piano, Ukulélé, Parapluie,* and *Caravan* (L'Association, 2002–5). These volumes, which range in length from 125 to 848 pages, constitute a tremendous intervention into the field. In 2003 alone, Sfar published more than 1000 pages of autobiographical comics through L'Association,

18 Pascin paints a portrait of Antanas. From *Pascin* volume 5, by Joann Sfar.

in addition to his other projects. The *carnets*, unfinished stream-of-consciousness sketchbook material, represent a serious departure from the traditions of comic book publishing. The *carnets* include not only sketches but hand-written essays, faxes, doodles, memos, and even musical tablature. In *Parapluie*, the third volume in the series, Sfar discusses work that he has undertaken in the film industry, developing a script for a movie based on his characters. He suggests that the difference between the two media revolves around the question of spontaneity. Sfar's drawings, particularly in the *carnets* series but elsewhere as well, are finalized in minutes and can develop without a set course, much like a conversation. His work in film, on the other hand, requires careful preplanning. Of course, the high-finance world of the film industry does not allow for the type of improvisation that Sfar is permitted in the world of comics, particularly in the world of small-press comics. In the end, Sfar conceptualizes comics as a medium of artistic freedom that permits experimentation and improvisation, an aesthetic which he developed in the small press but which he has sought to transfer to the larger houses.

Sfar's desire to work for the larger publishing houses – and to work within the field of genre-based comics – stemmed, he insists, from a realization that publishing through the large houses was a greater guarantor of financial success. Sfar told interviewer Hugues Dayez that: '*Le Petit Monde du Golem*, which is so close to my heart, sells terribly with 2000 copies at L'Association, while this *Troll* that I don't like sells more than 20,000.'[46] Accordingly, Sfar's work has increasingly become a blend of the two tendencies – that is, he produces books in the style that he likes but for the type of commercially oriented publishers who produced *Troll*. Sfar's solo work for Dargaud and Delcourt consists of a number of related but distinct series, including *Le Chat du rabbin* (Dargaud), *Le Minuscule Mousquetaire* (Dargaud), *Petit Vampire* (Delcourt Jeunesse), and *Grand Vampire* (Delcourt). Of these, *Le Chat du rabbin* has been the most successful. It was the serialization of the third volume in this series that placed Sfar on the cover of *Les Inrockuptibles* in the summer of 2003, and the books have appeared frequently on the bestselling albums list regularly compiled by *L'Express*.[47]

Le Chat du rabbin is Sfar's most explicitly Jewish-themed series. The stories revolve around a talking cat who challenges his master – a rabbi – to instruct him in the Jewish faith so that he might have his bar mitzvah. The fantastic element of the story is moderated by a keen desire for the books to be taken seriously as a novelistic enterprise. Individual volumes are introduced by forewords written by notable public figures, including

French novelist Eliette Abécassis and Algerian humorist Fellag, and the books deal with serious issues through the use of absurd humour. Sfar, who rejects the incorporation of historical language in books that are set in the past, structures these stories around self-conscious wordplay addressing cultural identity – as when the cat and an ass debate whether the root of the word 'Sfar' is Hebrew or Arabic – and issues of faith – as when the cat uses carbon dating to refute the rabbi's contention that the world is less than 6000 years old. The books themselves have narratives that could be characterized as extremely weak – with few points of high drama and no clear narrative drive. These are laconic, self-referential humour books dealing with serious issues, quite removed from the traditions of the Franco-Belgian school.

Sfar's other major solo works for the large publishing houses are more akin to his work for the small press, and deliberately so. *Le Minuscule Mousquetaire,* published by Dargaud, is simply a full-colour version of *Le Borgne Gauchet,* the character that appeared in two books from L'Association. Similarly, the conclusion of Sfar's children's book *Petit Vampire va à l'école* (Delcourt, 1999) – the first album in the *Petit Vampire* series – directs the readers to two possibilities: await the forthcoming publication of *Petit Vampire fait du Kung Fu* (Delcourt, 2000) or read the adult versions of the same characters that had already been published as *Le Petit Monde du Golem* (L'Association, 1998). Here Sfar deliberately confuses a number of issues, mixing the same characters into books published by small and large presses so that each serves as a referent for the other, and creating a continuity between work addressed to children and that intended for adults. This confusion is amplified by the addition of the *Grand Vampire* series from Delcourt in 2001. This series, clearly related to *Petit Vampire* but not intended for children, follows the adventures of the same character as an adult – with a complicated theory about how vampires age. Further, Sfar gradually introduces characters from a number of his other fantasy works until it becomes clear that his dozens of books in multiple series all contribute to a shared universe. At the end of the third *Grand Vampire* book, for example, Sfar includes notes indicating the origins of characters from other series (Professeur Bell, Ossour Hyrsidoux, Imhotep III) whose adventures were published by L'Association, Dargaud, and in books with art by Emmanuel Guibert.

The fourth *Grand Vampire* book, *Quai des brunes* (Delcourt, 2003), takes the connection to their semi-logical conclusion and introduces the author as a character who deliberately interrupts the story to create a false sense of suspense. Thus, Sfar – depicting himself in a fashion familiar from his autobiographical *carnets* series – links his numerous fantasy series from the small and large presses to his ongoing non-genre production. Sfar contends that this mode of intertextual weaving is a way for him to keep all of his various characters alive at once:

> The question is: what is a character for an author? For me, there are small voices in my head that are always speaking. There are some who say stupid things; there are some who say interesting things. And when these voices are developed, one has more and more. Me, I started to try to find their faces. I say to myself, 'Hold on, that's the voice that resembles that ... that's the voice that resembles that ...' and at the end of the moment, these voices, when I don't allow them speak regularly, they aren't happy.[48]

Needless to say, this is a radical departure in the field of traditional comics album publishing in Europe. While the idea of characters from one series appearing in another is not unheard of, it is rare that it occurs on such a comprehensive scale, or across so many publishing houses – and genres – at once. In this way, the complexity of Sfar's self-referential undertaking serves as a challenge to the dominant traditions extant in the field and acts as a deliberate provocation to the normative understanding of comic book series as distinct artifacts. In short, Sfar becomes his own industry. Just as publishers have long used genres, labels, and publishing lines to steer readers from successful series to similar undertakings by other authors, Sfar directs readers of any one of his series to the totality of his other work. In its magnitude – exemplified by his own two-pages-per-day credo – Sfar's oeuvre becomes a parody of traditional album publishing executed from within.

In assessing the impact of Sfar's work as a challenge to the traditions of the large-press publishing houses in France and Belgium, one must take into consideration the ways in which he acts as a nexus of a particular comic book scene. The scene that Sfar particularly characterizes is quite different from those previously discussed in that it is local not only to Paris but to a particular atelier, Atelier des Vosges. Here Sfar worked alongside a number of cartoonists who ultimately became his collaborators, including David B., Emmanuel Guibert, and Christophe Blain. Together these artists form the core of the *nouvelle bande dessinée* movement (indeed, all are interviewed in Hugues Dayez's book *La Nouvelle Bande dessinée*), with Sfar acting as something of a linchpin, although this may overstate his influence. Examining the four artists, for example, demonstrates the high degree of interconnectedness that exists between them. Sfar and David B. collaborated on *Urani* (Dargaud, 2000), David B. and Guibert worked together on *Le Capitaine écarlate* (Dupuis, 2000), and David B. wrote the two volumes of the *Hiram Lowatt and Placido* series that Blain drew (Dargaud, 1997, 2000). Sfar has worked with Guibert on three different projects: *La Fille du professeur* (Dupuis, 1997), *Sardine de l'espace* (Bayard, 2000–2003), and *Les Olives noires* (Dupuis, 2001–3). Similarly, he has worked with Lewis Trondheim and Blain on the *Donjon Potron-Minet* series (Delcourt, 1998–2003). Additionally, Guibert and Blain are each responsible for their own ongoing solo series, as are, of course, David B. and Sfar. Together these four men, working from the same atelier,[49] have sought to redefine the traditions of genre-based comics in Europe.

Emmanuel Guibert's first published comic, *Brune* (Albin Michel, 1992), is entirely atypical of the rest of his published work to date. Taking place against a backdrop of the rise of Nazism, *Brune* was done in the direct-colour style that more closely recalls the 1980s work of an artist like Liberatore than the small press of the early 1990s. Guibert has maintained in interviews that with his particular aesthetic interests he felt alone in the world of comics until he met David B., who introduced him to L'Association.[50] Guibert had trained at art school with a particular emphasis on art deco and art nouveau stylings, which was an awkward fit for *Brune*'s direct-colour styling. His later projects defined his unique visual style, with their emphasis on round, shadowy lines. His works fall generally into two categories: collaborations on fantasy projects and fact-based undertakings that are closer to solo works.

Guibert's fact-based works consist primarily of two series: *La Guerre d'Alan* (L'Association, 2000, 2001) (figure 19) and *Le Photographe* (Dupuis, 2003, 2004). *La Guerre d'Alan* is his only strong tie to the European small press. In April 1996 he began publishing short stories based on the life of his American friend Alan Ingram Cope in the pages of *Lapin*. *La Guerre d'Alan* was originally serialized in the pages of that magazine from the fifteenth issue (April 1997) onward and was subsequently collected in book form. Described by *Libération* as 'a major work, moving without hustling, that reconciles the old with the modern,' the story follows the recollections of Cope and his time spent in the U.S. armed forces during the Second World War.[51] Cope's is not a particularly glamorous tale. The first volume tells the story of his basic training and his departure for Europe after the D-Day invasion. He arrives in France in February 1945, and the second volume finds him and his company moving easily through a largely demilitarized Europe.

19 Alan Cope recalls the memory of another soldier. From *La Guerre d'Alan* by
Emmanuel Guibert.

La Guerre d'Alan is not in any way a traditional war comic. It is not about young men being forged in the fires of the battlefield, but rather a quiet reflection on how a young American came to define himself in relation to other cultures because of his experiences during the war. The book itself is part biography and part autobiography. The text is written in the first person, evoking Cope's words, but the illustrations are by Guibert. Moreover, the illustrations are not simple transcriptions of Cope's memories. Guibert uses a style that is built on grey washes and the deliberate suppression of extraneous detail. Many pages have no background illustrations of any kind, as figures move through blank white spaces that symbolize the absences of memory. As Hugues Dayez has noted, Guibert's drawings 'translate the subjectivity of the narrator: one really feels that it is the act of seeing the war, and not a historical report of it.'[52]

A similar effect is found in *Le Photographe*, based on the recollections of a trip taken by photographer Didier Lefèvre to Afghanistan to work with Médecins Sans Frontières in 1986. Here, however, Guibert's drawings co-exist on the page with Lefèvre's first-person narration (which is, nonetheless, credited to Guibert as 'the writer') as well as the photographic record of the trip. Switching from the 'reality' of the photographs to the 'reconstruction' of events on a panel-by-panel basis, Guibert's work confounds traditional notions of autobiography and biography, fact and fiction. Guibert's works are quasi-autobiographies that draw on the most common assumptions about the small press in order to signal a personal commitment that is both akin to and divergent from the norm.

Guibert's mostly widely read works are undoubtedly those he produced with Sfar and David B. With the latter he drew *Le Capitaine écarlate*, a fantasy story based on the writings of Marcel Schwob. The book follows Schwob's own adventures aboard a flying pirate ship filled with decapitated pirates. While the book grew out of a shared interest in the work of Schwob (the two had, along with Vincent Sardon, contributed stories to a tribute to the writer in *Lapin* #16 [July 1997]), the book's themes seem aligned more closely to David B.'s interests than to Guibert's.

Guibert's breakthrough book, however, was written by Sfar. The award-winning *La Fille du professeur* tells the story of a Victorian-era romance between a revivified Egyptian mummy and the daughter of the archaeologist who brought him to the British Museum. This is, to say the least, a highly unconventional comic book romance, and its references are primarily cinematic – from Harold Lloyd to Buster Keaton – rather than rooted in the world of comics. Critically celebrated, the book was seen to be breathing 'new life into the classic publishers.'[53] The book's success led to pressure from Dupuis to develop it further into a series, but the artists did not pursue this. Rather, Guibert and Sfar reversed roles and created a new series – *Sardine de l'espace* – for the children's magazine *Maximum*.

Sardine follows the outer-space adventures of a precocious young girl and her space captain friends as they struggle to thwart the villainy of Docteur Krok and Supermuscleman. As a series of monthly short stories with eternally recurring characters and little plot or character development, these books do not challenge the dominant orthodoxies of the field. Rather, they simply support the traditions of absurd, gross-out humour directed towards children. The same cannot be said, however, for *Les Olives noires*.

Les Olives noires, written by Sfar and drawn by Guibert, is a *péplum* set on the outskirts of Jerusalem during the Roman occupation. Unlike most historical epics in French comics, it does not concern itself with important biblical or historical figures but 'intelligently renovates the Alix genre.'[54] Specifically, the story deals with a small band of Jews existing on the fringes of Roman society, with a particular focus on the life of a young boy. The story unfolds as a series of forty-six-page books, none of which is complete in itself. Indeed, the page numbering for the second volume begins with forty-seven and the third volume begins with ninety-three, indicating that this is a single lengthy historical tale very much in line with Sfar's ideas about open-ended and improvisatory narratives. Another unusual aspect of the work is the fact that each page contains exactly six panels (three tiers of two panels). The regularity of this approach – which features fewer panels of a much larger size than those one would encounter in books by Hergé, Jacobs, or Van Hamme – recalls, as a number of writers have observed, a television screen. It is a particularly contemporary sense of pacing that provides neither cliffhangers nor tonal variation. Other contemporary elements in the series include the widespread use of contemporary French slang ('baiser,' 'connard'). With these modernizing touches, Vincent Bernière has suggested that the books more clearly resemble Monty Python's *Life of Brian* than Stanley Kubrick's *Spartacus*.[55]

More than modern dialogue, however, the series also incorporates modern characters into its settings. Two Roman soldiers who desert the army and come to live with the outcast Jews, for example, are drawn as Joann Sfar and Christophe Blain, while a particularly nasty character is drawn as Lewis Trondheim. Sfar has suggested that he uses real acquaintances in his books as a deliberate realist strategy:

> And if, in *Les Olives noires,* I put in the scene characters who physically resemble my friends, it is not for a love of the private jokes so that one might recognize Blain or Guibert, it is because making the person real inspires me to richer and more credible characters.[56]

In touching on the theme of credibility, Sfar brings the historical epic back to other issues that were more concretely addressed both in the reportage that characterizes Guibert's non-genre comics and in the autobiographical comics movement. Indeed, by locating their friends and – more importantly – their colleagues in the *nouvelle bande dessinée* movement within a largely disavowed but nonetheless classic Franco-Belgian comics genre, Sfar and Guibert are in the process of creating something that is akin to an autobiographical comic book set in the biblical era. As Gilles Ciment notes, the series seeks to resituate autobiography within the tradition of the *péplum:* 'In the heart of the Roman empire or the grand Greek mythology, the material seems *real* – the simple life of men, their environment, their way of thinking, their manners, their daily habits: the "Nouvelle Histoire" of the *Annales* school has passed by there.'[57] By inviting readers to seek connections between historically marginalized figures struggling against a vast and oppressive empire, and a group of Paris-based cartoonists seeking to transform French comic book production through the creation of ironic or semi-traditional genre comics, Sfar and Guibert take on a remarkably romantic conception of the author at odds with the field of production. Whether this provocation is serious or playful is difficult to determine because the work remains ongoing, but it is clear nonetheless that a key element in the *nouvelle bande dessinée* movement is a self-conscious reflection on the author's position within that movement – and within the larger publishing traditions generally – stemming from a self-identification of the author as existing both within and outside the systems of production.

Christophe Blain, depicted in *Les Olives noires* as a renegade Roman soldier, is another collaborator of Sfar's who has made a significant contribution to the *nouvelle bande dessinée* movement. Blain first came to the attention of the comic book–buying public as the artist on the David B.–written revisionist western *La Révolte d'Hop-Frog* (Dargaud, 1997), one of the first of the L'Association-inspired genre works to be issued by that publisher. Blain's art on *La Révolte d'Hop-Frog* marked a significant departure from the norms of the western comic book tradition. Drawn in a direct-colour style not generally associated with the small press, but also largely out of favour for the larger publishers, Blain's art was perceived to be somewhat alienating and difficult to appreciate for the typical comic book reader.[58] In interviews, Blain expressed an appreciation for the work of American underground cartoonist Robert Crumb as well as for the heritage of the Belgian cartoonists of the 1960s.[59] This unusual pairing of influences is evidenced most strongly in the artist's approach to genre works, which is thoroughly revisionist. Indeed, so pronounced is this element of Blain's work that the title given to Hugues Dayez's interview with him is 'Le Détourner de genres.' His radical take on genre comics stems, at least in part, from his collaboration with writers whose origins are in the awkward and often fraught relationship between the small press and the French comics mainstream, notably David B. and Joann Sfar. At the same time, however, Blain's solo work – most notably his revisionist pirate saga *Isaac le pirate* (Dargaud) – is one of the clearest expressions of a small-press aesthetic within the larger framework of the traditions of the Franco-Belgian comics industry, despite the fact that Blain himself is not a small-press cartoonist.

Indeed, Blain has never produced a book for any of the publishers associated with the small-press comics movement of the 1990s, opting to work exclusively for Dargaud, Dupuis, and Delcourt. In his interview with Dayez, Blain indicates that this is entirely a function of economics – while he is sympathetic to L'Association, the publisher does not pay advances and he therefore cannot afford to work for them.[60] Nonetheless, through his connections Blain is widely regarded as an exemplar of the small press. More accurately, his work characterizes the small press as a stylistic rather than economic choice within the larger field of production.

Blain's work with Sfar and David B. has helped to position him as an innovative artist working on ironic takes on established genre conventions. *La Révolte d'Hop-Frog*, Blain's first published comic, tells the story of a writer named Hiram Lowatt and his bizarre adventures in the American west. The book tells the story of an uprising among inanimate objects that come to life and are led in battle against their human oppressors by a pot that has taken his name from a collection of Edgar Allan Poe stories. The book, with its strong fantastic overtones, has a highly dreamlike structure accentuated by Blain's impressionistic illustrations. Paul Bleton has discussed the book's 'perplexing' take on generic conventions in which all the formal elements of the classical western are evident, but neither the book's plot nor its conclusion makes sense within the framework of the genre.[61]

Dargaud published a sequel, *Les Ogres,* three years later. The second book changes the visual register as Blain abandoned his direct-colour style in favour of more traditional linework. The second volume, which finds Lowatt and his faithful native companion Placido in Alaska for a conference, again introduces elements of the fantastic – including cannibalism – into a generic western setting, thereby stripping the first volume of some of its uniqueness and helping to establish the series itself as a new genre: the fantastic western.

Blain's work with Sfar on the *Socrate le demi-chien* series (Dargaud) is similar in the way it creates an unusual gloss on an established genre – this time an ironic reading of mythology through the eyes of a talking dog. Throughout his collaborations with other artists – and including his work on the *Donjon* series with Sfar and Lewis Trondheim – Blain has displayed an innovative take on the established traditions of the small-press sensibility, despite the fact that the books themselves are the product of a well-established publisher.

Blain's first solo work, *Le Réducteur de vitesse* (Dupuis, 1999), is a departure from his other work insofar as it does not explore an established comics genre in a new way. The book tells the story of life aboard a military destroyer, detailing the adventures of several severely seasick sailors who venture into the heart of the massive ship only to get lost. In the process of seeking their way out of the bowels of the ship, the sailors accidentally and irreparably damage the part of the ship's engine that allows it to retard its speed. *Le Réducteur de vitesse* is clearly the most personal of Blain's books and the one that most closely adheres to the small-press aesthetic. It is a personal story that recalls Blain's own service in the navy, where he worked as an artist. Some of his illustrations from that period were published in *Carnet d'un matelot* (Albin Michel, 1994). Those realistic images are transformed in the comic book to a highly expressionistic depiction of the homosocial world of the sailor, rendered using a highly charged colour palette of bold and unnatural hues. At the same time, the art is, as Blain observes in an interview, more narratively oriented than his work in *Hop-Frog.*[62] In short, *Le Réducteur de vitesse* performs a mediating role between the artist's realistic illustration work and his highly unconventional and pictorial first comics work with David B. The resulting narrative, described by Jean-Pierre Mercier as Kafkaesque but with an 'absolutely banal' resolution,[63] announces Blain's unique voice in the comics form. More importantly, the book signals its intentions to be read as a highly personal statement produced within the confines of the traditional French comic book industry rather than on its periphery. By the end of the 1990s, it seems, this possibility was increasingly open to cartoonists like Blain.

Blain's best-known solo work, however, is the award-winning *Isaac le pirate* series (figure 20) that is published in Dargaud's Poisson Pilote line. The first volume in this series, *Les Amériques* (2001), was awarded the prize for best album at the 2002 Festival International de la Bande Dessinée in Angoulême, the most prestigious prize in European comics. The critical success of the volume served to legitimate the newly launched Poisson Pilote line, consecrating Guy Vidal's editorial vision a mere two years after the creation of the imprint. Subsequently, the series has been promoted as a major undertaking in France, being serialized in the pages of the mainstream French television magazine *Télérama*. The series itself is a revisionist gloss on the traditional pirate genre and a seeming hybrid of Blain's non-traditional genre work and his own previous book about sailors.

The hero of the series is the eponymous Isaac, a painter who embarks on a grand adventure with a group of pirates. As with Sfar and Guibert's works, the stories in the series are not self-contained but seemingly endlessly ongoing. The books are, as Evariste Blanchet has argued, 'postmodern and hybrid *par excellence.*'[64] Blain's use of an artist as the lead within an otherwise well-established comics genre permits an incredibly high degree of referentiality throughout the narrative. Just as Blain is symptomatic of the efforts of small-press artists to work within the seemingly exotic and alien constraints of the large publishing houses, so too Isaac acts as a metaphor for this process. His attempts to navigate the seemingly bizarre and arbitrary world of the pirates serves as a meta-commentary on the process of artistic creation within unusual constraints. The cover image of the first volume, depicting Isaac drawing amid a shadowy gathering of intrigued ruffians, is an unusually adept visual metaphor for the relationship of these disparate elements of the field of production that have been brought together by a figure like Vidal.

In his interview with Dayez, Blain comments on the fact that his art differs significantly from the type of work that had long been championed by the largest French publishing houses. He suggests that artists like himself, Sfar, and Blutch come to the production of comic books from the perspective of visuality, with a love of drawing that precedes their love of the comics form. He suggests, on the other hand, that the generation of artists who came of age in the 1970s and 1980s came to the medium through a love of the form: 'For example, an author like Giraud is an artist who likes drawing, while his "heirs" are types who like Giraud more than they like drawing.'[65] The insular world of artists whose goal was the emulation of other comics artists has tended, Blain suggests, to alter the expectations of the comics-reading audience to such a degree that an unusual visual stylist such as Blain will seem maladroit in comparison with an artist from the classical school – such as the artists who collaborate with Jean Van Hamme.

Nonetheless, Blain sees the work produced by Van Hamme and his collaborators not as threatening to the cultural legitimacy of the comic book but as central to his own artistic freedom: 'I would add that, even if bestsellers like *XIII* are not my cup of tea, I am happy that such series exist and bring in so much money for Dargaud! Vive Van Hamme! Vive Vance! Continue along these lines, allowing Dargaud to finance lines like "Poisson Pilote"!'[66]

This celebration of Van Hamme, however delimited and partial, is quite at odds with the conception of the field as divided by a number of core oppositions. The vision of large-scale production that permits more marginal artists to survive is, I would argue, primarily associated with a disposition such as Blain's, which is a function of a small-press ideology that exists outside of the small press in actuality. Blain's success – minor as it may be in comparison with a figure like Van Hamme – is symptomatic of the ability of artists to survive in the space carved out of the largest publishing houses by the small-press revolution of the 1990s. Further, it testifies to the way in which the boundaries between small and large presses have become increasingly irrelevant over a short period of time.

The charge that artists like Sfar, Guibert, and Blain represent a watering down of the small-press explosion of the 1990s or, more tellingly, a betrayal of the revolutionary thrust of those efforts remains somewhat common, but unproductive. Yet what the examples of these artists point out most concretely is the fact that many cartoonists of the 1990s did not conceive of the small-press renaissance as an end in itself or as an absolute moral good. Sfar is an example of an author who had long desired to work for the largest publishing houses but who was not welcomed by editors whose success in the 1980s had been derived from copying the bestsellers of a previous age. For Sfar, the small press was a semi-professional venue in which to establish a name before moving on to other publishers, a process which, in any case, he left incomplete by

20 Isaac paints a portrait of his hostile captain in Christophe Blain's *Isaac le pirate: Les Amériques.*

continuing to work for L'Association. Guibert and Blain, on the other hand, represent artists whose entry into the small-press world is partial (in the case of Guibert) or non-existent (Blain), but who nonetheless benefited by the opening up of the field by the artists associated more systematically with the small press.

Bourdieu notes that 'the opposition between the two markets, between producers for producers and producers for non-producers, entirely determines the image writers and artists have of their profession and constitutes the taxonomic principle according to which they classify and hierarchize works.'[67] Artists like Sfar, Guibert, and Blain mediate in various ways the opposition of which Bourdieu writes, but it is clear nonetheless that each conceptualizes certain aspects of their work as more appropriate for the small presses like L'Association or the larger publishing houses. The tendency to exist in both worlds problematizes the rigidity of Bourdieu's formulation but more accurately accounts for the realities of artistic production in the dramatically altered field of contemporary European comic book production in which artists can wear multiple hats. Guy Vidal addressed this issue when he noted

> In the last *Lettre Dargaud,* I posed these same questions to David B., one of the founding fathers of L'Association, who has just published *Le Capitaine écarlate* (with Emmanuel Guibert) at Dupuis and who published in June, with Christophe Blain, *Les Ogres,* in the Poisson Pilote collection, at Dargaud. Here is his answer: 'I do not feel recuperated, I continue to work regularly for L'Asso, I take part in decision-making, I represent them at certain festivals. I have not become a Dargaud author, I am an author who, to earn a living and for my pleasure, following a line of encounters, works with plenty of publishers.'[68]

David B.'s self-identification as an author, rather than as an author of a certain type of book or for a certain type of publisher, is, I would argue, an assessment that is highly dependent on the particular revolution that characterized the small-press explosion of the 1990s as it intersected with the dominant traditions in the field.

The intrusion of a small-press sensibility into the structures of the largest publishing houses is predicated not on claims to authorial authenticity – as with autobiographical comics – but on the selective mobilization of certain aspects of the visual register championed by the small press and avant-garde within the confines of the literary traditions of the previous generation. Sfar summarizes the tendency explicitly:

I believe that comics is above all in the writing and that the battle for the fine arts is lost in advance. My masters were Fred, Goscinny, Tardi or Pratt. In the current French literature, it seems to me that we have lost the sense of the epic. With the people at the Atelier des Vosges, Blain and Guibert, Emile Bravo, David B., Trondheim or Marjane Satrapi, we tried to put our experiments with autobiography, or introspection, in the service of epic stories. It is necessary that the reader be able to inhabit a character in order to test a vision of life.[69]

This tendency has become so quickly dominant in the small-press tradition that cartoonists whose previous works challenged the format of the comic book (BüLB and Drozophile's Frederick Peeters and Wazem) and the normative illustratorly aesthetics of comics (Fréon's Denis Deprez) have been recruited to do work for publishers like Humanoïdes Associés and Casterman, respectively. From the perspective of the largest and best-established publishing houses, this constitutes a tremendous degree of aesthetic liberalization. However, from the point of view of many artists who continue to define avant-gardist tendencies, it threatens to define the small-press revolution of the 1990s as nothing more than a marketing category.

Chapter 7

The Strange Case of Lewis Trondheim

La chose fabuleuse avec les vrais artistes, c'est qu'ils ne se rendent pas
compte eux-même à quel point ils font avancer les choses.

Lewis Trondheim, *Pichenettes*[1]

Two strips by Lewis Trondheim (Laurent Chabosy) published in the
small-press anthology *Rackham Poutch* (Rackham, 1991) succinctly sum-
marize the artist's initial intervention into the field of comics production
in the early 1990s and foreshadow the development of his career over
the next decade and a half. The first, 'Emmaüs,' visually reproduces four
panels from Art Spiegelman's award-winning comic book *Maus*. In the
scene, Art and his father, Vladek, have a discussion at a kitchen table. Art
suggests to Vladek that his life as a Holocaust survivor is so interesting
that he'd like to turn it into a film. Unfortunately, Vladek informs him,
Art's cousin David is already doing that. How about a television mini-
series then? Cousin Rebecca has bought those rights. A novel perhaps, a
thirty-volume epic? No, that is already being written. Art casts his eyes
downward and says, 'And what about me? I'm not going to do one of
those comics.'[2] The second strip, 'Les Gouts et les couleurs,' reproduces
one panel of Moebius's *Garage hermétique* eight times over two pages. The
dialogue finds a man debating the merit of that book with a fairy. The
fairy doesn't recognize the black-and-white edition of the material, having read it in colour. The man, however, finds the colour edition to be an
aberration, since the original was not conceptualized for colour printing. He argues that the colour edition is nothing more than a self-
evident concession to market forces, that this masterpiece has no inherent
need for colour. The fairy responds, 'You're saying that you are jealous

and that you would prefer that this masterpiece remain appreciated only by a small elite, of which you are a part.' After a pause, the man replies, 'I really don't like it when you try to prove that you're smart.'[3]

These strips highlight two particular attitudes towards comic books that have run through the pages of this book. First, comics are themselves an unimportant medium that pales in comparison with the written word, the cinema, and even television. The humour is largely derived from the reader's awareness that *Maus* is frequently cited as the greatest comic book of all time, and Spiegelman's grudging agreement to undertake such a project seems to suggest that achieving greatness in this field is no real accomplishment. As was the case with many of the cartoonists discussed in this volume, Trondheim's concern with the legitimacy of the field is foregrounded here. Second, Trondheim spotlights the debate between commerce and the integrity of artistic vision, giving a quick précis to the arguments of both sides before fundamentally deflating the pretensions of the fan who regards comics as art.

No single artist so decisively highlights the central themes of this book as does Lewis Trondheim. Beginning as a comic book writer in the 1990s who taught himself how to draw while publishing in fanzines and with the small press (including, most notably, L'Association, of which he was a co-founder), Trondheim emerged by the mid-1990s as one of the first small-press artists to move to the larger publishing houses. By the end of the 1990s he was one of the most celebrated names in French comics, regularly appearing in a variety of magazines and newspapers, having created more than one hundred albums in the first fifteen years of his career. Trondheim is a veritable industry unto himself, working for presses both small and large, in genres of all sorts, and in dozens of formats. Indeed, the entire transformation of the European comic book industry that occurred in the 1990s can be read from his work. In particular, the way his career carefully balances the commercial and the artistic as he seeks to legitimize the status of comics in relation to the other arts can be seen as an ongoing thread from *Rackham Poutch* to his current celebrity.

As the foreword to *Jeux d'influences,* a collection of essays by thirty cartoonists who recount the comic books that had the greatest influence on their thinking about the medium, Trondheim presents a twelve-panel strip depicting himself (in the anthropomorphized form that he uses in his autobiographical work) reading a copy of the Jean-Christophe Menu–edited anthology *Lynx* that has arrived in the mail. He notes that the drawings are really bizarre and not very pretty. While he doesn't like the work of Mattt Konture, he decides to continue reading the book since he's already paid for it. Suddenly, a moment of recognition. He realizes that the comics in *Lynx* are poorly drawn but nonetheless interesting. In that case, even he could do comics if he wanted to; all he would have to do is try.[4]

As an origin story, this single page gets the job done. It provides the 'eureka' moment central to the development of the artist's aesthetic rooted in a do-it-yourself ethos. It hints at the future connection between Trondheim and his collaborators in L'Association: Menu and Konture. And it spells out an entire point of view rooted in the notion of the badly drawn but interesting work. Indeed, for the most part the fanzine and small-press movements have always championed non-traditional (non-commercial) drawing styles so long as the content was of interest. Trondheim's realization here, placed by the title in 1987, is one of dozens of such epiphanies that must have taken place all over Europe around this time to launch this movement. By examining Trondheim's exceptional – and in no way representative – development since that epiphany, we can encapsulate the thrust of the small-press movement.

Trondheim's earliest publications in the French small-press/fanzine scene took the form of both mini-comics and formal comics experiments. The latter appear in retrospect as an effort to transform a limitation into a strength. His drawing skills in the early 1990s were, by most standards of the form at that time, highly unpolished and unprofessional. He developed a number of strategies to work around this lack of drawing ability. Most importantly, he often worked as a writer for other artists, as with *Gare Centrale* (Rackham, 1994) with Jean-Pierre Duffour, or with his unauthorized collaborations with Spiegelman and Moebius.

Trondheim's early experiments as a writer can be seen in his *Moins d'un Quart de seconde pour vivre* (L'Association, 1991). In this book, he worked from eight panels created by Jean-Christophe Menu. These panels are deployed by Trondheim as a series of four-panel gag strips, with the writer adding comic dialogue. The repetitive nature of the book places it in the experimental comics camp, and the second edition of the book (L'Association, 1996) includes a preface indicating that it should be considered a proto-OuBaPo book (that group was not created until after the publication of the first edition), as well as an introduction by OuLiPo president Noël Arnaud.

Trondheim carried out a number of similar experiments around this same time, although with art by the author himself. *Psychanalyse* (Lézard, 1990) (figure 21), Trondheim's first book, is a fifteen-page volume

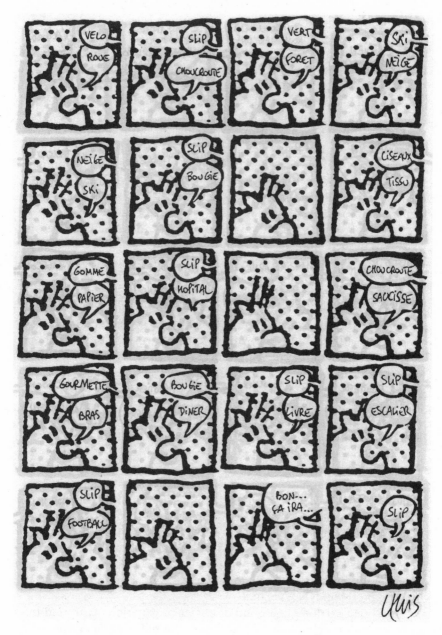

21　Word play from *Psychanalyse,* an early effort by Lewis Trondheim.

consisting of just two images, endlessly repeated using a photocopier. The images, of a bloblike creature with its mouth open and with its mouth closed (silent/speaking), form the basis of a dialogue with an off-panel voice that takes the form of a psychoanalytic session. *Monolinguiste* (Lézard, 1992) and *Le Dormeur* (Cornélius, 1993) use similar aesthetic strategies, though *Le Dormeur* reduces the number of images to one. The lack of visual interest in these books, with their crudely drawn and repetitive images, challenges the logics of visuality and serves to privilege the ability to write well as the most important aspect of comic book creation. Indeed, these four experimental volumes utilize images simply as markers of pacing. Little narrative information is imparted through the images except for the identification of the speaker through the use of word balloons and the imposition of a narrative rhythm, particularly through the use of wordless panels representing pauses. *Moins d'un Quart de seconde pour vivre* with its eight panels has the greatest visual sophistication of the four books, but even here Trondheim creates the majority of the strips using only one of the images. Insofar as they articulated a nascent experimental aesthetic that privileged the writer, these comics inverted the traditional dichotomy of the comics market in the 1980s that tended to favour technical drawing skills as the hallmark of sophisticated comics for adults.

As Trondheim started to draw his own comics, he tended to work primarily in fanzine styles and formats. His first 'traditional' comic book was *Un Intérieur d'artiste* (L'Association, 1991), a mini-comic in the first *Patte de Mouche* line that remains one of the few Trondheim creations that is out of print. Over the course of the next decade, however, Trondheim continued to produce mini-comics in L'Association's Patte de Mouche format, including *Imbroglio* (1992/1995), *Nous sommes tous morts* (1995), *Diablotus* (1995), *Les Aventures de la fin de l'épisode* (1995), *Non non non* (1987), and *Galopinot* (1998). These mini-comics continued his experimental tendencies but drove them in a different direction. Rather than playing with form, these comics toyed with generic conventions, signalling an engagement with the medium on a very different level. *Diablotus* and *Non non non,* for example, are inversions of Trondheim's earliest works, being totally wordless. Moving from comics that were entirely dependent on their text to comics that completely relied on their images in so short a period demonstrates how quickly Trondheim became confident in his ability to tell a story visually and how quickly his work acceded to the logic of visual rather than narrative forms of distinction.

Trondheim's other mini-comics are more traditional, addressing humorous topics through generic transformation. *Imbroglio,* for example, tells the story of two men and a woman who endlessly pretend to kill each other – one pair will kill the third only to have the death revealed as a ruse, with a new pairing uniting against someone else. The book is a nearly unending series of double-crosses and false accusations that parodies the ending of so many similar books, films, and comic books where the real plot is revealed only at the end. Similarly, *Les Aventures de la fin de l'épisode,* with art by Frank Le Gall, provides only the ending of a supernatural detective story. A tweed-wearing British detective unmasks a man dressed as a werewolf, but when his explanation has an inconsistency he unmasks the man again, and again, and again. Ultimately the story is resolved when every participant has been unmasked, revealing the culprit as the sidekick, the sidekick as the real detective, and the detective as none other than the werewolf. These short works, which present only a fraction of a total narrative in order to parody generic constructions, serve as a sort of commentary on the traditions of the field as it existed at that time. Moreover, these fanzine productions are the first indication of Trondheim's interest in examining generic questions raised by traditional album publishing, something that will be central to his work as it develops over the course of the next decade.

The culmination of these initial small-press efforts was a wordless book that demonstrated Trondheim's ability to think through generic conventions in new and unusual ways. *La Mouche* (Seuil, 1995) is a lengthy graphic novel featuring the adventures of a housefly. The book, which was a one-hundred-page elaboration of a four-page short piece published in *Lapin* #2, marked a radical departure from Trondheim's previous work insofar as it contained no text. For a cartoonist whose career had been celebrated until that time for the notion that the quality of his writing overcame the limitations of his drawing, a book that relied primarily on the visual plane to carry the reader's interest was a daring gesture.

La Mouche follows the adventures of a common housefly from birth as it explores a typical domestic space. The fly interacts with a series of other insects – a worm, a spider – but spends most of its time exploring the world and eating. Late in the book, the fly is magically transformed into a being of tremendous size and power, growing larger than the humans who seek to kill it with a swatter. Eventually the fly becomes gargantuan, destroying skyscrapers and eating entire city waste sites, before growing to cosmic scale. Much of the humour in the book stems from the panel transitions, which are often skewed and semi-arbitrary, alternating between great compositional depth and narrow close-ups. These transitions recall the unpredictable flight trajectories of house-flies, and, later, as the fly grows larger than planets, humour is derived from the ability of the comics form to play with scale. Although the fly remains at all times a little black ball with crudely drawn features, its force is magnified by alterations to backgrounds and highlighted by the regularity of Trondheim's nine-panel grid. Thus, Trondheim demonstrates for the first time that he is able to conceive a full-length narrative in predominantly visual terms, and thus makes the transition from the purely literary side of comics production to a more integrated position that brings him more fully into the visual traditions.

In a 1998 profile of the artist, Jean-Batiste Harang described Trondheim to readers of *Libération:* 'Lewis Trondheim is a thirty-three-year-old man, fine like a bird, a crooked yellow beak, a white crest with three tufts, four fingers on each hand, a thick and continuing brow marking his glance, and when he laughs, the ladies envy the seven or eight teeth in his mouth.'[5] While not strictly accurate, Harang has absolutely captured the image of the artist as it is presented in Trondheim's autobiographical comic *Approximativement* (Cornélius, 1995) (figure 22). This book, which collects the six issues of his *Approximate Continuum Comics* (Cornélius, 1993–4), placed Trondheim near the centre of the autobiographical comics movement of the early 1990s as it existed particularly around L'Association and Cornélius at the time.

Trondheim's approach to autobiography differs significantly from the methods of Dupuy and Berberian, David B., and Fabrice Neaud. Trondheim, first and foremost a humorist, places his primary emphasis on an excavation of his own personality quirks through caricature, not unlike a stand-up comedian. Specifically, Trondheim depicts himself as an anthropomorphized bald eagle, and he embodies his own worst personality traits throughout the book as a giant snake that follows him around, chastising him. The book is filled with fantasy sequences featuring the artist vanquishing evil-doers (such as the man who insists on boarding the subway car before all the people have gotten off) and placing Trondheim's anxieties and desires at the nexus of the book's construction. These include his trepidations about becoming a father, moving to Montpellier from Paris, and throwing away insignificant personal items because of his attachment to the past. Throughout the book, Trondheim depicts himself as a series of Trondheims – the stupid comics fan, the bitter artist, the starstruck dreamer – visually enacting his constantly changing state of mind. Indeed, the book's cover, which depicts

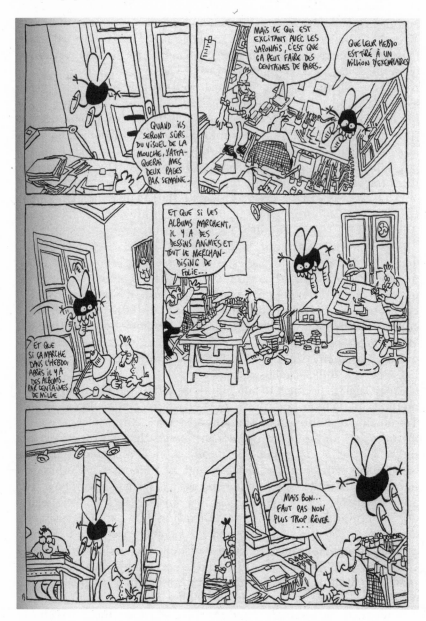

22 Trondheim's La Mouche circulates through his atelier. From *Approximativement.*

hundreds of versions of his self-caricature interacting, speaks directly to these shifts, which characterize so much of the work.

Trondheim's self-image as an artist is developed and enunciated through the pages of *Approximativement* in relation to two distinct poles. First, Trondheim portrays cartooning as a particular struggle between collaborative inspiration and self-expression. In a number of instances he depicts his own internal struggle to be creative and demonstrates how new ideas are developed in relation to the work of his peers. Second, he shows cartooning as a form of professionalization quite at odds with the more romantic portrayals discussed previously, specifically when he discusses his work in terms of a career trajectory rather than as a particular form of artistic growth. These tendencies mean that his participation in the myth of the romantic artist working towards self-expression is severely compromised throughout *Approximativement*.

During the period in which he was working on this book, Trondheim shared the Atelier Nawak with Jean-Christophe Menu, Émile Bravo, David B., Brigitte Findakly (his wife), and others. Throughout the book, he discusses problems with writer's block, which he surmounts by interacting with the cartoonists with whom he shares his working space. In one instance, for example, he is distracted from his work by David B., who reports that a mutual friend and professional contact in Japan is going to watch a sumo match. Trondheim inserts himself into a fantasy scene in which he is a deadly martial artist throwing kicks and punches against a yokozuna. This sequence breaks up a longer sequence in which he is struggling to find something interesting to draw and serves as a commentary on the way his ideas are developed from the spontaneous stimuli that transpire in a shared work setting. Similarly, he includes a nine-page story early in the book that is inspired by Menu's work on an autobiographical comic on the theme of guilt. Trondheim's story on the same theme, which details his participation in a childhood prank that goes awry, shifts the action of the book to the past, allowing him to move through differing modes of autobiographical address. More importantly, these instances demonstrate how the development of an individual style is the result of complex social factors that are not always acknowledged in other autobiographical works.

The development of Trondheim's professional career is also addressed throughout *Approximativement* in relation to the central character of his 1995 book *La Mouche*. In *Approximativement* he explains that *La Mouche* first appeared in a slightly different form as 'Les Aventures de la mouche à merde' in *Lapin* #2 (1992). This story was then expanded again for the

Japanese publisher Kodansha in the magazine *Afternoon,* although with
several 'frustrating compromises.'[6] The Japanese publishers had requested
that the fly be rendered as more 'cute' without its protruding teeth, that
it be coloured white rather than black, and that the pacing be extended
to more closely mirror manga storytelling traditions. He finds the editorial suggestions annoying, but is told by his agent in Japan that it is
impossible to comprehend the editorial directives of manga publishers
and that he should simply do as they request. His interest in working
within these constraints is depicted as purely economic. He is excited by
the fact that *Afternoon* sells millions of copies, that the book collections
from *Afternoon* sell hundreds of thousands of copies, and that success in
the Japanese market can mean animated television shows and product
licensing that could make him a rich man. As he speaks, Trondheim
recedes into the background of his own page, and the foreground is
occupied by the French version – the more personal version – of his fly,
who hovers above the action before flying through an open window. The
following mute page presents the same static image of the Paris skyline,
with the fly disappearing and then slowly being replaced by a riot of
planes, blimps, and balloons celebrating and promoting the *La Mouche*
phenomenon before dissipating in a blast of Trondheimian cynicism.

Later in the book he depicts himself as literally floating on air when he
learns that his strip has tested positively with the Japanese readership,
but he is brought back to earth by a demand that he introduce a female
fly to the story and develop a romance. He rationalizes these demands –
'Don't contradict the Japanese. They're the bosses. They're the ones
who are right. Don't try to understand. Their logic is different. They're
crazy'[7] – but his expression and placement in the panel demonstrate
that his agreement is, at best, partial. In the book's final chapter, he
wonders to himself – alongside a flurry of cute, white, de-toothed Japanese flies – 'must I accept making these filthy and compromising stories
to become a billionaire?'[8]

Trondheim's foregrounding of these kinds of economic concerns –
the explicit discussion of the process of 'selling out' – is unusual within
the field of autobiographical comics, signalling as it does a primary
submerged tension in the small press of the early 1990s. Ultimately,
however, his breakthrough into mainstream success came not through
La Mouche (which, ironically, did become a French-Canadian animated
television co-production in 1999 despite its lack of success in Japan), but
through the character of Lapinot, whose origins reside with L'Association
but whose fame came from Dargaud.

The Lapinot books are a particularly instructive comics success story, not only because of their small-press origins but also because of how they trouble traditional generic conventions. While the majority of the Lapinot stories are collected in Dargaud's *Les Formidables Aventures de Lapinot* series of traditional full-colour forty-six-page albums, the work does somewhat confuse straight classification by publisher.

The first Lapinot book, *Lapinot et les carottes de Patagonie* (L'Association/ Lézard, 1992), stands as one of the early hallmark books of the new comics revolution of the 1990s. Extending over a then-unheard-of 500 pages, the volume is a picaresque adventure told in a rambling, improvised style. Trondheim created the book as a learning tool, setting out to create a single 6000-panel story (500 twelve-panel pages) in which the writer would teach himself to draw, to become a cartoonist rather than simply a writer. The book, while tremendously unpolished in the earliest pages, became a cult success and spurred his rise to prominence in the world of independent comics production. Indeed, in some circles the book became synonymous with the independent comics scene of the early 1990s, a symbol of the aspirations to novelistic size that the small press was preaching at the time. It was impossible, as *Libération* observed, to imagine a book like this one from a traditional press: 'There is only L'Association to publish a thing like this.'[9]

Lapinot et les carottes de Patagonie introduced his best-known character to the reading public. A retiring anthropomorphic rabbit-everyman character lacking a strong personality, Lapinot (the character's name recalls both Jean-Christophe Menu's character Lapot and L'Association's anthology *Lapin*) served as a strong base upon which he was able to explore a number of generic tendencies. The Lapinot universe is somewhat confused and confusing because of this.

The first major work to engender the Lapinot world in a comprehensive manner was *Slaloms* (L'Association, 1993; re-edition Dargaud, 1997). This book reintroduced Lapinot in a contemporary setting and established the key relationships in his life with his friends Richard (the immature and slightly irritating best friend), Titi (the womanizer), and Pierrot (the reserved intellectual), as well as Nadia (the love interest). The story itself unfolds entirely at a ski resort, with a minimal plot. While there is some intrigue created by the rumoured presence of a predatory wolf – a particular concern for the rabbit-like Lapinot – for the most part the book deals exclusively with the relationships among this group of friends. The book was a success when it was initially released, winning the Alph'Art Coup de Coeur (for best first book) at the Salon International de la Bande Dessinée in Angoulême in 1994, a prize that helped to consecrate the efforts of Trondheim, L'Association, and the small press generally at that time. *Slaloms* demonstrated to many the possibility that an album-sized book (forty-six pages) could be produced by the small press – in black and white – and become a widely heralded success despite its lack of generic elements, or rather despite its use of the contemporary slice-of-life fiction genre, a set of conventions almost totally absent from French comics of the period. The fact that *Slaloms* cemented an association between the small press and slice-of-life fiction can be seen by *Le Monde*'s choice of *Slaloms* (the colour re-edition from Dargaud) as the most important comic of 1997. In an article noting the twenty-five most important comics for the twenty-fifth anniversary of the Angoulême festival, the paper placed Trondheim alongside Hugo Pratt, Jacques Tardi, Moebius, Will Eisner, and Art Spiegelman in the pantheon of great cartoonists. *Le Monde* summed up Trondheim's contribution to the world of comics: 'Trondheim is distinguished by his mastery of dialogue and his sense of observation. *Slaloms,* initially published by L'Association, then reprinted by Dargaud, is a good introduction to his universe: one meets his fetish character, Lapinot, preyed upon by his existential doubts and by the troubles of everyday life. A lucid and falsely naïve author.'[10]

The Lapinot stories that followed *Slaloms* serve to reinforce that volume's association with the quotidian and to utterly undermine that same association. *Mildiou* (Seuil, 1994) is a 140-page volume that depicts Richard as the usurper of a medieval crown and Lapinot as the peasant who fights him to the death. The book is the first to suggest the possibility that the Lapinot characters move easily through genres and historical eras, for despite the temporal and generic change, Lapinot, Richard, and Titi (Pierrot and Nadia are absent from the book) all remain true to their personalities as they had been established in the earlier *Slaloms*. The book, little more than an elaborate chase and fight sequence, is actually more akin to Trondheim and Sfar's *Donjon* material than to the other Lapinot books.

Le Crabar de Mammouth, on the other hand, returns the series to a realistic setting. The story, rejected by a number of publishers as a stand-alone album and published in its entirety in *Lapin* #7 (1995), is set in the childhood of Richard, Titi, and Pierrot and details their youthful misadventures in a manner that recalls Trondheim's own childhood recollections in *Approximativement*.

The foursome reappear in the Thierry Groensteen–edited anthology

Noire est la terre (Autrement, 1995) in a story entitled 'Promenade.' This work is extremely similar to *Slaloms,* placing the four primary characters from that book in the countryside and following them as they take a walk. The story is extremely minimalist, with most of the emphasis placed on the way Trondheim generates drama from conversations among his characters while introducing few story elements. 'Promenade' is perhaps the purest expression of the Lapinot world as a realist landscape, and the story – along with *Slaloms* – forms the basis for much of the 'real' continuity of the Lapinot series. That it was published by a prestigious literary publishing house further serves to affirm the presumed solidarity of the small press's connection to 'serious' non-genre literature.

In 1995, however, Trondheim shattered all of these existing presumptions with the publication of *Blacktown*. First, he transferred the Lapinot stories to a large publishing house, Dargaud, seemingly removing one of the most visible independent comics successes from the small press. Second, he worked entirely within the traditions of the established houses, producing a forty-six-page, full-colour, hardcover album as part of an ongoing series with recurrent characters. Finally, the work that he produced was a western, a well-established genre associated with Dargaud through series such as Giraud and Charlier's *Blueberry*.

Blacktown (ironically titled given the fact that it is Trondheim's first work in colour) presents a parodic take on the conventions of the American Wild West. The story revolves around a Boston-based stranger (Lapinot) who arrives in town slightly ahead of a gang that is chasing him. Here he falls into an intrigue involving the discovery of a possible goldmine, which he has to resolve before he is able to escape the men who are hunting him. Richard and Titi appear as townsfolk, with Trondheim himself playing the role of town marshal. Nadia appears in the role of the schoolmistress with whom all the men are in love. Trondheim's use of ironic humour can be seen when Nadia's attempts to lead a seminar on non-violence are interrupted when a lynching breaks out or when Richard uses deductive logic to outwit a gunfighter. Overall, the book is only marginally a western. Although it includes gunfights, horses, and other trappings of the genre, the narrative thrust is laconic and irreverent, displaying an unwillingness to fully engage with the conventions.

The third book in the series, *Walter* (Dargaud, 1996), takes a similar tone. This volume is a turn-of-the-century monster tale featuring Lapinot as a medical student, Richard as a reporter, and Titi as a police detective, all of whom become embroiled in a case in which a mad scientist has discovered the ability to turn people into monsters. Both of these volumes mark a radical departure from the small-press emphasis on slice-of-life material and can be read as a refutation of that aesthetic. At the same time, however, both books tend to advance the central ongoing plots in the 'real' Lapinot series. Indeed, both books fill holes in the relationship between Lapinot and Nadia that is developing more specifically in the books set in contemporary Paris. Lapinot and Nadia meet in *Slaloms*. They meet again (in the past) in *Blacktown*, although their possible relationship is disrupted by Lapinot's need to flee the town and Nadia's temporary insanity.

In the third volume, *Pichenettes* (figure 23), Lapinot and Nadia meet for a second time, now in Paris. She – or her stand-in – is absent from the fourth book, *Walter*, and that absence is explicitly commented upon in the fifth book, *Amour et intérim*. Thus, read as a series of ten discrete books, the Lapinot series can be regarded as a collection of contemporary volumes interrupted by a set of 'unreal' generic adventures. On the other hand, read as a continuing saga, the non-contemporary Lapinot books can be seen as highlighting the central romantic tension in the series in an innovative manner as they relegate key romantic elements to the realm of fantasy genres.

Nonetheless, the core of the Lapinot series remains focused on the characters as they were introduced in *Slaloms*, and their adventures play out across the ten volumes of the complete Dargaud saga. Throughout these books, genre elements never completely disappear from the work. *Pichenettes* (Dargaud, 1996), for example, finds Lapinot relocating to Paris to live temporarily with Richard. While there he intervenes to help a cursed man by accepting an ancient stone which will bring bad luck to whomever receives it. Lapinot's luck does not change, but Richard feels he has received the curse when, among other things, he can't find his dictionary. Throughout the book it remains unclear as to whether Richard is genuinely cursed or simply bringing bad luck upon himself through his belief in the curse and his own boorish behaviour. In the end the book is a slice-of-life tale with strong overtones of the 'ancient curse revisited in the present day' generic conventions.

Similar overtones appear in all of the Lapinot books set in the contemporary period. *Amour et intérim* (Dargaud, 1998) is a conspiracy novel in which Lapinot becomes embroiled with an organization bent on improving the world through social interventions. *Pour de Vrai* (Dargaud, 1999) has elements of a ghost story, complete with Lapinot and Richard being

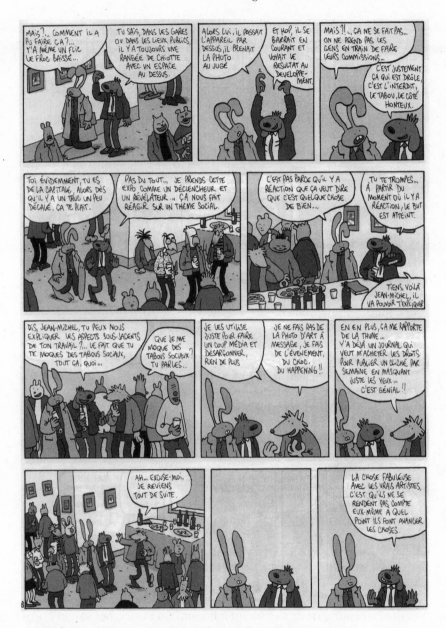

23 Lapinot and Titi at a vernissage in *Pichenettes*. David B., Trondheim, and
Jean-Christophe Menu appear in the fourth panel.

possessed by demonic spirits (illustrated with highly expressionistic images) after they buy a lottery ticket based on numbers provided by the dead. *La Couleur de l'enfer* (Dargaud, 2000) includes conventions from the spy thriller, focusing as it does on an activist group that spray-paints circles on the sidewalk to highlight dog droppings that have not been curbed by pet owners. Throughout each of these volumes Trondheim stays true to the narrative arc established by his small-press work (*Slaloms* and 'Promenade' in particular) but gradually tweaks that tradition by including small bits taken from other genres. Indeed, none of the Lapinot books set in the contemporary world could truly be termed a spy thriller or a ghost story. Rather, they incorporate minor elements that give the slice-of-life material a generic tinge, in much the same way as the generic stories (*Blacktown, Walter,* and the Frank Le Gall–written Victorian romance *Vacances de printemps* [Dargaud, 1999]) incorporate elements of the quotidian that keep them from becoming real genre works. The Lapinot stories, therefore, stand as model character-driven series comics for the 1990s: meshing the publishing expectations of both small and large houses through a selective and hybrid use of genre strategies with a highly ironic stance.

In 2003 and 2004 Trondheim radically altered the stakes in the large-press publishing field through two important volumes in the Lapinot series: *L'Accélérateur atomique* (Dargaud, 2003) and *Le Vie comme elle vient* (Dargaud, 2004). Although it was published first chronologically, *L'Accélérateur atomique* is numbered ninth in the series (*Slaloms,* the first volume, is numbered zero because it was only published in full colour after the release of *Blacktown* and *Pichenettes* in the Dargaud series, which were numbers one and two), and *La Vie comme elle vient,* the last book to be released, is number eight.

La Vie comme elle vient is set in the contemporary Lapinot world – confirmed for the first time as our world when Lapinot and Nadia condemn the American reaction to the events of 11 September 2001 – at a party gone horribly wrong. When a guest uses Tarot cards and predicts that a guest will die, the party gets off on the wrong foot. When four romantic relationships come to an end, including, accidentally, that of Lapinot and Nadia, things go from bad to worse. In the end, the lives of all the characters are threatened to a certain degree (by ferocious dogs, street punks, and a house fire), while Richard winds up in a coma as a result of a beating from an irate neighbour, Titi undergoes surgery on a cancerous lung, and Lapinot is struck by a taxi and killed. With this gesture, Trondheim breaks with the traditions of classical French cartooning for good. While the heroes of classical adventures were often imperilled, the most important generic rule was that they never died. Centrally, the possibility of continuing the stories existed for all time, and, indeed, some characters – such as Spirou – have continued for generations, even past the deaths of their authors. By killing Lapinot, Trondheim signals the end of the classical tradition and the birth of a modern, or postmodern, heroic narrative in which the old rules are forgotten.

On the last page of *La Vie comme elle vient*, Lapinot's friends walk from the cemetery to his apartment. As they walk past a news kiosk, one notices a prominent ad for *Spirou* magazine, which had not been published in this world – or Lapinot's – for a decade. This single, subtle gesture marks the transition from the classical to the postmodern era of French comic book characters, but, further, it acts as a bridge to the ninth volume of the series.

Published the year before Lapinot's death, *L'Accélérateur atomique* is a departure even by the standards of the Lapinot series, as it sets the character in the world of the *Spirou* comics, long published by Dupuis. *L'Accélérateur atomique* opens with a note indicating that it is an homage from the author to Spirou and his creators and further that this Dargaud book is published with the friendly authorization of Dupuis. Lapinot is placed in the role of Spirou, the bellboy character created in 1938 by Rob-Vel (Robert Velter) as a copy of the more successful *Tintin* series. Rob-Vel oversaw the adventures of Spirou for only a few years before turning over the reins briefly to Jijé (Joseph Gillain), who in turn handed the series to André Franquin in 1946. Franquin would be the creative force behind Spirou for twenty-two years, creating many of the best-known supporting characters (the citizens of Champignac, Zantafio, Zorglub, and Marsupilami) while creating some of the most highly regarded adventure-comedy comics in Belgian history. Franquin left the Spirou stories in 1968 to focus on the character Gaston, which had made him increasingly famous. In the intervening years Spirou and his friends have been drawn by Fournier, Nic Broca, and most recently by Tome and Janry, but it is Franquin's work on the character that is generally held as the standard.

L'Accélérateur atomique sets out to ape the work of Franquin, paying homage not only in terms of story construction and imagery, but in not-so-subtle references to the Château Sain-Frinquan Millésime 1924 wine that signifies the presence of a true connoisseur. Nonetheless, it is in terms of formal construction that *L'Accélérateur atomique* is of most interest.

The book tells the story of Spirou (Lapinot) and Fantasio (a role not played by any of the established Lapinot cast) as they accidentally become embroiled in a jewel heist. Seeking to investigate the crime, they get dragged into a story in which a mad scientist has invented suits that allow the wearer to become invisible and to alter time. Along the way they make a number of assumptions about the guilt and innocence of a variety of suspects, each of which in turn is shown to be incorrect. Ultimately the villain is revealed to be not the mad scientist but the neighbour of the mad scientist (Richard), and the story is resolved with a large explosion that seemingly kills the villain. All of this unfolds within a context of a number of recurrent jokes regarding sound effects and a can of carrot juice, as well as a series of set action pieces that establish the generic conventions. What is interesting about the book is not how it so ably imitates the classic Spirou tales, but how it creates its own space. While Spirou and Fantasio are drawn in a precise fashion (factoring in the extreme difference in style between Franquin and Trondheim), the lead characters are never referred to by name. This makes the book both a Spirou book and self-evidently not a Spirou book. Similarly, smaller elements of the Spirou books have been altered to make the book more akin to a Trondheim book. Spip, Spirou's attendant squirrel friend, is here transformed into a rabbit, making him a more appropriate fetish animal for Lapinot. Thus, while the book is self-consciously an homage to the Spirou universe, it also maintains an arm's-length distance. Further, the book is removed from the traditions of Trondheim's own series by the absence of so many of the Lapinot cast, who can generally be found even in those books set in other generic worlds. Thus, *L'Accélérateur atomique* acts as a sort of afterlife for Lapinot. Having died in his own continuity, he is reborn in the tenth book as a classic character that, importantly, can never be killed. The contemporary adventure character is reincarnated in a classical universe, constructed as a postmodern pastiche of that classicism.

Trondheim thus has things both ways. He has created in Lapinot a marketable character whose image can be used to sell T-shirts and books, but he also gets to stand at a distance from the heteronomous traditions that would celebrate legitimation through commercial success. Through the construction of a skewed temporality in the Lapinot universe that allows the character to appear in any type of genre story, Trondheim is able to maintain an autonomous disposition within the realm of heteronomous production. Further, Trondheim is able to draw on the processes of legitimation that are afforded to him as an author in the

Dargaud family, a group that has included celebrated artists such as E.P. Jacobs, Morris, and Jean Giraud. Thus, it is clear that through Dargaud Trondheim is able to have his cake and eat it too, as the artist and publisher work to contribute their respective cultural capitals one to the other.

Trondheim's participation with Dargaud in the Lapinot series may have been his first encounter with the large publishing houses, but it was hardly his last. Since 1995 he has launched no fewer than fifteen different ongoing album series with publishers like Dargaud, Delcourt, and Dupuis. Many of these series are more traditionally generic than the boundary-smashing Lapinot series. Yet at the same time, his willingness to work in a variety of genres at the same time – either individually or in collaboration with other artists – has become a hallmark of his artistic practice. While his various narrative universes do not circle in on each other to the same degree as those of Joann Sfar, he does nonetheless present a striking example of creative productivity placed in the service of monumental output.

Trondheim's first traditional album outside of the *Formidables Aventures de Lapinot* series was the first installment of the *Formidables Aventures sans Lapinot, Les Aventures de l'univers* (Dargaud, 1997). It is this particular book that is the true link between Trondheim's work in the small press and his work for the established houses. While the Lapinot series represents the transformation of a formerly small-press character and its consecration in the world of commercial publishing through a process of conversion and adaptation, *Les Aventures de l'univers* is itself a straight transplantation of small-press aesthetics to Dargaud. The strips in this book are collected from the pages of *Les Inrockuptibles,* the French music magazine. Each strip is a single page, and, for the most part, they deal with Trondheim and his family in an autobiographical mode (using the visual style from *Approximativement*). The non-autobiographical material in the book consists primarily of short gag strips of the type that he generally placed in the pages of *Lapin.* Thus, a book like *Les Aventures de l'univers* demonstrates how he had, by 1997, escaped the small-press/large-press dichotomy through the mediating institution of a French music magazine. As a publication implicitly built upon the navigation of notions of authenticity and legitimacy within commercial culture, *Les Inrockuptibles* confers commercial status on his small-press aesthetic, allowing it to be transformed into material that is most appropriate for a well-established publisher like Dargaud.

Two additional volumes in the 'Formidables Aventures sans Lapinot' series have followed, each of which deals with the subject of computers. As with the previous volume, these strips were originally serialized in a mass-market magazine, *SVM Mac*. These primarily single-page strips are set on the edges of the Lapinot universe and demonstrate how that story-world is permeable in relation to commercially derived projects. The two books again speak to the competing generic impulses in Trondheim's work. The first volume, *Ordinateur mon ami* (Dargaud, 1998), is a mixed bag of material. The book features a number of single-page strips using a variety of character types and drawing styles that are akin to his work for *Lapin* in their refusal to cohere as a traditional package. At the same time, he has inserted a number of longer stories featuring two immature computer gamers named Patrick and Félix. These characters, drawn in a style very much akin to the Lapinot stories, actually exist on the periphery of his larger narrative project. Indeed, in the last story in the book the characters meet up with Richard and Titi. The next volume, *Cyberculture mon amour* (Dargaud, 2001), focuses exclusively on Félix and Patrick as they work to develop a video game that will make them rich. Trondheim's parody of the world of high-concept creative pursuits seems an apt self-commentary on his own position in relation to the structures of economic power, particularly insofar as it recalls the author's own fixation on video games, evidenced in *Approximativement*. Trondheim further integrates this work into the Lapinot world when he uses Félix as a supporting character in *Pour de Vrai* as a friend of Richard. The introduction of Félix in that context acts to close the circle in the Lapinot universe and subsumes the connections between the small-press, the non-comics mass media, and the large press in a manner that privileges the mass market ideal.

Once he was established as a legitimate large-press artist at Dargaud, Trondheim quickly expanded into other realms of the comics market. His remaining album series can be divided into a number of categories: work undertaken in collaboration with other artists, solo works, works for children, works for adults, and semi-experimental works. His 'mature' or traditional album series include several collaborations. In 2000 Trondheim created, with artist Manu Larcenet, *Les Cosmonautes du futur* (Dargaud). This science-fiction series focuses on the exploits of two school-aged children and their adventures negotiating a daily life that is constantly interrupted by aliens. The books draw humour from the presentation of fairly standard French sci-fi comics tropes that are subtly mocked by the presence of children. Another science-fiction series, *Kaput & Zosky*, was launched at Delcourt in 2002. Based on characters that originally appeared in *Journal de Mickey*, and later in *Lapin* #16, these books follow the adventures of two aliens who struggle to conquer new worlds, always with hopeless results. The figures are mean-spirited tyrants who always end up with the short end of the stick. Trondheim published one volume of this series as a solo artist; the second volume was a collaboration with Stakhano co-founder Eric Cartier. The books have subsequently been developed as a series of animated short films which air on French television, bringing Trondheim to a far larger public than the books themselves. Additionally, he has authored, with artist Fabrice Parme, a series of adventure books set in the espionage world of Renaissance Venice, *Venezia* (Dargaud, 2001). These books, which depend heavily on stories of mistaken identity for their humour, demonstrate something of the breadth of the writer's interests, which range from the distant past to the distant future.

The vastness of the Trondheimian project is further demonstrated by the six series that he has undertaken specifically for children. These books, written in a slightly different register from the hip cynicism that characterizes much of his adult satire, further solidify Trondheim's interest in trans-generic exploration. With artist Fabrice Parme, he has created a series entitled *Le Roi catastrophe* (Delcourt Jeunesse, 2001). These are short albums, each composed of three stories, featuring a petulant child king. The books are extremely colourful, more closely resembling the open-paged structure of a great deal of children's literature. Completely the opposite of this is *Papa raconte* (Delcourt Jeunesse, 2001), a book created with artist José Parrondo. *Papa raconte*, which tells the tale of a father inventing a story for his children while he struggles to watch his football game on television, is constructed of thirty pages of thirty-five identically sized panels in a five by seven grid. The colours are extremely basic, as are the figures and the integration of the textual elements.

The extremely wordy *Papa raconte* is the total opposite of the *Petit Père Noël* series (Dupuis, 2000), with artist Thierry Robin, which are entirely wordless. These books, set at the North Pole and featuring the exploits of Santa Claus and his friends, recall Trondheim's wordless experiments in the small press, now recast as material for children. The variety of the approaches taken in these books – ranging from wordlessness to high-density text – is indicative of the scope of Trondheim's reach. In constructing a series of children's books with a number of collaborators, he has expanded the genre in a number of formal directions at the same time, considerably blurring the traditionally understood distinction between the avant-garde and comic books for children.

In particular, Trondheim has aggressively problematized this distinction in three different series. The first of these series, *Monstrueux* (Delcourt Jeunesse, 1999), particularly situates the small press in a unique fashion. The first *Monstrueux* book, *Monstrueux Bazar* (1999), established the tone of the series. The book features Trondheim, his wife, and their children in slightly more cartoony versions of the way they had been depicted in the artist's autobiographical material. The book, told from the point of view of the children, focuses on magic powder that is able to turn the parents' drawings into real objects. When the children pour the powder on their own drawings of monsters, trouble erupts. Central to the book's conceit is the fact that the artist incorporates his children's extremely crude drawings of monsters into the text – subtly manipulating them on the page with the aid of computers.

The fourth book in this series, *Monstrueux Dinosaure* (2001), introduces a new element. This book, which is concerned with a tournament of fighting dinosaurs, includes art not only by his children but also by his friends. In the endpapers he thanks the proprietors of the Sfarodactyle, the Davidbnodon, and the Tomdieckosaure (among many others). Once again, Trondheim manipulates these figures on the computer in order to incorporate the drawings of more than a dozen small-press stars into a children's book. The net result is a volume of fantasy autobiography that incorporates the small-press publishing scene into the realm of children's literature – the end result, it could be argued, of the development of the small-press comics revolution of the 1990s.

Not only has Trondheim incorporated the small-press movement into the field of children's publishing, but he has also moved that field towards avant-gardism through the use of OuBaPienne elements in his work. *Mister O* (Delcourt, 2002), for example, features the deeds of a crudely drawn circular figure (little more than a stick figure) in thirty wordless single-page strips as he attempts to cross a crevasse. Each page is identically formatted in a six-by-ten panel grid, and the end result of almost every strip is failure. The strips, six of which originally appeared in *Libération* in 1999, demonstrate Trondheim's interest in minimalism and in panel transitions. The comics are reduced to basic elements, and the emphasis is placed on sequentiality.

A very different version of sequentiality is provided by a series of books entitled *Les Trois Chemins* (Delcourt Jeunesse, 2000, 2004). Created with artist Sergio Garcia, *Les Trois Chemins* are books that follow three narrative lines simultaneously. In each book, images are composed across two-page spreads, with no panel boundaries. A single background image across the two pages hosts a series of sequentially arranged figures, demonstrating the movement of characters through space. On each page three different characters move through the space, each creating a line that traces their movement across the page. Occasionally these figures intersect, or an element used by one character will move into the realm of another. The books can be read as a series of three narratives at once or as three single stories that can be read semi-independently. Nonetheless, the books demonstrate a lack of fixity with regard to the book page and present a complex and innovative take on sequentiality in the form of a book for children. Throughout these various series, therefore, it is clear that Trondheim's primary interest lies in shattering traditional boundaries. His work is remarkably hybrid, combining genres, forms, and aesthetic dispositions in order to create a style of production that is uniquely his own.

Writing on the relationship of the autonomous and heteronomous spheres in cultural production, Pierre Bourdieu has noted that breaks from past practice often take the form of parody, a strategy that serves to confirm the artist's emancipation from the past. Bourdieu argues that newcomers 'get beyond' the dominant mode not by explicitly denouncing it but by rendering it incongruous and absurd.[11] Certainly this is the case with the work that Trondheim has produced with Joann Sfar at Delcourt. Delcourt, a publishing house started by Guy Delcourt in 1990, is the most notable comics success story of the 1990s, having risen from nothing to a position as one of the largest publishers of comics in France. One of Delcourt's most notable strategies has been to recruit young talents from art schools and to specialize in a popular – if long neglected – genre, historic fantasy. Trondheim and Sfar's first work for the publisher was one such series, *Donjon*.

Set in a dungeons-and-dragons-style fictional universe featuring bizarre monsters (such as a vegetarian fire-breathing dragon), the *Donjon* story follows an inept, sword-wielding duck and his adventures in a magical castle and its dungeon. The book, primarily written by Sfar with art by Trondheim, is not precisely a parody of knights-and-dragons-style comics, but it is not played straight either. Clearly humorous, the books are highly self-aware – as they would be in a parodic voice – but can also be read as somewhat playful, traditional adventure books. For example, in *Donjon* the hero, an anthropomorphic duck named Herbert, is compelled to complete a series of tasks before he is even permitted to wield the magic sword that he has looted from the corpse of an adventurer he has accidentally killed. On the one hand, the requirement that the protagonist prove his mettle is a characteristic of the genre. On the other hand, however, the circumstances by which he accomplishes this task are ludicrous, as is the petulant belt that guards the sword. When the tasks are ultimately accomplished, no one – including Herbert – actually notices. A subsequent requirement that Herbert unite the 'objects of destiny' goes completely ignored as the characters regard this as too much of a hassle to be bothered with.

Clearly, the use of humour suggests a parodic mode, but the fidelity to generic conventions also suggests what Fredric Jameson has termed 'the nostalgia mode,' or a mass cultural form of pastiche interested in retrospective styling. Jameson describes this form of pastiche as an allusive plagiarism of older plots and styles within a contemporary sensibility.[12] This tendency is evident in *L'Accélérateur atomique* as well as in the *Donjon* books, which relentlessly foreground in a knowing way both the conventions of the sword-and-sorcery genre and the economic structure of the French comics-publishing industry that relies upon ongoing series as a guarantee of financial stability.

This economic structure is derived explicitly from the confusion that accompanied the rapid expansion of the *Donjon* line in the years that followed its initial success. Sfar and Trondheim announced early on that the *Donjon* series would run to a length of one hundred novels before it played out but soon renounced that plan. In 1999 the artists added two new series to the *Donjon* line. The first of these, *Donjon Crépuscule*, functions as an inversion of the first series (rechristened *Donjon Zénith*), as Trondheim is primarily responsible for the writing and Sfar for the art. If one accepts the first *Donjon* book (*Coeur de canard*) as the 'present' starting point of the series, then the *Crépuscule* stories take place in the future. This sense is literalized in the structure of the books. The earliest *Donjon Zénith* books (figure 24) are numbered sequentially starting with volume one, but the *Donjon Crépuscule* books begin at 101. This indicates that the primary story in the *Zénith* series has more than ninety books remaining in its continuity before the *Crépuscule* story begins. The connection between the stories is rendered even more explicit by the continuous page numbering, which finds *Le Cimetière des dragons* beginning with page number 4601. Further, many of the same characters that appear in the *Zénith* stories are present in these volumes, but they have been transformed over time. The hapless lead, Herbert, has emerged as a despotic ruler who has united the objects of destiny and transformed the Dungeon into a post-apocalyptic nightmare.

Here the difference in Sfar and Trondheim's visual styles plays an

24 Herbert is put to the test by a sword-wielding mouse. From *Donjon: Le Roi de la bagarre* by Lewis Trondheim and Joann Sfar.

important role, as Sfar's sketchier linework contributes to a sense of decay entirely absent from the Trondheim-rendered *Zénith* series, which is more frivolous and brightly coloured. Laurent Gerbier, in a review in *9e Art*, has drawn attention to how the tones of the various series are made distinct from each other through the use of colour, noting that the *Zénith* stories use colours that are 'luminous' while the *Crépuscule* stories are 'faded, dull, they limit the palette to degraded forms of mauve, orange, and brown.'[13] The humour in the *Crépuscule* series is similarly downbeat, contributing a more tragic sensibility.

Having established a 'present' and 'future' continuity for the *Donjon* series, the artists also launched a third continuity in 1999, set in the past. For this series they recruited Sfar collaborator Christophe Blain to produce the art on the *Donjon Potron-Minet* series. This series, whose first book was numbered −99 and which is presumably to run to 0, follows the adventures of the Dungeon's guardian, Hyacinthe, as a young man. A number of the characters from the *Zénith* continuity are introduced as their younger selves in this series, which is again quite different in tone from the other books.

The *Potron-Minet* books are not set in the Dungeon, but in a Renaissance city-state to which Hyacinthe has been sent by his father. Here he becomes embroiled in a series of palace intrigues, falls in love with a female assassin, and takes the streets at night as a masked adventurer bent on righting wrongs. Blain's art, a sort of hybrid of the Sfar and Trondheim styles in the series, again conveys a different temporal moment. The *Potron-Minet* series parodies entirely different sets of conventions, and each of the three series serves as a vehicle in which the artists are able to explore different conventions in the heroic-fantasy genre. The key here is in the establishment of a comprehensive world in which no single character is absolutely central. This allows tremendous flexibility in the creation of a 300-part ongoing story told simultaneously with art by three different artists.

Yet these three series are not the end of the project, which has expanded in a number of other ways. The *Donjon* series, far from being simply an ironic or postmodern take on a popular French comics genre, intersects with the structure of the field of European comic book production in more important ways. The first of these is the publication of the *Donjon Parade* series. These books, illustrated by Manu Larcenet (Trondheim's collaborator on the *Cosmonautes du futur* series), are shorter albums (thirty pages) that tell stories set in the continuity between the first and second *Donjon Zénith* books. Situated as straightforward humour, these works are serialized in Delcourt's magazine *Pavillon rouge*. The short comedic stories, therefore, serve as a way of keeping the *Donjon* series before the public even at times when no new volume in the main series is forthcoming. In a sense then, these minor works act as a form of advertising for the more central primary texts and bring Sfar and Trondheim fully into the traditions of the traditional European album production format that had existed for generations.

A second offshoot, *Donjon Bonus,* moves the creators even more forcefully into the world of commerce. *Donjon Bonus* is a black-and-white volume by Trondheim, Sfar, and Arnaud Moragues that acts as a role-playing game guide for the *Donjon* universe. Thus, the parody of dungeons-and-dragons-type games comes full circle to become a dungeons-and-dragons-type game itself, albeit infused with considerable ironic humour. Relative to the careers of Trondheim and Sfar, it is clear from *Donjon Parade* and *Donjon Bonus* that the series allows the artists not only to reap the benefits of the large-scale commercial publishing venture in a well-established genre but also to stand outside that genre through the deployment of a detached, ironic disposition to the arena of commerce that the books so assiduously court.

A final *Donjon* series is the fastest-growing to date: *Donjon Monsters.* These books, which are stand-alone albums, feature the adventures and back-story of various supporting characters in the *Donjon* universe. Set in each of the primary historical epochs of the Dungeon, the books are illustrated by various cartoonists from scripts by Sfar and detailed roughs by Trondheim. Among the artists who have contributed to the *Donjon Monsters* series to date are Mazan, Andreas, Stéphane Blanquet, Jean-Emmanuel Vermot-Desroches, Carlos Nine, Killoffer, and Yoann. Individual books are tailored to the strengths of the various artists, with different volumes taking on widely divergent visual tones depending on the inclinations of the collaborators, and foregrounding the visual as a key distinguishing feature of each. These books, which serve as background material against which the three-hundred-volume epic unfolds, allow Trondheim and Sfar to create not only a fully realized fictional world but an alternative comics publishing empire at whose centre they reside. The creation of the *Monsters* series brings with it the possibility of incorporating all of the artists from the so-called *nouvelle bande dessinée* movement – or, indeed, all comics artists if their expansive reach is fulfilled – into a particularly postmodern vision of genre publishing. As each new artist is added to the collection, however, the project itself is subtly changed.

The second *Donjon Monsters* book, *Le Géant qui pleure* (2001), is illustrated by Jean-Christophe Menu. Menu, best known as an autobiographical cartoonist and as the outspoken anti-genre comics publisher of L'Association, is not an artist generally sympathetic to this particular type of project. Having never created a traditional album, and having released his work almost exclusively in self-published fanzines at Futuropolis and at L'Association, Menu would not seem an obvious choice for this series, despite the visual appropriateness of his cartoony art style. Nonetheless, Menu's participation in the process, about which he says, 'I gave pleasure to the little ten-year-old Menu who dreamed of nothing but that ...,'[14] does little to destabilize or challenge the commercial publishing industry against which the artist had long campaigned. Instead, the book seems to mark a distinctive shift in emphasis in the ongoing struggle between the large- and small-press publishers in France. Menu's use of in-jokes – for example, making all of the books in the magician's library part of L'Association's publishing line – does little to mitigate the sense of co-optation.

The seventh book in the *Monsters* series, *Mon Fils le tueur* (2003), illustrated by Blutch, further signals the change that has taken place over the course of the decade-long rise of the small-press artists to mainstream significance. Blutch, whose work is split somewhat evenly between the pages of *Fluide glacial* and small-press publishers such as Cornélius and L'Association, contributes a book that was published by Delcourt in two editions. The 2004 edition is a standard-sized full-colour album that visually matches the rest of the *Donjon* line. The 2003 advance edition, however, is physically larger than the standard *Donjon* book and is printed in black and white. Further, the cover – with its barely perceptible title – suggests that it is only partially akin to the other books in the series. The black-and-white edition hearkens back to the idea of an artist's edition of the work or the *tirage-de-tête*, and the lack of colour is intended to highlight the beauty of Blutch's original drawings, unfettered by the intervention of a colourist. Further, the black-and-white edition was limited to four thousand copies, highlighting its scarcity even if it is much more widely available than the artisanal works published by the likes of Drozophile and BüLB. Indeed, the fact that the book was artificially limited to four thousand copies – a sum that artists like Trondheim, Sfar, and Blutch had struggled to attain only a decade before – is indicative of how the field of European comics had been transformed by these artists in the intervening years.

Yet more than simply illustrating the transformation of the field of production, a project such as *Donjon* transforms notions of generic conventions and, even more to the point, alters the perception of the comic book series as a fixed object. By incorporating six distinct series within the framework of a larger project, Trondheim and Sfar have embraced trans-generic renewal in a truly aggressive manner. Further, in telling the same story from distinct points (*Potron-Minet, Zénith,* and *Crépuscule*) in the ongoing narrative, the authors offer a significant avant-gardist challenge to traditional notions of narrative development. Indeed, this approach to the narrative seems more closely aligned to the formal experimentation of OuLiPo than it does to the traditions of the *bande dessinée* market. Further, this idea of an avant-garde parodic sword-and-sorcery series has as its primary impact the dislocation of traditional notions of mastery that are central to so much of comics fandom.

Donjon illustrates, in a strong manner, the impossibility of complete fan knowledge. For instance, because the 101st volume of the series shows Herbert to have united the objects of destiny, but the fourth volume shows him having no interest in such an undertaking, the reader is aware that somewhere in the intervening volumes – as yet unwritten – Herbert will complete this task and substantially alter his destiny and his reality, but it is unclear how this will happen. Further, because the reader is aware that this quest will ultimately be undertaken and resolved, when an object of destiny is mentioned casually in one of the *Donjon Monsters* books it becomes a fact to be mentally catalogued for future reference. In short, the story elements set in the future of the characters signal to the reader knowledge gaps that will have to be filled at a later time: the books tell the reader enough to let them know that there is much that they do not know.

Yet, at the same time, the pace of publication for the series – twenty-two books in the first eight years (1998–2005), and only ten of those in the three primary continuities – makes it impossible for the fan to comprehend the entire structure of the narrative in all of its complexity. Thus, Sfar and Trondheim resituate themselves as artists at a distance from their readers. At the established pace of just under three books per year, and less than two books in the main story per year, *Donjon* cannot be completed in much less than two centuries. Of course, the books will never be finished – there will never be a volume 100 that serves as a transition from *Donjon Zénith* to *Donjon Crépuscule*. Trondheim and Sfar have created the ultimate postmodern adventure tale, structured around so many knowledge gaps and incorporating so many diverse voices that it becomes ludicrous to think of *Donjon* as a series at all. Indeed, *Donjon* puts the lie to the idea of the open-ended, eternally developing comic book series originated by Hergé and those who followed him. By structuring their series within a formal framework they have demonstrated the impossibility of the project, destabilizing the foundation of the commercial publishing houses through an elaboration of the core values.

Trondheim's success with the *Donjon* and *Lapinot* books has helped to position him as one of the most significant figures in the contemporary French comics field. His emergence as a star of the *nouvelle bande dessinée* movement has largely been a function of his ability to maintain the celebrity that he has accrued through his large-scale publishing projects and the authenticity of the small-press artist, despite the fact that the weight he places on undertakings in each area is increasingly disproportionate. The shift in his publishing base is demonstrated by his bibliography. From 1990 to 1995 (when he published *Blacktown* with Dargaud), Trondheim published twenty-four books with small presses (L'Association, Cornélius, Lézard) or with presses not traditionally associated with comic book publishing (Seuil), and one with a large press (Dargaud). In the next five years, however, this ratio reversed. He published six books with small presses (L'Association) and non-comics publishers (Autrement) and twenty-two with the large presses (Dargaud, Delcourt). Since 2001 that trend has accelerated, with five small-press publications and an incredible thirty-seven from the large publishers. Given the fact that, since 1996, his publications with established houses outnumber his small-press work by a margin of approximately seven to one, how has he maintained a reputation as a small-press cartoonist?

L'Association president Jean-Christophe Menu has sarcastically drawn attention to the shift in Trondheim's reputation. In a signed editorial in *Lapin* #23, Menu included a vicious caricature of his friend, with the tag line 'Lewis! the ass on how many chairs?!'[15] Here Menu mocks Trondheim by suggesting that he only works with L'Association now when Dargaud rejects his book proposals. At the same time, and from a completely opposite perspective, Dupuis's website suggests that he has only become an artist insofar as he has been able to shed his associations with his more autonomous past. His biography on the Dupuis site says of Lapinot, 'The character will become a hit and evolves from pure aesthetic self-indulgence ('Slaloms,' for L'Association in 1993, then 'Mildiou,' for Seuil a year later) into a much more commercial and traditional concept with his return in new adventures for Dargaud from 1995 on.'[16] For Menu, Trondheim's creation of too many projects for too many publishers threatens his status as a legitimate artist. For Dupuis, *Lapinot*'s shift from L'Association to Dargaud is an evolution from the autonomous principle ('pure aesthetic self-indulgence') and a capitulation to the heteronomous principle of the marketplace. Both argue the same point to the same conclusion, although Menu condemns the result while Dupuis celebrates it.

Trondheim himself problematizes his professional standing in much of the small-press work that he has published since becoming a successful artist for the established houses. His return to autobiographical comics in 2002, for example, highlights his personal and family life, but also his professional status. In 2002 Trondheim began publishing 'logbooks' of travels in his *Carnet de bord* series. These books, four of which have been published to date, are presented as less-formal comics storytelling. Done in a diaristic tone, and drawn in a looser, sketchier form, the *Carnet* series is akin to a form of direct expression in the comics form. These books depict his efforts to navigate his own career success and to balance his personal interests with his professional responsibilities.

The first of the *Carnet* books details a trip that he took to a comics festival in Saint-Denis de la Réunion, off the coast of Africa. The second includes two trips, one to the Festival International de la Bande Dessinée in Angoulême and a ski vacation with his two young children taken in the Alps. The third *Carnet* volume also details two trips, one with his family to Granada, and one in which the entire family moves to a new home. While each of these books addresses the same broad themes (because they deal with the artist's daily life and his feelings about his life), the second most forcefully enunciates his professional tensions.

Because they are told in a diaristic fashion, Trondheim's *Carnet de bord* volumes unfold in an episodic manner, without the traditional trappings of narrative. Elements are introduced and dropped quickly, and no single moment takes up more than a few drawings or a few pages before it is resolved. The *Carnet de bord* for 22–8 January 2002, the Angoulême Festival, does not break this pattern. Indeed, the story (such as it is) follows Trondheim's efforts to carve out a professional niche for himself in accordance with his gruff personality. The book begins with Trondheim pleased to find himself in a first-class rail seat, taking the train from his home in Montpellier to Paris. This is the first of several indications that his lifestyle has been somewhat altered by the success of his commercial undertakings. That success is thrown into question by the artist's dismissal of the book that he had brought to read on the train. He discards it after only forty-six pages, noting that this will be the first and last time he buys a book on the recommendation of *Télérama,* a magazine that has published (among others) colleagues of Trondheim's such as Christophe Blain. While this scene serves to establish Trondheim's general distemper, it also invokes an unease with the processes of the dominant or orthodox model of book publishing in France – a system in which he is intricately caught up and the system that is responsible (at least in part) for his current first-class seating assignment.

Arriving in Paris, Trondheim meets with Joann Sfar, and together they take part in a roundtable (with Will Eisner) on the question of Judaism in comics. He finds the conference boring, and this one particularly so due to the necessity of time-consuming French–English translation. In Angoulême he and Sfar take part in another roundtable on children's comics, and he makes it perfectly clear that this aspect of the professional cartoonist's career is completely unpleasant for him. One other aspect that he dismisses in the comic is the social networking that happens in conference hotels and bars. He describes, for example, a method that he has devised to 'teleport' himself out of conversations with people whom he finds uninteresting at parties. In addition to these aggravations, he outlines his work responsibilities at the festival. He depicts himself at the L'Association stand, where artists sign their books, although he is not signing but playing a small accordion by himself. Significantly, this is the only time he depicts the L'Association space, and other partners in L'Association are depicted in the book only incidentally. Nonetheless, his relationship with Dargaud is not depicted on far better terms. He shows himself at a Dargaud dinner playing a (much larger) accordion with Sfar and others, to the general displeasure of many of the gathered cartoonists and employees. Indeed, throughout this particular travel diary he makes repeated reference to the distinction between music and comics and the pleasures that he derives from the former, which are clearly set at odds with the psychic pain brought about by the latter.

The most telling commentary on his professional career occurs when he has lunch with David B. (himself emblematic of the tension between the two poles of the French comics market) and Philippe Druillet and Nikita Mandryka, two of the artists involved with the creation of the highly influential publishing house Humanoïdes Associés in the 1970s. Dining with Mandryka and Druillet, artists whose impact on the French comics scene in the 1970s is comparable to that of Trondheim and David B. in the 1990s, forces him to consider his long-term legacy and that of his partners. He depicts the founders of L'Association as they might look in twenty-five years, unchanged except for their physical years. Through-out *Carnet de bord* he keeps his professional career at arm's length. While it is clear that he sees his place in history affiliated with the creation of L'Association, his more commercial work is given nearly equal weight in the book, although neither apparently provides him much pleasure. Indeed, the diary ends with him back home in Montpellier in bed with his wife, only to be roused from his sleep by passing comics fans who saw his name on the doorbell and decided to find out if he really lived there. In short, cartooning is presented as a constant source of aggravation for Trondheim. This allows him the opportunity to play the traditional role of the tormented artist even while engaging with the advantages that his work within the cultural system has afforded him.

Aside from his autobiographical comics Trondheim has continued to produce new works for L'Association that are atypical of his larger oeuvre. Many of these projects have limited commercial potential. He has revived his interest in the form of the daily comic strip in *Le Pays des trois sourires* (L'Association, 1997), a series of four-panel comic strips, and *Politique étrangère* (L'Association, 2000), a series of four-panel gag strips that he wrote for Jochen Gerner. He also collaborated with Mattt Konture on *Galopinot* (L'Association, 1998), a mini-comic in the *Patte de Mouche* line that featured Lapinot and Konture's Galopu wandering the streets of Paris. At the same time, he continues to produce short works for *Lapin* – where he appears in every issue – and his frequent publications for L'Association ensure that he continues to regard it as his artistic home and his outlet for highly 'personal' material. What is clear is how his ongoing participation with the most significant artist-run comic book publisher in Europe provides a foundation for artistic legitimation and credibility. Thus, Trondheim – and by extension Dargaud and Delcourt – is inoculated against charges of 'selling out' through his ideological alignment with the quintessential French small-press publisher.

In 2004, having produced more than one hundred books in a fifteen-year span, Trondheim indicated in the fourth volume of his *Carnets* and in interviews that he would be taking a hiatus from comics. While still continuing to write for a few of his series (including *Donjon* and *Le Roi catastrophe*), he would otherwise move on to other pursuits. This an-nouncement was formalized in January 2005, with, ironically, the publi-cation of a comic book announcing the artist's disillusionment with comic books. *Désoeuvré* (figure 25), one of two books that launched a new collection of essays from L'Association (Collection Éprouvette), traces the evolution of the artist's thinking about his own career. In the

25 Lapinot returns from the dead to confront his author. From *Désoeuvré*.

essay, Trondheim explores his belief that cartoonists age poorly. Noting that serialization emphasized repetition to the point of creative sclerosis, Trondheim struggles to find examples of great cartoonists who maintained a high level of quality in their later years. Instead, what he encounters is a depressing list of failures: the depression of Franquin, the suicides of LeLong and Degotte, Gotlib's total work stoppage, and Carl Barks's lack of comics production for the last forty years of his life. While the counter-example of Jean 'Moebius' Giraud, a cutting-edge artist who has remained innovative for almost four decades, is constantly suggested, Trondheim is unable to generate the enthusiasm for comics that he attributes to his colleagues, like Edmond Baudoin and Joann Sfar. Instead, he depicts himself withdrawing from comics production and moving on to new projects in his life.

On the one hand, *Désoeuvré* is simply the depiction of one man's disillusionment with the comics movement that I have described in this book, a movement in which he played a central role. On the other, to many it might signal the beginning of the end of that same movement, the first marker of a generational shift that is inevitable in all forms of cultural production. There can be no doubt that, over the course of a decade and a half, the small-press comics movement has dramatically restructured our conception of the field of comic book production. The stars of the movement have become the stars of the industry, celebrated award-winners whose new works are highly anticipated. The small press has arrived, and just as L'Association is no longer a do-it-yourself fanzine publisher run out of Jean-Christophe Menu's apartment, many of the authors associated with the movement are now consecrated artists with mortgages, families, and responsibilities. The revolutionary energy that marked the initial burst of small-press excitement has, in the case of Trondheim and some of his contemporaries, given way to meetings with representatives of the Walt Disney Company. In his book, Trondheim offers a graph illustrating the rise and fall of the comics artist in six phases: simple notoriety, renown, glory, stardom, has-been, big has-been.[17] If this leaves Trondheim one step removed from 'has-been,' can the same be said of the movement with which his career was so closely aligned?

Trondheim marks his departure with the definitive statement that only a death can engender. His retirement from the field of comics production, however circumscribed or short-lived it may wind up in the end,[18] is one sign that the comics-producing generation that came of age in the 1990s is being supplanted by a newer generation. Nonetheless, the success of Lewis Trondheim is emblematic of the possibilities opened by the small-press renaissance in European comics since 1990. That an artist who, by his own admission, had no ability to draw could become one of the most prolific, popular, and financially successful cartoonists of his generation was conceivable only given the redefinition of the field by the artists of the small press. Few cartoonists involved in the movement have yet matched his success, and his victories are not entirely shared. However, the ascension of Trondheim to the top ranks of European cartoonists and his ongoing success in a number of related fields and international markets symbolize the importance of the entire small-press revolution and the transformation of the comic book field that it put into motion.

In an article in *The Comics Journal,* Paul Gravett speculated on the reason why Lewis Trondheim opted for such a bizarre nom de plume. Gravett suggests that the name may be an anagram for 'The World is Mine,' a megalomaniacal gesture entirely fitting with the artist's expansive publishing efforts.[19] I would suggest, however, that while he rose to a position of prominence within the world of comics, Trondheim's accomplishments were not his alone, but the product of an entire cultural movement rooted in the small-press renaissance. In the end, the world is theirs.

Conclusion

L'Association president Jean-Christophe Menu concluded his 2005 book-length essay, *Plates-bandes,* with the following question: 'Will the years 1994–2004 mark the dates of a golden age, recalled in time and in memories, which we will soon evoke with nostalgia and bitterness, as others recall 1969–1979?'[1] This question summarizes Menu's assessment of comics production after more than a decade of sustained efforts to transform it. While Menu pauses to take stock of what has been accomplished over the course of this productive period, it is clear that he remains apprehensive about what the future holds, both for the publishing house to which he has dedicated so much of his professional life and to the artistic movement for which he has often been a reluctant spokesperson. In the sixty-six pages of *Plates-bandes,* Menu provides a retroactive manifesto of the small-press comics movement (a term, significantly, to which he does not subscribe) and a forward-looking attack on the processes of co-optation by the forces of commercialization. It is somewhat serendipitous that this essay appeared when it did, because it speaks to so many of the issues outlined in this book. Thus, I want to conclude by briefly responding to his claims and outlining not only the important legacy of this passing era, but its possibilities for future directions in both the cultural production of art comics and our critical understanding of them.

Menu begins *Plates-bandes* by questioning exactly what L'Association, and related French publishers, have accomplished over the past ten years. He rejects various labels relating to the political economy of the publishers (independent, alternative, or underground), arguing instead that L'Association constituted a true avant-garde. In chapter three of this book, I placed the locus of the contemporary comic book avant-garde at a remove from L'Association (with the notable exception of the OuBaPo experimentations), positioning it more fully with Fréon and Amok. Menu's suggestion that L'Association is an avant-garde is derived from his observation that they were inspired by the advances made by literary surrealism and that the group brought many of the avant-gardist innovations of surrealism to the field of comics for the first time, including dream stories and collective processes like the exquisite corpse, thereby elevating the overall status of the field.[2] But Menu's position-taking is not merely affirmative. He juxtaposes what he sees as the comic book avant-garde with a 'soft avant-garde.' Borrowing the term from the subtitle of the first French issue of *Black* (Coconino/Vertige Graphic, 2004), Menu notes that the editor of *Black*, the Italian cartoonist Igort, is also an editorial director for Casterman, one of the large publishing houses that has been most aggressive in terms of co-opting the small-press aesthetic. Through the introduction of this binary (L'Association as the avant-garde, *Black* as soft avant-garde) Menu seeks to highlight an autonomous/heteronomous split in the field that is not necessarily as apparent as he might argue.

Indeed, as the examples of Lewis Trondheim and the authors associated with *la nouvelle bande dessinée* ably demonstrated, by 2005 the relative success of the small-press comics movement, both financially and aesthetically, threatened to problematize the significance of their intervention into the field of production. Increasingly, the small-press comics movement is, in the simplest terms, a victim of its own success. Specifically, while it must be noted that many of the artists associated with the small-press comics movement in Europe are enjoying personal successes, that very success has served to destabilize the movement, both financially and aesthetically.

Menu dedicates much of *Plates-bandes* to the financial threat posed to L'Association, and to publishers like them, by the soft avant-garde and the faux-avant-garde. The death of Futuropolis was one of the important spurs in the creation of the French small-press comics movement in the early 1990s. However, the sudden revival of that publishing house is held by Menu to be a signal that the movement may be on its last legs. In 2005, Futuropolis was resurrected as a publishing imprint by Sébastien Gnaedig, under the joint auspices of the comic book publisher Soleil and the book publisher Gallimard, with whom Étienne Robial had worked from 1987 until the official demise of the label in 1994. Gnaedig's decision was loudly criticized by many in the small-press comics movement, perhaps most vocally by Menu, who described the move as a cynical marketing ploy, indicative of the consumerist ethos of the French comics industry. Menu pointed out that, within the field of French comics production, no publisher was more dedicated to commercial imperatives than Soleil, and few were less praised for the quality of their publications. By acquiring the name of the most celebrated comics imprint, 'the avant-garde itself,'[3] Soleil dons a magic hat that will allow it to co-opt the cultural capital that had accrued to the long-dead publisher. For Menu, this is akin to reviving the Miles Davis Quartet with four stars taken from *Star Academy*,[4] a marketing ploy pure and simple.

While threatening to some parts of the small-press comics movement, the resurrection of Futuropolis, a move notably condemned by Robial himself, is also, at least in part, recognition of that movement. It is clear that by 2005 the small-press comics movement was significant enough economically and culturally that the largest comic book publishers would try to masquerade as small-press enterprises. Gnaedig described the new Futuropolis as a mid-sized publisher, straddling the border between the small press and better-established houses: 'Futuropolis is situated between these "small publishers" and the "large ones." I obtained the possibility of having an author-centred policy while also having the financial means of a large publisher.'[5] At the rhetorical level, the hybrid model proposed by Gnaedig is seriously at odds with that of L'Association. Similar efforts to launch contemporary 'literary' comic book lines were also initiated around this time by the book publisher Actes-Sud, as well as by Denoël Graphic, which, like Futuropolis, is affiliated with Gallimard.

While traditional book publishers rushed to enter the 'literary' comics market in 2004, the most significant threat to the L'Association legacy, according to Menu, came from the long-established comic book publishers seeking to abandon their reliance on the traditional album (what Menu calls the 48CC book, defining the page count, the visual aesthetic [*couleurs*] and the hard-bound format [*cartonné*]). Significantly, Menu exempts from this criticism Dargaud's Romans BD line, which included the work of Joann Sfar and David B., as well as the 48CC albums produced by L'Association members and colleagues at Dargaud and Delcourt – a list that would, notably, include his own contribution to the *Donjon* series. Menu notes that L'Association and the other avant-garde publishers of the 1990s had no intention of creating full-colour albums. They are not publishers, like Glénat in their earliest days, compelled to produce black-and-white books while aspiring to full colour, but publishers genuinely dedicated to a different aesthetic sensibility. That some of their authors might want to work, either full or part time, in the traditional album field was not a problem, so long as each side respected the other in a spirit of peaceful co-existence. Casterman, Menu argues, violated this spirit.

For Menu, and for Frémok's Yvan Alagbé, whom Menu quotes in support of his observations, the Écritures book series at Casterman is a naked attempt to knock off L'Association. Publishing North American small-press authors in translation (Seth, Chester Brown, and Craig Thompson), the books in the Écritures line adopt a visual presentation reminiscent of the books published by L'Association, with their distinctive size and cover graphics. Menu suggests that the Casterman books are themselves second-rate knock-offs of the L'Association catalogue, specifically highlighting the work of Craig Thompson. In 2004, Casterman translated Thompson's 600-page autobiographical graphic novel *Blankets* (Top Shelf, 2003) as *Blankets: Manteau de neige*. Menu notes in his essay that the book was originally offered to L'Association and that they were Thompson's preferred French publisher, as he was strongly influenced by the books that they had produced. Nonetheless, L'Association rejected the book, feeling that it was too derivative of the work of Blutch, and it wound up at Casterman, where it became a major success. Thompson's follow-up, *Carnet de voyage* (Top Shelf, 2004), was, as its name suggests, a 224-page travel diary explicitly inspired by L'Association's Carnets collection. This book, which was not offered to L'Association, was translated by Casterman as *Un Américain en balade* (2004) and reformatted for the Écritures collection.

From Menu's point of view, Thompson's books with Casterman represent a double victimization of the small press, introducing the aesthetic threat in addition to the financial one. Not only has Casterman moved to imitate the L'Association book model, but they are doing so by publishing artists who are seen to be copying the L'Association 'look.' For Menu, this development threatens to destabilize the autonomy of the small-press comics movement altogether. However, while Menu sees the French success of *Blankets: Manteau de neige* as an affront to French comic book production, there is more at play here. Thompson's comic is a decidedly American work repackaged to align it with a specifically French aesthetic tradition. Thus, it speaks to the breadth and scope of the small-press movement and to how 'European values' have infiltrated the international market. A more generous reading of the situation than Menu's might see Thompson's work as the inevitable outgrowth of the internationalization of the small-press European comics movement to the United States.

Throughout this book I have been reluctant to dwell on the connections that exist between European comics and the comic book production of the United States. This has had the effect of forcing a separation on the two fields that does not, in fact, exist as clearly as my narrow focus might lead one to surmise. Clearly, there are a large number of cartoon-ists who exist simultaneously in both worlds. Julie Doucet, to take but one example, began publishing fanzines in Montreal before being picked up by Drawn and Quarterly, where she started her own American-sized English-language comic series. L'Association subsequently translated her work, although her most recent work, *Journal* (2004), was published originally by L'Association before being translated into English by Drawn and Quarterly. For an artist like Doucet, who exists in both worlds simultaneously, it is largely irrelevant which publisher is the first to bring her work to the market.

Yet, even in cases that are not quite so hybrid, the exchange between American and European cartoonists can be significant. Indeed, similari-ties to the small-press revolution that occurred in Europe can be found in the United States and Canada. While significant differences exist between the two movements relating to storytelling format, publishing systems, and distribution channels, a similar, though differently articu-lated, aesthetic disposition unites the two cultures. It is difficult to find European small-press publishers who have not translated works by Ameri-can cartoonists such as Debbie Drechsler (L'Association), Ben Katchor (Amok), James Kochalka (Ego Comme X), Dan Clowes (Cornélius). The prevalence of this material in translation highlights a shared aes-thetic and unites cartoonists across linguistic and cultural barriers. From this vantage point, it is easy to see Thompson as an artist on the front line of this cultural exchange. Visually influenced by the work of Blutch, but telling a distinctly American story of romantic and sexual awakening within the confines of fundamentalist Christian middle America, a work like *Blankets* demonstrates the increasing range of the European small press. Rather than being seen merely as symptomatic of a new form of co-optation, Thompson's work can be viewed as a sign of the vitality of the aesthetic that Menu champions.

It is clear that, after a decade of missteps, the products of the Euro-pean small press are finally finding their place in English translation. While the mid-1990s were marked by a period of disinterest from Ameri-can comic book publishers towards their European counterparts, the 2000s have witnessed a significant expansion across the Atlantic. Car-toonists like Jason, Francesca Ghermandi, and Igort are translated by

Fantagraphics; Guy Delisle and Dupuy and Berberian by Drawn and Quarterly; and NBM has translated several works from the *nouvelle bande dessinée* end of the spectrum, including selections from Dargaud's Poisson Pilote line, notably Christophe Blain's *Isaac the Pirate* (2003) and Manu Larcenet's *Ordinary Victories* (2005), as well as Delcourt's *Donjon* books. By making these materials available to an entirely new audience, the translation process has had the effect of broadening the influence of the European small-press comics movement to the United States, where it has intersected with the existing post-underground comics scene to create new avenues for artistic exploration. On this front, Craig Thompson is only one artist influenced by the turn to new forms of visuality, as the experimental aesthetics and non-traditional formats of the European small press have begun appearing in innovative American publishing ventures such as the Jordan Crane–edited *Non* and the Sammy Harkham–edited *Kramer's Ergot.*

Undoubtedly the small-press cartoonist who has had the largest impact in the United States is the one who has also had the greatest success in Europe: Marjane Satrapi. I have already noted the tremendous success of Satrapi's four-volume autobiographical novel *Persepolis* (figure 26), which sold more than 100,000 copies. Subsequently, the books were translated by Pantheon, a division of Random House, in two volumes (2003, 2004), where they met with similar success. What is most interesting about Satrapi's career is how it highlights a range of assumptions about the field of comics as it currently exists. Writing in a special issue of *Beaux Arts Magazine* dedicated to comics, Romain Brethes argues that Satrapi's success owes little to the anti-commercial avant-garde tendencies identified by Menu:

> Doubly remarkable for her status as a woman and as an exiled Iranian in an artistic world that singularly lacks figureheads, Marjane Satrapi became an icon because the topic of *Persepolis* – schematically, her relationship to Iran and to the Islamist dictatorship – took steps towards the treatment of this subject. Comics as a cultural object are not directly valorized here because they disappear behind an individuality that is ideally wed to topicality, as is attested by the business relating to the Islamic hijab or the attribution of the Nobel Peace Prize to Chirine Ebadi, for which they consulted, a little thoughtlessly, the young cartoonist.[6]

Brethes's assumption that Satrapi's success owes more to the intersection of her subject with contemporary French political and cultural debates,

26 Marjane discusses the Iran/Iraq war with her parents. From *Persepolis* volume 2 by Marjane Satrapi.

that she is the right woman in the right place at the right time, is thoroughly dismissive of her accomplishments, which are themselves frequently the subject of debate.

Satrapi's reception in the United States ran at least partially along similar lines. While *Persepolis*, and her follow-up book *Embroideries* (Pantheon, 2005), were widely reviewed in the book pages of American newspapers, critics often had difficulty coming to terms with her work. Several critics followed a line similar to that which Brethes suggests, celebrating the book for the light that it sheds on Iran during the United States's imperial crusade in neighbouring Iraq. *USA Today*'s Christopher Theokas notes that *Persepolis* 'offers readers another link to understanding a country whose politics is gaining attention in the American media,[7] and the *San Francisco Chronicle* suggests that 'a revolution by definition takes itself too seriously. Every revolution needs a chronicler like Satrapi to bring it down to earth.'[8] At the same time they praised the content of the story, critics like Theokas condemned Satrapi's artwork, arguing 'the simplicity of the artwork lacks the texture of *Maus*, thus keeping *Persepolis* from rising above a child's point of view.'[9] While this sentiment was not universally shared – the *New York Times* praised the artwork, noting that it communicates in an unmediated way, 'like a letter from a friend'[10] and the *Observer* suggests that 'her drawings are as packed as Persian miniatures'[11] – the debate about the quality of Satrapi's art highlighted the difficulty that many literary critics have when evaluating a narrative form that is primarily visual.

Terming Satrapi's art 'sloppy,'[12] as the *Orlando Sentinel* did in a review of *Embroideries*, fails to acknowledge that the book was produced for L'Association's sketchbook-inspired Carnets series. Yet this lack of attention to a foreign comics culture is not nearly as grave as the fact that it also fails to take account of how comics exist as a visual language. Thierry Groensteen, whose *Système de la bande dessinée* has done more to advance the subject of the semiotics of comics than any other book, draws a crucial distinction in comics between narrative and illustrative modes of drawing. For Groensteen, it is inappropriate to evaluate comics with the aesthetic criteria that are applied to non-narrative images, because the drawing in comics is fundamentally a narrative process. Where contemporary comics have edged closer to the visual concerns of the contemporary plastic arts, as is the case with many of the artists whom I discussed in chapter three, it is because they have aligned their personal visual aesthetics with appropriately innovative narratives:

The aesthetic evolution of comics for the past quarter of a century has moved in the direction of liberating the image. The traditional narrative drawing, from Töpffer to Franquin, and from Milton Caniff to Mézières, is seen to be concurrent with writing that is freer, more pictorial, and more poetic. From Moebius to Alagbé, from Loustal to Barbier, from Baudoin to Vanoli, comics have shown that they can accommodate the illustrative drawing, and can even completely abandon the linear drawing, to the profit of a play with surfaces and colours, lights and intensities ... The narrative themes *par excellence* (the voyage, the pursuit, the investigation, the disguise, the metamorphosis ...), which traditional comics have used and abused, while not abandoned, have at least been relativized by the conquests of new story spaces: more literary, more immobile, more poetic, more sensual, and more introspective.[13]

While I have not engaged with comics as a semiotic system in this book, preferring to approach it as a field of cultural production rather than as a language of artistic creation, I wish to signal my agreement with Groensteen's observation. Central to the transformation of the field of European comics in the 1990s has been the reconceptualization of the form in terms of its expressivity. This newly emergent understanding has brought comics into a closer alignment with more consecrated forms of artistic practice. In the United States, as many of the reviews of Satrapi's work demonstrate, comics are still largely regarded as a sub-set of literature. In Europe, despite new 'literary' comics lines launched by book publishers like Actes-Sud and Gallimard, comics are increasingly regarded as a branch of the visual arts. This is evidenced by the art shows that are incorporated into comics festivals from Angoulême to Luzern and, increasingly, by the incorporation of comic book art into museums and gallery spaces that had long excluded them. In the end, despite Menu's fears of competition emanating from well-established book publishers, the transformation of European comics in the 1990s revolved around a destabilization of the concept of the literary (the book) and a renewed emphasis on the visual (the image). As comics are still widely held to be an inferior cultural form, it is clear that this revolution is far from completed. But the generation of cartoonists who came of age in the 1990s have laid a foundation for a new conceptualization of the form, removing it from its former domain and creating the possibility that comics will be seen as a primarily visual, rather than literary, form of communication.

Notes

Introduction

1 Antoine de Gaudemar, 'La Nouvelle Bande à part,' *Libération* 25 January 1996: 2–3.
2 'Santé, prospérité, bonheur ... et Astérix,' *Libération* 25 January 2001: 4.
3 Eric Loret, 'Nadia Raviscioni l'affiche bien,' *Libération* 25 January 2001: 11. 'Quand je suis arrivée aux Beaux-Arts, je voulais déjà faire de la BD et les profs voulaient de l'abstrait. Je faisais des sens interdits, et quand j'ai commencé à mettre des couleurs, on m'a dit: "Une couleur, c'est déjà beaucoup."'
4 De Gaudemar 2. 'Après une sérieuse crise d'identité marquée par un académisme certain et un fléchissement du marché, une nouvelle bande dessinée est-elle en train de naître en France? On est tenté de le croire si l'on considère le nombre d'initiatives prises depuis quelques années, au départ en marge des circuits traditionnels. Une nouvelle génération de dessinateurs et d'illustrateurs s'est rassemblée autour de revues à petit tirage – sans être pour autant des fanzines – comme *Lapin, le Cheval sans tête*, et de structures éditoriales aussi légères que rudimentaires, telles l'Association, Cornélius, les Requins marteaux ou encore Amok.'
5 Gilles Ratier, *Avant la Case* (Paris: PLG, 2003).
6 Pierre Bourdieu, *The Field of Cultural Production* (New York: Columbia UP, 1993) 60.

Chapter One: L'Association and the '90s Generation

1 *Le Rab de lapin* 5 October 1996: 4.
2 Pierre Bourdieu, *The Field of Cultural Production* (New York: Columbia UP, 1993) 29–73.

3 Bourdieu, *Field* 38.

4 Luc Boltanski, 'La Constitution du champ de la bande dessinée,' *Actes de la recherche en sciences sociales* January 1975: 37–59.

5 Thierry Groensteen, *Astérix, Barberella & Cie: Trésors du Musée de la Bande Dessinée D'Angoulême* (Paris: Somogy éditions d'art, 2000) 148.

6 Boltanski 39.

7 Boltanski 40.

8 Boltanski 40.

9 Thierry Groensteen, 'Les Années 90: Tentative de récapitulation,' *9e Art* 5 (2000): 13. '*Largo Winch*, le *Joe Bar Team*, le *Petit Spirou*, *Lanfeust de Troy* ou encore *Titeuf* ont attesté, dans cette décennie [1990s], que la industrie de la BD a conserver intacte sa capacité à fabriquer les bestsellers.'

10 'Association a la Pulpe,' *Le Rab de lapin* October 1993: 4. 'Les labeurs communs, comme la confection manuelle des albums à tirage limité, sont rémunérés sous forme d'un repas au restaurant consommable le jour même.'

11 Antoine de Gaudemar, 'La Nouvelle Bande à part,' *Libération* 25 January 1996: 2. 'L'Association revendique d'être 'un espace à part' et imprime sa marque: des ouvrages de fabrication extrêmement soignée, délaissant le papier glacé pour du papier épais, et la couleur pour le noir et blanc, se distinguant par un format plus petit et par des thèmes plus littéraires (notamment l'autobiographie) ou plus expérimentaux (dans le graphisme).'

12 Jean-Philippe Martin, 'L'Irrésistible Ascension de l'édition indépendante,' *9e Art* 5 (2000): 22. 'Resolument alternatif à la bédé en place.'

13 Jean-Christophe Menu, 'L'Art de tous les paradoxes,' *LABO* (Paris: Futuropolis, 1990) 91. 'Concernant ce fichu contexte, on ne va pas revenir sur le fait que les années 80 semblent avoir été catastrophiques pour la bande dessinée.'

14 'Éditorial,' *L'Association Bulletin* January 1991: n.p. 'Notre engagement de longue date dans la défense de l'expression d'une Haute idée de la Bande Dessinée ne pouvait attendre plus longtemps, ce second souffle. L'Association sera la nouvelle structure indépendante au sein de laquelle se poursuivra désormais cette aventure. Une structure dont les principes de base seront: Intégrité et Long Terme.'

15 'Avis important aux libraires et aux particuliers,' *L'Association Bulletin* January 1991: n.p. 'Nous sommes avant tout des auteurs, et nous envisageons l'Edition comme un creation supplémentaire. Nous ne sommes donc pas vraiment des professionnels de la gestion et des relations commerciales.'

16 Bourdieu, *Field* 115.

17 'Compte-Rendu,' *Le Rab de lapin* July 1995: 2. 'L'Association n'a de toute façon pas l'intention de publier trop d'albums, mais uniquement les albums qui continueront à lue paraître indispensables.'

18 *Le Rab de lapin* 1 November 1995: 4. 'L'Association n'est plus la seule sur le terrain de l'édition de band dessinée créative et intelligente ... Il vaut probablement mieux être en saine concurrence avec d'autres éditeurs talentueux défendant les mêmes idées (puisque c'est le cas avec Le Seuil, Cornélius ou Amok) que d'être éternellement seuls à se battre contre des moulins à vent.'

19 Jean-Christophe Menu, *Plates-bandes* (Paris: L'Association, 2005) 37–40.

20 *Le Rab de lapin* 1 December 1994: 1. 'Enfin bref, tout ça commence à fichtrement ressembler à une véritable Maison d'Édition.'

21 'Compte-Rendu' 3.

22 *Le Rab de lapin* 1 November 1995; 14 July 1996; 8 October 1997; 25 November 1998.

23 Menu, 'L'Art' 92. 'Où est le *Spirou* de notre enfance, où sont le *Métal* et *l'Echo* de notre jeunesse, où est la revue de bande dessinée adulte de notre maturité qui n'a jamais existé?'

24 Quoted in Jean-Christophe Menu, 'Lapin n'est toujours pas une revue,' *9e Art* 4 (1999): 44. 'Une poignée de fonctionnaires inconnus auraient ainsi donc le pouvoir souverain de décider ce qui est un moyen d'expression et ce qui ne l'est pas? Et ces adjutants-là auraient décidé en septembre 1978 que la bande dessiné n'est pas un moyen d'expression.'

25 Menu, 'Lapin' 44–5.

26 *Le Rab de lapin* 14 July 1996: 4. 'Après le scandale *Pilote,* le scandale *Lapin?*'

27 *Le Rab de lapin* 1 January 1995: 3.

28 *L'Association catalogue* (Paris: L'Association, 2004) 13. 'Trouve aujourd'hui sa place définitive.'

29 Bourdieu, *Field* 133.

30 Jean-Christophe Menu, 'Foreword,' *Comix 2000* (Paris: L'Association, 1999) ii.

31 Vincent Bernière, 'Comix 2000: Un livre intelligent,' *9e Art* 5 (2000): 129–31. 'Certaines pages ne sont que figuratives – je veux dire infra-narratives – comme le travail du peintre Ricardo Mosner ou celui de la Carlos Nine.'

32 Bourdieu, *Field* 107.

Chapter Two: The Shifting Terrain of the Comic 'Book'

1 David Hume, 'Of the Standard of Taste,' *Of the Standard of Taste and Other Essays,* ed. J.W. Lenz (New York: Bobbs-Merrill, 1965) 3–24.

2 Noël Carroll, *Beyond Aesthetics: Philosophical Essays.* Cambridge: Cambridge UP, 2001) 38–41.

3 Donna Stein, 'When a Book Is More Than a Book,' *Artists' Books in the Modern Era 1870–2000: The Reva and David Logan Collection of Illustrated Books,* ed. Robert Flynn Johnson (San Francisco: Fine Arts Museums of San Francisco, 2001) 27.

4 Stein, 'When a Book' 40.

5 Lucy R. Lippard, 'The Artist's Book Goes Public,' *Artist's Books: A Critical Anthology and Sourcebook,* ed. Joan Lyons (Rochester, NY: Visual Studies Workshop P, 1985) 45.

6 Dick Higgins, 'A Preface,' *Artist's Books,* ed. Lyons, 11.

7 Richard Kostelanetz, 'Book Art,' *Artist's Books,* ed. Lyons, 28–9.

8 Steven Bury, *Artists' Books: The Book as a Work of Art, 1963–1995* (Aldershot, UK: Scolar P, 1995) 1.

9 Clive Phillpot, 'Books by Artists and Books as Art,' *Artist/Author: Contemporary Artists' Books,* ed. Cornelia Lauf and Clive Phillpot (New York: Distributed Art Publishers, 1998) 47.

10 Robert C. Morgan, 'Systemic Books by Artists,' *Artist's Books,* ed. Lyons, 211.

11 Shelley Rice, 'Words and Images: Artists' Books as Visual Literature,' *Artist's Books,* ed. Lyons, 60.

12 *Le Rab de lapin* 1 April 1996: 2. 'Plus beau s'adaptant au format un peu carré des originaux, plutôt qu'avec des blancs disproportionnés au dessus de chaque page.'

13 Pascal Lefèvre, 'The Importance of Being "Published": A Comparative Study of Different Comics Formats,' *Comics & Culture: Analytical and Theoretical Approaches to Comics,* ed. Ann Magnussen and Hans-Christian Christiansen (Copenhagen: Museum Tusculanum P, 2000) 92–5.

14 Claude Moliterni, Philippe Merlot, and Michel Denni, *Les Aventures de la BD* (Paris: Gallimard, 1996) 124.

15 *Le Rab de lapin* 15 May 1993: 3.

16 Eric Loret, 'Pince-moi, Genève,' *Libération,* 25 January 2001: 10. 'Mais, comme ils avaient tous préparé des trucs à l'avance, le résultat était trop bon, alors on a fait une revue de luxe.'

17 Betsy Davids and Jim Petrillo, 'The Artist as Book Printer: Four Short Courses,' *Artist's Books,* ed. Lyons, 157.

18 Alexis de Tocqueville, *Democracy in America* (New York: Vintage, 1990).

19 Gary Kornblith, 'Becoming Joseph T. Buckingham: The Struggle for Artisanal Independence in Early Nineteenth-Century Boston,' *American Artisans: Crafting Social Identity 1750–1850,* ed. Howard B. Rock, Paul A. Gilje, and Robert Asher (Baltimore: Johns Hopkins UP, 1995).

Chapter Three: The Postmodern Modernism of the Comic Book Avant-Garde

1 Lionel Tran, 'L'Électron belge,' *Jade* 18 (1999) (http://www.pastis.org/jade/cgi-bin/reframe.pl?http://www.pastis.org/jade/avril/freon1.htm).

2 Eric Loret, 'Collectif Self Service,' *Libération*, 7 September 2001: 29. 'Réponse ironique, poétique et bédéistique au marché et à la globalisation.'

3 Pierre Bourdieu, *The Rules of Art: Genesis and Structures of the Literary Field*, trans. Susan Emanuel (Stanford, CA: Stanford UP, 1995) 157.

4 Bourdieu, *Rules* 225.

5 Sally Everett, 'Introduction,' *Art Theory and Criticism: An Anthology of Formalist, Avant-Garde, Contextualist and Post-Modernist Thought*, ed. Sally Everett (Jefferson, NC: McFarland, 1991) x.

6 Richard Kostelanetz, *Dictionary of the Avant-Gardes* (Chicago: A Cappella Books, 1993) xiv.

7 Donald Kuspit, *The Cult of the Avant-Garde Artist* (Cambridge: Cambridge UP, 1993) 2.

8 Bourdieu, *Rules* 120.

9 Diana Crane, *The Transformation of the Avant-Garde: The New York Art World, 1940–1985* (Chicago: U of Chicago P, 1987) 1.

10 John Ashberry, 'The Invisible Avant-Garde,' *Art Theory and Criticism*, ed. Everett, 135.

11 Bridget Fowler, *Pierre Bourdieu and Cultural Theory: Critical Investigations* (New York: Sage, 1997) 73.

12 Thomas Crow, 'Modernism and Mass Culture in the Visual Arts,' *Modernism and Modernity*, ed. Benjamin H.D. Buchloh et al. (Halifax: The Press of the Nova Scotia College of Art and Design, 2004) 253.

13 Clement Greenberg, 'Avant-Garde and Kitsch,' *Art Theory and Criticism*, ed. Everett, 31.

14 Crane, *Transformation* 109.

15 Greenberg, 'Avant-Garde' 31.

16 Greenberg, 'Avant-Garde' 32.

17 Fowler, *Pierre Bourdieu* 73–4.

18 Clement Greenberg, 'Modernist Painting,' *Art Theory and Criticism*, ed. Everett, 112.

19 See, for example, Scott McCloud, *Understanding Comics: The Invisible Art* (Northhampton, MA: Kitchen Sink P, 1993).

20 François Ayroles, 'Hybridation entre *Placid et Muzo font du judo*, de Nicolaou, et les *Premiers dialogues*, de Platon (*Premier Alcibiade* 107 d),' *OuPus* 1 (Paris: L'Association, 1997): 4.

21 Pascal Ory, 'Relecture de *Tintin en Amérique*,' *Lire* December 2002: 27. 'Fait

penser à un Miró cavernicole qui pourrait n'être que décoratif s'il n'en transpirait pas une sorte d'angoisse moderne, bien ajustée.'

22 Jochen Gerner, '*TNT en Amérique:* Jochen Gerner par lui-même' (2002) (http://www.bulbe.com/fr/sous-titres/jochengerner.php). 'Cette nuit est une nuit américaine : un filtre sur une image tournée le jour pour donner l'illusion de la nuit. Car avec le deuxième degré de lecture intervient le souvenir d'une lecture : Tintin en Amérique de Hergé. À partir de ce livre, utilisé comme support matériel, j'ai choisi des mots qui me semblaient significatifs et des zones de couleurs dans lesquelles découper de nouvelles formes illustrant l'enchaînement des mots précédemment choisis. Puis, j'ai recouvert de noir le reste de la planche de bande dessinée.

   Avec ce type d'intervention graphique, je parle de l'Amérique en utilisant une bande dessinée de Hergé. Mais je parle également du travail de Hergé par le biais d'un travail thématique sur l'Amérique. Car ces deux univers, la ligne claire de Hergé et la société américaine, peuvent être interprétés de façon similaire : deux mondes riches, beaux et lisses en apparence, troubles et violents en profondeur.'

23 Andreas Huyssen, 'Mass Culture as Woman: Modernism's Other,' *Art Theory and Criticism*, ed. Everett, 233.

24 Huyssen, 'Mass Culture' 233.

25 Bourdieu, *Rules* 240.

26 'Le Frémok: Un dieu vivant' (n.d.) (http://www.fremok.org/fremok/fremok-presse.html). 'Face à la globalisation, Amok et Fréon font bloc et retrouvent leur entité primordiale, le Frémok (FRMK).

   Dans les mers du sud et la mer des nords, de sauvages indigènes s'opposent aux chiens de race du marché. Contre la médiocrisation galopante, ils font mieux que résister : ils proposent. Ils élèvent des totems, s'inscrivent contre les lois et la bonne société. Ils inventent leurs propres langues et font des livres.'

27 'Le Frémok: Un dieu vivant.' 'Assurer l'éternelle et toujours fragile victoire du sens sur l'argent et les forces incultes du KOMERF.'

28 Tran, 'L'Électron belge.' 'C'est qu'au début des années 80 il y avait derrière le travail des gros éditeurs vraiment une ambition quelque part artistique. Je pense surtout à *(À Suivre)*, cette idée de roman dessinée. Il y avait une pensée derrière tout ça et j'ai l'impression que c'est complètement disparu. *Métal*, Les humanos c'était des gros éditeurs, c'était des sociétés commerciales, pas comme ce qui se passe actuellement dans le milieu indépendant, c'est des associations, c'est vraiment quelque chose de très curieux en fait.'

29 Mona Chollet, 'En Orbite du monde' (1998) (http://www.peripheries.net/

g-amok.htm). 'Yvan et moi, on a toujours été décentrés, dans tout ce qu'on a fait ... Par nos origines, déjà, et aussi parce que ni l'un, ni l'autre, nous ne sommes issus d'un milieu lettré. Ce qu'on représente, y compris dans notre travail, c'est l'impureté. On n'est pas des puristes, on ne travaille pas pour un public de puristes – ce que sont les fans de bande dessinée: des "purs et durs." Nous, on a toujours tout mélangé. On a toujours été en décalage.'

30 Tran, 'L'Électron belge.' 'J'aime les possibilités qu'on y voit, cela m'intéresse en tant que langage. Jusqu'ici, la bande dessinée a beaucoup fonctionné en circuit fermé, comme si elle voulait définir un territoire très restreint, pour se donner une sorte d'identité, en refusant de trop s'aventurer au dehors.'

31 'Avant-Propos,' *Frigorevue* 3 (Geneva: Atoz Éditions, 1994) 3. 'Frigo ce serait la quête d'auteur sur les moyens qu'ils utilisent. Tu fais allusion aux moyens matériels. Oui, quels papiers, quels moyens de production, quels outils de travail... tout ça c'est expérimental, à chaque fois que tu abordes un nouveau travail, tu mets en place une nouvelle technique, que ce soit l'eau forte, le collage, ou n'importe quel autre procédé. Oui mais cette approache signifie quelque chose, l'expérimental n'est pas une fin en soi. Non bien sur. Tu expérimentes parce que tu cherches des overtures.'

32 'Le manifeste des nomades,' *Frigobox* 5, December 1995: 6–7. 'Nous sommes des nomads en quête de territories impossibles.'

33 Eric Loret, 'Parlez-moi d'Amok,' *Libération,* 25 January 2001: 11. 'Quand on parle du genre d'ouvrage que nous publions, c'est toujours pour dire que c'est mieux que de la BD ou moins bien. Dire, par exemple, de *Berlin 1931,* par Raúl et Cava, que chaque vignette est comme une peinture, c'est méconnaître à la fois la peinture et la BD.'

34 Frédéric Paques, 'Fréon, éditeur de bandes dessinées d'art et d'essais' (2002) (http://www.art-memoires.com/lettre/lm1820/20ulgfreon.htm).

35 Tran, 'L'Électron belge.' 'Je pense que la réflexion sur le récit chez nous elle est prépondérante. La critique qui revient pas mal par rapport aux indépendants c'est "oui mais il n'y a pas d'histoire, c'est le dessin." C'est inconcevable, parce que la première réflexion elle est sur le récit et pour nous la Bande dessinée c'est vraiment un langage, un vocabulaire qui est hyper, hyper riche, qui nous intéresse à fond et je pense qu'il faut ramener des choses d'ailleurs dans le champ de la bande dessinée.'

36 Jan Baetens, 'Gloria Lopez: Une réflexion sur le langage de la bande dessinée,' *Image and Narrative* 3 (2001). (http://www.imageandnarrative.be/illustrations/janbaetens.htm). 'Dans le scalpel du médecin-narrateur on reconnaîtra ainsi sans problème l'un des instruments du dessinateur Thierry Van Hasselt. Et la quête des policiers ressemble à s'y méprendre à celle des lecteurs du livre, confrontés eux aussi à plus de questions que de réponses.'

37 Thierry Van Hasselt, 'Historique du projet *Brutalis*' (2003) (http://www.
fremok.org/entretiens/projetbrutalis.html).
'Le livre se lit seul. Il se suffit à lui même.
Le livre se lit comme une extension du spectacle.
Après avoir vu le spectacle, lire le livre prolonge l'intimité avec le corps.
Le spectacle se suffit à lui même.
Le spectacle se voit comme une extension du livre.
Assister au spectacle prolonge l'intimité avec la matière.'

38 Vincent Bernière, 'Entretien avec Vincent Fortemps' (2003) (http://
www.fremok.org/entretiens/vfortemps.html).

39 Bernière, 'Entretien.'

40 For an example of this type of argument, see R.C. Harvey, *The Art of the
Funnies: An Aesthetic History* (Jackson: UP of Mississippi, 1994).

41 Pierre Polomé, 'Entretien avec Dominique Goblet' (2001) (http://
www.fremok.org/entretiens/souvenirgoblet.html). 'Oui, une fois de plus
dans mon approche personnelle, le récit a tenté de se distancier d'un
rapport autobiographique, ce qui l'en a en fait rapproché.'

42 Huyssen, 'Mass Culture' 233.

43 'Qu'est-ce qui vous manque?' *Amok Catalogue, 1996–1997* (Paris: Amok,
1996) 2.

44 Harold Rosenberg, 'The American Action Painters,' *Art Theory and Criticism*,
ed. Everett, 59.

45 Richard Murphy, *Theorizing the Avant-Garde: Modernism, Expressionism, and the
Problem of Postmodernity* (Cambridge: Cambridge UP, 1988) 30.

46 Loret, 'Parlez-moi d'Amok.' 'Il s'agissait en fait pour moi de montrer comment des gens marginalisés, au lieu de s'entraider, finalement s'oppriment
les uns les autres.'

47 Tran, 'L'Électron belge.' 'Je n'ai pas envie de réduire ce que nous faisons à
des questions socioculturelles. Récemment, quelqu'un nous disait à ce sujet:
Ah, c'est bien ce que vous faites ... Non! Cela n'a pas à être bien. Ce côté
"socialiste" m'énerve.'

48 Loret, 'Parlez-moi d'Amok.' 'Retranscrire les intterogations plutôt que
délivrer un message.'

49 'Entretien avec Olivier Bramanti' (2004) (http://www.fremok.org/
entretiens/obramanti01.html). 'Je voulais savoir, si j'avais été serbe, si
j'aurais pu être manipulé par tous ces poèmes et toute la littérature qu'ont
suscités cette histoire.'

50 Ironically, Del Barrio's work for Amok under the pen name Silvestre –
Rélations (1999) and *Simple* (2000) – are highly experimental in a mode akin
to the OuBaPo exercises in panel transitions and page design.

51 Eric Loret, 'Hortus sanitatis,' *Libération*, 6 July 2001: 31.
52 'Éditorial,' *Frigobox* 2 (1995): 3. 'De ce mythe du nouveau pout le nouveau, nous devons nous en déprendre. Comme pôle d'une modernité toujours à redéfinir choisissons le pôle des formes et de leur inlassable pouvoir de combinaisons, vive l'hyperconstruction! Donc, militons non pas pour une noveauté dans l'allure mais pour une qualité dans l'agencement. La bande dessinée, les bandes dessinées devrait-on écrire, a (ont) certainement un coin, fût-il modeste, à enforcer dans une histoire des raports entre l'art et les villes, ou l'inverse.'
53 Olivier Deprez, 'Entretien avec Pedro Nora' (2003) (http://www.fremok. org/entretiens/pedronora.html). 'Je pense qu'il faut s'imbiber d'un maximum de disciplines. Je crois que c'est une approche postmoderne de la bande dessinée.'
54 Deprez, 'Entretien.' 'Je n'ai pas de problème avec les dessinateurs de bande dessinée qui exposent dans les galeries et les peintres qui utilisent la bande dessinée et j'apprécie de plus le bénéfice de telles démarches. Regardez Raymond Pettibon, Mark Beyer ou David Schringley.'
55 Deprez, 'Entretien.' 'Je ne suis pas peintre.'
56 Walter Benjamin, quoted in Markus Huber, *Promenade à Saturnia*, trans. Waltraud Spohr (Paris: Amok, 2000): n.p. 'Langue incomparable de la tête de mort: elle unit l'absence totale d'expression (noir des orbites) à l'expression la plus sauvage (grimace de la denture).'
57 Aarnoud Rommens, 'Comics & Culture: A Step towards Comic "Absolution"?' *Image and Narrative* 3 (2001) (http://www.imageandnarrative.be/ illustrations/aarnoudrommens.htm).
58 Martin tom Dieck, 'Dada,' *Cheval sans tête* 2.4 (Paris: Amok, 1997): 15.
59 Karel Vanhaesebrouck, 'Entretien avec Martin tom Dieck' (2002) (http:// www.fremok.org/entretiens/tomdiecknouvelles.htm). 'Cette structure répétitive me permet de présenter un problème complexe dans une forme accessible. Grâce aux dessins, le lecteur n'a plus besoin d'explications supplémentaires, c'est ça qui est important pour moi. J'espère que les gens qui achèteront les deux livres sur Deleuze les achèteront parce qu'ils aiment la BD et non pas parce qu'ils connaissent Deleuze.'
60 Vanhaesebrouck, 'Entretien.' 'La forme classique de la BD rend la philosophie accessible.'
61 'Bande dessinée: Vient de paraître,' *Libération*, 26 September 2002: 12. 'Une exégèse précise de l'oeuvre du philosophe.'
62 Jan Baetens, 'Autarcic Comix,' *Frigobox* 5 (1995): 31–7.
63 Peter Bürger, *Theory of the Avant-Garde*. (Minneapolis: U of Minnesota P, 1994) 83.

64 Bourdieu, *Rules* 267.
65 Loret, 'Parlez-moi d'Amok' 11. 'Quand on a fait la revue *Cheval sans tête*, au début d'Amok, on l'a ouverte à des gens qui n'avaient jamais fait de BD – "Ben, ils n'en ont toujours pas fait," c'est ce que certains doivent penser.'

Chapter Four: From Global to Local and Back Again

1 Julien Bastide, 'Manga: Le deuxième souffle,' *9e Art* 10 (2004): 69.
2 Ulf Hannerz, *Transnational Connections: Culture, People, Places* (London: Routledge, 1996) 132.
3 Howard S. Becker, *Art Worlds* (Berkeley: U of California P, 1982) 364.
4 'Asuntos Internos,' *Nosotros somos los muertos* 5 (1998): 106. 'Unas premisas son claras: comic de autor, de calidad y que es difícil que tenga cabida en otras publicaciones. Pero la relacíon con el mercado no está tan definida. Hay términos que rondan por ahí y que ya no sabemos exactemente lo que significan y que a veces enturbian: independiente, alternativo, y cosas parecidas.'
5 Hannerz, *Transnational* 128.
6 'Destination Comicon' (2005) (http://bdangouleme.fr/actualites/index.ideal?action=consulter&id=835). 'Il me semble qu'Angoulême a un ancrage beaucoup plus tourné vers la création artistique et la culture. À la ComicCon de San Diego, on sent très nettement l'aspect business de tout cela, parfaitement assumé par tous les participants, y compris le grand public. Le marketing, après tout, fait complètement partie de la culture de base de tous les Américains.'
7 Internationales Comix Festival – Luzern (n.d.) (http://www.fumetto.ch/main_en.htm).
8 Internationales Comix Festival.
9 Internationales Comix Festival.
10 Benedict Anderson, *Imagined Communities: Reflections on the Origin and Spread of Nationalism* (London: Verso, 1983) 16.
11 Rolf Classon, 'Cartoons from the Nordic Countries in the 90s,' *Gare du nord* (NordiComics, 1997) 2.
12 Hannerz, *Transnational* 102.

Chapter Five: Autobiography as Authenticity

1 Fabrice Neaud, 'Réponses à huit questions sur l'autobiographie,' *9e Art* 1 (1996): 80.

2 Philippe Dupuy, 'Lundi 23 Août 1993,' *Journal d'un album*, Philippe Dupuy and Charles Berberian (Paris: L'Association, 1994) n.p.

3 Fabrice Neaud, *Journal (III)* (Angoulême: Ego Comme X, 1999) 241. 'Le "Journal d'Anne Frank" moi, ça me fait chier. Je trouve ça mal écrit.'

4 Lewis Trondheim, 2001. 'Journal du journal du journal,' *Le Rab de lapin* 26 (2001): 33. '"XIII" moi, ça me fait chier. Je trouve ça mal écrit.'

5 Philippe Lejeune, *On Autobiography*, trans. Katherine Leary (Minneapolis: U of Minnesota P, 1989) 4.

6 William C. Spengemann, *The Forms of Autobiography: Episodes in the History of a Literary Genre* (New Haven, CT: Yale UP, 1980) 207.

7 Paul de Man, 'Autobiography as De-Facement,' *Modern Language Notes* 94 (1979): 919.

8 Linda Anderson, *Autobiography* (London: Routledge, 2001) 6.

9 Timothy Dow Adams, *Telling Lies in Modern American Autobiography* (Chapel Hill, NC: U of North Carolina P, 1990) 9.

10 Lejeune, *On Autobiography* 22.

11 Monique Yaari, 'Who/What Is the Subject? Representations of Self in Late Twentieth-Century French Art,' *Word and Image* 16.4 (2000): 363.

12 Thierry Groensteen, 'Les Petites Cases du moi: L'autobiographie en bande dessinée,' *9e Art* 1 (1996): 65.

13 Janet Staiger, 'Authorship Approaches,' *Authorship and Film*, ed. D.A. Gerstner and Janet Staiger (New York: Routledge, 2003) 27.

14 Michel Foucault, 'What Is an Author?' *The Foucault Reader*, trans. Josué V. Harari, ed. Paul Rabinow (New York: Pantheon, 1984) 107.

15 Nancy Hartsock, 'Foucault on Power: A Theory for Women?' *Feminism/Postmodernism*, ed. Linda J. Nicholson (New York: Routledge, 1990) 163–4.

16 Julia Swindells, *Victorian Writing and Working Women* (Cambridge: Polity P, 1985) 7.

17 'Élaboration permanente,' *L'Association Catalogue* (Paris: L'Association, 2004).

18 'Instantané,' *Libération*, 12 February 2003, 7. 'Star persane de la bande dessinée.'

19 'La lutte des cases,' *Libération*, 23 January 2003, 11.

20 Groensteen, 'Petites Cases' 66.

21 Thierry Groensteen, 'Petit Manuel d'introspection graphique,' *Ego Comme X* 1 (1994): 2. 'Naguère encore, la bande dessinée déroulait sur papier glacé les aventures en couleurs de héros sans reproche. Elle négligeait le réel, se tournant de préférence vers n'importe quel ailleurs, pourvu qu'il fût synonyme d'évasion, promesse de divertissement. Mais c'est fini tout ça! La bande dessinée a changé.'

22 Thierry Leprévost, 'Édito,' *Ego Comme X* 1 (1994): 2. 'Une bande dessinée qui réfléchit, s'interroge sur ses moyens, réalisée par des auteurs conscients de ne pouvoir s'exprimer autrement avec autant de justesse, devient un langage propre.'

23 Groensteen, 'Petites Cases' 66.

24 'Interview David B.: *L'Ascension du Haut Mal*' (2000) (http://www. bdparadisio.com/intervw/davidb/intdavid.htm). 'Souvent, les gens, dans la bd autobiographique, racontent leur vie. Point. Enfin, racontent des faits concrets ... Moi, j'essaie de raconter autre chose, je raconte ce qui est arrivé à ma famille, je raconte aussi des souvenirs sur mes grands-parents, des choses que j'ai entendu racontées, une espèce de mythologie familiale, des souvenirs sur des grands-parents, des arrières grands-parents. Par exemple, la guerre de 14 dans le cas de mon grand-père, ou la colonisation de l'Indochine dans le cas de mon arrière grand-père ... des choses comme ca ... Et puis, j'essaie de raconter, parallèlement à ça, la construction de mon imaginaire et l'influence que tout ce que j'ai vécu a pu avoir sur cet imaginaire.'

25 'David B.,' *Tao* 5 (n.d.): 12. 'Bien sûr, ce n'est pas un travail que j'ai entrepris tout seul, égoïstement. C'est un travail, que je fais aussi pout ma soeur, pour mes parents et pour mon frère.'

26 David B., *L'Ascension du Haut Mal*, vol. 2 (Paris: L'Association, 1997) 7.

27 David B., *L'Ascension du Haut Mal*, vol. 1 (Paris: L'Association, 1996) 19.

28 'David B.,' 67.

29 David B., *L'Ascension du Haut Mal*, vol. 6 (Paris: L'Association, 2003) 52.

30 'David B.,' 67. 'Menu dit très souvent: On ne fait pas le même que ces gens là. Au contraire. Je pense qu'on fait exactement le même métier. Mais on ne le fait pas de la même manière.'

31 'Interview David B.' '*L'Ascension du Haut Mal* donne des clés au lecteur qui ne sont pas dans les autres livres.'

32 'David B.,' 67. 'Pour moi l'autobiographie n'est pas une fin en soi. J'ai envie maintenant de raconter des choses importantes et qui, à mon avis, peuvent intéresser des lecteurs. Parce que ce qui nous est arrivé n'arrive pas tous les jours et parce que c'est en même temps un témoignage sur une époque, des gens etc. En plus c'est une autobiographie un peu élargie puisque je parle de mes grands parents, de mes arrières grand parents, de gens que je nai pas connu. Je ne parle pas uniquement de moi, j'essaie de parler autour du cercle familial. C'est vrai que j'ai l'intention ensuite de faire des fictions.'

33 David B., '*L'Ascension*,' vol. 6, 14.

34 David B., '*L'Ascension*,' vol. 6, 63.

35 Charles Berberian, 'Une Lettre de Charles Berberian,' *9e Art* 1 (1996): 83. 'Alors voila, j'ai un sujet à traiter. Si je peux le développer en utilisant un personnage autre que moi, je le fais. Je transpose, par exemple, dans Monsieur Jean. Je peux dire "nous," parce que dans ce cas-là, Dupuy et moi utilisons ensemble Monsieur Jean comme paravent.

Mais dans le cas du *Journal d'un album,* le sujet (entre autres) était mon rapport à la bande dessinée. Là, il faillait que j'aille en première ligne. Je me suis alors traité comme un personnage. Je me suis caricaturé, et à partir de là, aucun problème pour m'envoyer balader dans quelques cases. En fait, j'ai cerné un personnage qui incarne une certaine idée de moi.'

36 Philippe Dupuy and Charles Berberian, *Journal d'un album* (Paris: L'Association, 1994) front cover. 'Nous sommes dessinateurs, nous faisons des bandes dessinées.'

37 Philippe Dupuy, 'L'Année dernière,' *Journal d'un album,* by Philippe Dupuy and Charles Berberian (Paris: L'Association, 1994) n.p. 'Je comprends parfaitement votre engouement pour l'Association, nous le partageons! Mais les Humanos ont aussi la vocation de sortir des livres atypiques (à partir du moment où nous les jugeons intéressants). Pensez également à ce que nous pouvons apporter: diffusion, impact groupé avec l'album de M. Jean ... et pour finir, il faut être logiques: on ne peut prétendre avoir une politique d'auteur et ne pas vouloir sortir ce journal!'

38 Anderson, *Autobiography* 34.

39 Fabrice Neaud, *Journal (4)* (Angoulême: Ego Comme X, 2002) 176. 'La proportion de pages attribuées aux hommes dans ce journal est non-repreésentative en diable de la présence de ces derniers dans ma petite vie ... Mais elle l'est totalement de la place qu'ils occupent pour moi. Si j'étais plus juste, plus objectif, plus arithmétique, je devrais plutôt dessiner du vide. Tâcher de représenter leur absence.'

40 'L'Interview! Fabrice Neaud 1/2' (2001) (http://www.bdselection.com/php/?rub=page_dos&id_dossier=9). 'Il n'y a pas plus difficile, au contraire, que de supprimer la distance, surtout avec un dessin comme le mien. Il faudrait une écriture minimale pour parvenir à tenir un journal qui prétendrait à l'abolition de la distance, ce qui resterait une illusion. Il y a toujours transposition.'

41 'L'Interview! Fabrice Neaud 2/2' (2002) (http://www.bdselection.com/php/?rub=page_dos&id_dossier=73).

42 John L. Ward, *American Realist Painting, 1945–1980* (Ann Arbor, MI: UMI Research P, 1989) 2.

43 'L'Interview! Fabrice Neaud 1/2.'

44 Lejeune, *On Autobiography* 110.

45 Neaud, *Journal (III)* 185. 'La plus grande souffrance n'excuse pas La médiocrité littéraire, si on ne lui adjoint pas du talent ... Alors, l'autobiographie en B.D.'

46 'L'Interview! Fabrice Neaud 2/2.'

47 'David B.,' 71. 'Par exemple, [François] Boucq dans un débat auquel je participais avait dit: "Ouais, L'Asso, c'est des gens qui racontent comment on se lave les dents."'

48 'Persepolis tome 2,' *Libération* 16 November 2001, 12. 'ironie et tendresse, loin du didactisme et de l'héroïsme sclérosés qui caractérisent la BD historique.'

Chapter Six: From the Small Press to *La Nouvelle Bande Dessinée*

1 'Interview David B.: *L'Ascension du Haut Mal*' (2000) (http://www.bdparadisio.com/intervw/davidb/intdavid.htm).

2 Thierry Groensteen, 'Genres et séries,' *9e Art* 4 (1999): 78.

3 Groensteen, 'Genres' 81.

4 Groensteen, 'Genres' 84.

5 'Success Séries,' *Libération* 22 January 1998: 12.

6 'Marché de la BD en 1994: Légère reprise,' *Libération* 26 January 1995: xiv.

7 Fabrice Tassel, 'Spécial bande dessinée,' *Libération* 22 January 1998: 16.

8 'Planches à billets,' *Libération* 27 January 2000: 5.

9 'La BD ne bulle pas,' *Libération* 3 January 2002: 5.

10 'La lutte des cases,' *Libération* 23 January 2003: 11. 'Chaque Angoulême apporte son lot de statistiques industrielles. Mais l'ennui, dans les sondages de ce genre, c'est qu'on ne sait pas trop de quoi on parle quand on soupèse "la BD." Est-ce qu'un film de Cédric Kahn, c'est la même chose qu'un navet hollywoodien lambda? Est-ce que, dans les statistiques sur les ventes de roman, on met aussi la Bibliothèque rose? Et le fait que la Star Ac' vende plus de disques que Brigitte Fontaine, est-ce que ça doit nécessairement inspirer des commentaires éberlués ? On apprend donc que les meilleures ventes de BD en 2002 ressemblent à celles des dix dernières années, avec au palmarès Titeuf, XIII, Largo Winch, Titeuf, Titeuf, Titeuf, Titeuf, Titeuf et Titeuf (vu qu'il y a plusieurs tomes).'

11 'La lutte des cases.' 'C'est Marjane Satrapi qui fait péter le plafond avec 100 000 exemplaires de ses trois premiers Persépolis, suivie de près par Christophe Blain.'

12 Bruno Canard, 'Jean Van Hamme: Autopise d'un succès,' *9e Art* 5 (2000): 54.

13 Canard, 'Jean Van Hamme' 54.

14 Lewis Trondheim, 'Journal du journal du journal,' *Lapin* January 2001: 33–5.
15 Pierre Bourdieu, *The Field of Cultural Production* (New York: Columbia UP, 1993) 108.
16 Canard, 'Jean Van Hamme' 58.
17 Groensteen, 'Genres' 84. 'Les éditeurs alternatifs apparus dans les années 1990s (L'Association, Cornélius, Amok, Fréon, Ego Comme X ...), peu sensibles aux "charmes de la série," ont réinventé la bande dessinée d'auteur en renouant avec les éphémères conquêtes des années 1970 ... À vingt ans de distance, ce n'est pourtant pas même pièce qui est rejouée. À travers la conception même du support (caractérisé par une plus grande diversité de formats), la volonté affichée d'organiser la jeune création au plan international, et certain tendances de la création même (illustrative, formaliste, littéraire, sociale ou autobiographique), c'est une nouvelle approche du médium qui, progressivement, s'affirme.'
18 Keith Negus, *Music Genres and Corporate Cultures* (London: Routledge, 1999) 25.
19 Steve Neale, *Genre* (London: British Film Institute, 1980) 19.
20 Bourdieu, *Field.*
21 David Hesmondhalgh, *Cultural Industries* (New York: Sage, 2002) 71.
22 David Hesmondhalgh, 'Indie: The Institutional Politics and Aesthetics of a Popular Music Genre,' *Cultural Studies* 13.1 (1999): 35.
23 Negus, *Music Genres* 91.
24 Charlie Gillet, *The Sound of the City: The Rise of Rock and Roll* (New York: Outerbridge and Dienstfrey, 1970) 79–131.
25 Hesmondhalgh, 'Indie' 36.
26 Stephen Lee, 'Re-examining the Concept of the "Independent" Record Company: The Case of Wax Trax! Records,' *Popular Music* 14.1 (1995): 26.
27 Steve Chapple and Reebee Garofalo, *Rock 'n' Roll Is Here to Pay: The History and Politics of the Music Industry* (Chicago: Nelson-Hall, 1977) 306.
28 Negus, *Music Genres* 32.
29 Lee, 'Re-examining' 13.
30 Lee, 'Re-examining' 26.
31 Negus, *Music Genres* 51.
32 Bourdieu, *Field* 127.
33 Herman Gray, *Producing Jazz: The Experience of an Independent Record Company* (Philadelphia: Temple UP, 1988) 120.
34 Keith Negus, *Producing Pop: Culture and Conflict in the Popular Music Industry* (London: Edward Arnold, 1992).
35 'Poisson Pilote' (n.d.) (http://www.imaginet.fr/universbd/dossiers/poissonpilote/). 'Il y a un indiscutable air de famille entre eux, nous avons

pensé les réunir sous un même pavillon pour mieux les défendre commercialement.'

36 'Interview David B.' 'Les grands éditeurs qui nous ont sollicités, nous ont demandé de venir faire chez eux la même chose que ce qu'on faisait à L'Association. Enfin, la même chose, avec les concessions nécessaires. On ne faisait pas forcément que du noir et blanc, on faisait des albums 46 pages en couleurs ou 54 pages en couleurs. Il y avait ces passages obligés. Mais en dehors de ça, pour le contenu, moi j'ai toujours été absolument libre de faire ce que je voulais chez Dargaud, chez Dupuis.'

37 'Interview de Guy Vidal, Directeur éditorial chez Dargaud' (2002) (http://www.bdparadisio.com/intervw/vidal/intvidal.htm). 'Mais il y a toujours une révolte contre les choses établies. Je citais Goscinny et Charlier ... eux aussi se sont un peu révoltés dans les années 60 par rapport à ce qu'était la presse de bande dessinée. De même, dans les années 70–75, Mandryka, Brétécher, Gotlib ... se sont, eux, révoltés contre Goscinny qui représentait l'ancienne école ... De même, ces jeunes qui viennent de l'Association se sont révoltés contre les schémas dominants dans les années 80–90 et ont créé ce qu'ils ont créé et ont élargi, à mes yeux, le champs de la bande dessinée. La bande dessinée s'est considérablement enrichie par rapport à mes début dans les années 60. Quand j'étais gamin, la bande dessinée c'était pour les enfants ... Maintenant, ça l'est peut-être toujours et heureusement – je pense à Boule et Bill, à Titeuf ... – mais le champs d'investigation et d'exploration de la bande dessinée s'est considérablement enrichi et je trouve cela formidable.'

38 'Interview de Guy Vidal.' 'Ces auteurs ont intelligemment réalisé que Dargaud n'était pas l'Association et que Dargaud était une relativement grosse machine dans l'univers éditorial. Nous ne pouvons pas avoir le même fonctionnement qu'une structure telle que l'Association qui est une petite structure et qui peut se permettre des choses que Dargaud ne peut pas se permettre.'

39 Jean-Pierre Mercier, 'Le Vaste Monde du Joann Sfar,' *9e Art* 6 (2001): 114.

40 Mercier, 'Le Vaste Monde' 115

41 Benoît Mouchart, 'Joann Sfar Debordement Graphique,' *Beaux Arts Magazine Hors Série: Qu'est-ce que la BD aujourd'hui?* (2003) 114. 'Sensuel et protéiforme.'

42 Hugues Dayez, 'Sfar: Le Conteur intarissable,' *La Nouvelle Bande Dessinée* (Paris: Éditions Niffle, 2002) 193. 'Je pense que la bande dessinée a définitivement perdu le combat des baux-arts car une planche accrochée au mur restera toujours mons impressionnante qu'u tableau. Et à chaque fois qu'on essaiera de faire des musées avec la bande dessinée, on n'arrivera jamais à la cheville du Louvre! Par contre, le combat que la BD dot gagner,

c'est celui de l'écriture. Car, indubitablement, une bande dessinée, c'est un livre, c'est une objet que a un contenu litteéraire et culturel souvent plus intéressant que ce qui se produit en littérature contemporaine.'

43 Mercier, 'Le Vaste Monde' 117.

44 Mouchart, 'Joann Sfar' 114. 'La part la plus personnelle de son approche de la bande dessinée.'

45 Dayez, 'Sfar' 184.

46 Dayez, 'Sfar' 195. '*Le Petit Monde du Golem* qui me tient tant à coeur tire péniblement à 2 000 exemplaires à L'Association, tandis que ce *Troll* que je n'aime pas se vend à plus de 20 000.'

47 In July 2003, when Sfar appeared in *Les Inrockuptibles,* for example, the first and second books in the series placed 18th and 26th respectively on the bestseller list. 'Palmarès des meilleures ventes de bandes dessinées,' *L'Express* 14 July 2003: 33.

48 'Interview de Joann Sfar' (2001) (http://www.bdparadisio.com/Intervw/ sfar/intsfar.htm). 'La question c'est: qu'est-ce qu'un personnage pour un auteur? Pour moi, on a des petites voix dans la tête qui parlent en perma- nence. Il y en a qui disent des conneries, il y en a qui disent des choses intéressantes. Et quand on cultive ces petites voix, on en a de plus en plus. Moi, je me suis mis à essayer de leur trouver des visages. Je me dis "Tiens, ça c'est la voix qui ressemble à ça ... ça c'est la voix qui ressemble à ça ...' et au bout d'un moment, ces voix-là, quand on ne les fait pas parler régulière- ment, elles ne sont pas contentes.'

49 The fullest elaboration of the history of the Atelier des Vosges can be found in Dominique Hérody, 'En Atelier,' *9e Art* 8 (2003): 76–86.

50 Gilles Ciment, 'Conversation,' *9e Art* 8 (2003): 52.

51 Eric Loret, 'L'Art de la guerre,' *Libération* 25 April 2002: 12. 'Une oeuvre majeure, émouvante et sans esbroufe, qui réconcilie les anciens et les modernes.'

52 Hugues Dayez, 'Guibert: Le Dessin comme mémoire,' *La Nouvelle Bande Dessinée* (Paris: Éditions Niffle, 2002) 146. 'Traduire la subjectivité du narrateur: on sent bien qu'il s'agit d'une vision de la guerre, et non d'un compte rendu historique de celle-ci.'

53 'Du 9 critique' (n.d.) (http://www.pastis.org/joann/filleprof/ filleduprof.html). 'Donner du sang neuf aux éditeurs classiques.'

54 Eric Loret, 'Les Olives noires,' *Libération* 15 June 2001: 31. 'rajeunir intelligemment le genre Alix.'

55 Vincent Bernière, 'Genre Peplum,' *9e Art* 7 (2002): 141.

56 Dayez, 'Sfar' 183. 'Et si, dans *Les Olives noires,* je mets en scène des personnages qui ressemblent physiquement à mes copains, ce n'est pas par

amour des private jokes pour qu'on reconnnaisse Blain ou Guibert, c'est parce que le fait de partir de personnes reélles m'inspire des personnages plus riches et plus crédibles.'

57 Gilles Ciment, 'Les Nouveaux Avatars du péplum,' *9e Art* 8 (2003) 99. 'Au coeur de l'épopée impériale romaine ou de la grande mythologie grecque, la matière même du *réel* – la simple vie des hommes, leur environnement, leurs mentalités, leurs moeurs, leurs gestes quotidiens: la 'Nouvelle Histoire' des *Annales* est passée par là.'

58 Hugues Dayez, 'Blain: Le Détourner de genres,' *La Nouvelle Bande Dessinée* (Paris: Éditions Niffle, 2002): 25.

59 Jean-Pierre Mercier, 'Christophe Blain: Odyssée loufoques,' *Beaux Arts Magazine Hors Série: Qu'est-ce que la BD aujourd'hui?* (2003): 52.

60 Dayez, 'Blain' 18.

61 Paul Bleton, 'Piste de signes,' *9e Art* 8 (2003): 90.

62 Dayez, 'Blain' 20.

63 Mercier, 'Christophe Blain' 52.

64 Evariste Blanchet, 'Pirates!' *9e Art* 8 (2003): 101. 'Post-moderne et hybride par excellence.'

65 Dayez, 'Blain' 26. 'Par exemple, un auteur come Giraud est un artiste qui aime le dessin, tandis que ses "héritiers" sont des types qui aiment Giraud avant d'aimer le dessin.'

66 Dayez, 'Blain' 29. 'J'ajouterais que, même si des best-sellers comme XIII ne sont pas ma tasse de thé, je suis ravi que de telles séries existent et rapportent autant d'argent à Dargaud! Vive Van Hamme! Vive Vance! Continuez ainsi, ça permet à Dargaud de financer des collections comme "Poisson Pilote."'

67 Bourdieu, *Field* 130.

68 'Poisson Pilote.' 'Dans la dernière *Lettre Dargaud*, j'ai à peu près posé cette même questions à David B., un des pères fondateurs de l'Association, qui vient de publier "Le Capitaine écarlate" (avec Emmanuel Guibert) chez Dupuis et qui a publié en juin, avec Christophe Blain, "Les ogres," en collection Poisson Pilote, chez Dargaud. Voila sa réponse: "Je ne me sens pas récupéré, je continue à travailler régulièrement pour l'Asso, je participe aux prises de décision, je la représente dans certains festival. Je ne suis pas devenu un auteur Dargaud, je suis un auteur qui, pour gagner sa vie et par plaisir, au fil des rencontres, travaille pour plusieurs éditeurs."'

69 Eric Loret, 'L'Ami Sfar cerebral,' *Libération*, 25 January 2001: 6–7. 'Je crois que la BD, c'est avant tout de l'écriture et que le combat pour les beaux-arts est perdu d'avance. Mes maîtres, ce sont plutôt Fred, Goscinny, Tardi ou Pratt. Dans la littérature française actuelle, il me semble qu'on a perdu le

sens de l'épique. Avec les gens de l'Atelier des Vosges, Blain et Guibert, Emile Bravo, David B., Trondheim ou Marjane Satrapi, on essaie de mettre notre expérience de l'autobiographie, de l'introspection, au service de récits épiques. Il faut que le lecteur puisse s'incarner dans un personnage pour éprouver une vision de la vie.'

Chapter Seven: The Strange Case of Lewis Trondheim

1 Lewis Trondheim, *Pichenettes* (Paris: Dargaud, 1996) 35.
2 Lewis Trondheim, 'Emmaüs,' *Rackham Poutch* (Paris: Rackham, 1991) 39. 'Et moi alors? ... Je vais quand meme pas en faire une bédé.'
3 Lewis Trondheim, 'Les Gouts et les couleurs,' *Rackham Poutch* (Paris: Rackham 1991) 45. 'Dis plutôt que tu es jaloux et que tu aurais preferé que ce chef d'oeuvre reste apprécié par une petite elite dont tu aurais fait parti. Je n'aime vraiment pas quand tu essaies de te montrer intelligent.'
4 Lewis Trondheim, '1987,' *Jeux d'influences* (Paris: PLG, 2001).
5 Jean-Baptiste Harang, 'Trondheim, du lapin sur la planche,' *Libération* 22 January 1998: 7. 'Lewis Trondhein est un homme de 33 ans, fin comme un oiseau, le bec jaune et crochu, une crête blanche de trois houpes, quatre doigts à chaque main, un trait épais et continu marque son regard, et quand il rit, les poules lui envient sept ou huit dents dans le bec.'
6 Lewis Trondheim, *Approximativement* (Paris: Cornélius, 1995) 12. 'Quelques compromis frustrants.'
7 Trondheim, *Approximativement* 80. 'Ne pas contrairer les Japonais. C'est eux les patrons. C'est eux que ont raison. Ne pas chercher à comprendre. Leur logique est autre. Ils sont fous.'
8 Trondheim, *Approximativement* 140. 'Est-ce que j'aurais accepté de faire des histoires merdeuses et compromettantes pour être milliardaire?'
9 Harang, 'Trondheim' 7. 'Il n'y a que L'Association pour éditer un truc pareil.'
10 '25 Ans de BD en 25 albums,' *Le Monde* 21 January 1998: 4. 'Trondheim se distingue par sa maîtrise des dialogues et son sens de l'observation. Slaloms, paru d'abord aux éditions L'Association, puis repris par Dargaud, est une bonne introduction à son univers : on retrouve son personnage fétiche, Lapinot, en proie à ses doutes existentiels et aux prises avec la vie quotidienne. Un auteur lucide et faussement naïf.'
11 Pierre Bourdieu, *The Field of Cultural Production* (New York: Columbia UP, 1993) 31.
12 Fredric Jameson, 'The Cultural Logic of Late Capitalism,' *Postmodernism, or, The Cultural Logic of Late Capitalism* (Raleigh, NC: Duke UP, 1991) 1–54.

13 Laurent Gerbier, 'Donjon, les 3 âges de l'héroïsme,' *9e Art* 5 (2000): 136. 'Fanées, ternes, elles limitent la palette aux degrades de mauve, d'orange et de brun.'

14 'Donjon People' (n.d.) (http://www.pastis.org/donjonland/news/people/peoplemenu.html). 'J'ai fait plaisir au petit Menu de 10 ans qui ne rêvait que de ça ...'

15 Jean-Christophe Menu, 'L'Aérophagie, mal des mangeurs d'air,' *Lapin* 23 (April 1999): 6. 'Lewis! Le cul entre combien de chaises?!'

16 'Lewis Trondheim' (2005) (http://www.dupuis.com/servlet/jpecat?pgm =VIEW_AUTHOR&lang=UK&AUTEUR_ID=167).

17 Lewis Trondheim, *Désoeuvrée* (Paris: L'Association, 2005) 6. 'Légère notoriété. Renommée. Gloire. Vedettariat. Has-been. Gros has-been.'

18 Significantly, the final page of *Désoeuvré* does not depict the artist riding off into the sunset, but labouring at his drawing table, and, at the end of 2005, his website listed twelve forthcoming books through the end of 2006.

19 Paul Gravett, 'Side by Side by Trondheim,' *The Comics Journal Special Edition* (Summer 2002): 52.

Conclusion

1 Jean-Christophe Menu, *Plates-bandes* (Paris: L'Association, 2005) 66. 'Les années 1994–2004 vont-elles marquer les dates d'un âge d'or révolu dans le temps et les mémoires, que nous évoquerons bienôt avec nostalgie et amertume, comme d'autres les années 1969–1979?'

2 Menu, *Plates-bandes* 12.

3 Menu, *Plates-bandes* 41. 'l'Avant-Garde même.'

4 Menu, *Plates-bandes* 40.

5 Nicolas Anspach, 'Sébastien Gnaedig parle de Futuropolis,' *ActuaBD* (January 2005) (http://www.actuabd.com/article.php3?id_article=2106). 'Futuropolis se place entre ces "petits éditeurs" et les "grands." J'ai obtenu la possibilité d'avoir une politique d'auteur, tout en ayant des moyens de grand éditeur.'

6 Romain Brethes, 'Bande dessinée et culture,' *Beaux Arts Magazine Hors-série: 32 bandes dessinées pour 2004* (2004): 19. 'Doublement remarquable pour son statut de femme et d'exilée iranienne dans un monde artistique qui manque singulièrement de figures de proue, Marjane Satrapi est devenue une icône parce que le sujet de Persepolis – schématiquement son rapport à l'Iran et à la dictature islamiste – a pris le pas sur le traitement de ce sujet. La bande dessinée en tant qu'objet culturel n'est pas directement valorisée ici puisqu'elle disparaît derrière une individualité qui épouse idéalement

l'actualité, ainsi que l'attestent les affaires relatives au foulard islamique ou l'attribution du prix Nobel de la paix à Chirine Ebadi, pour lesquelles on a consulté à tout va, et un peu inconsidérément, la jeune dessinatrice.'

7 Christopher Theokas, 'Persepolis Paints Iran from a Kid's Perspective,' *USA Today* 6 August 2003 (http://www.usatoday.com/life/books/reviews/2003-08-06-persepolis_x.htm).

8 Sandip Roy, 'Back Home, Feeling Homeless,' *San Francisco Chronicle* 29 August 2004 (http://www.sfgate.com/cgibin/article.cgi?f=/chronicle/a/2004/08/29/RVGS18B17S1.DTL).

9 Theokas, 'Persepolis Paints.'

10 Luc Sante, 'She Can't Go Home Again,' *New York Times* 22 August 2004 (http://query.nytimes.com/gst/fullpage.html?res=9A01E7DF173FF931A1575BC0A9629C8B63).

11 Samantha Ellis, 'Less of Your Lipgloss,' *The Observer* 7 November 2004 (http://observer.guardian.co.uk/print/0,3858,5056926–102280,00.html).

12 Rebecca Swain Vadnie, '"Embroideries": Rich Family Yarns Give Rise to Warmhearted Sampler,' *Orlando Sentinel* 17 April 2005 (http://www.orlandosentinel.com/features/lifestyle/orl-livembroideries_bkrv041705apr17,1,2858496.story?coll=orl-living-headlines&ctrack=1&cset=true).

13 Thierry Groensteen, *Systéme de la bande dessinée* (Paris: Presses Universitaires de France, 1999) 192–3. 'L'évolution esthétique de la bande dessinée depuis un quart de siècle a été dans le sens d'une libération de l'image. Le dessin narratif traditionnel, tel qu'il avait prévalu de Töpffer jusqu'à Franquin et de Milton Caniff jusqu'à Mézières, s'est vu concurrencer par des écritures plus libres, plus picturales, plus poétiques. De Moebius à Alagbé, de Loustal à Barbier, de Baudoin à Vanoli, la bande dessinée a montré qu'elle pouvait s'accommoder du dessin illustratif, et qu'elle pouvait même abandonner complètement le dessin linéaire, au profit du libre jeu des surfaces et des couleurs, des lumières et des intensités ... Les thèmes narratifs par excellence (le voyage, la poursuite, l'enquête, le déguisement, la métamorphose ...), dont la bande dessinée traditionelle usait et abusait, s'ils n'ont pas été abadonnés, ont été du moins relativisés par la conquête de nouveaux espaces du récit: plus littéraires, plus immobiles, plus poétiques, plus sensuels et plus introspectifs.'

Works Cited

'25 ans de BD en 25 albums.' *Le Monde* 21 January 1998: 4.

Anderson, Benedict. *Imagined Communities: Reflections on the Origin and Spread of Nationalism.* London: Verso, 1983.

Anderson, Linda. *Autobiography.* London: Routledge, 2001.

Anspach, Nicolas. 'Sébastien Gnaedig parle de Futuropolis.' *ActuaBD* (January 2005). http://www.actuabd.com/article.php3?id_article=2106.

Ashberry, John. 'The Invisible Avant-Garde.' *Art Theory and Criticism: An Anthology of Formalist, Avant-Garde, Contextualist and Post-Modernist Thought.* Ed. Sally Everett. Jefferson, NC: McFarland, 1991. 132–8.

'Association a la Pulpe.' *Le Rab de lapin* October 1993: 1–4.

'Asuntos Internos.' *Nosotros somos los muertos* 5 (1998): 106.

'Avant-Propos.' *Frigorevue* 3. Geneva: Atoz Éditions, 1994. 3.

'Avis important aux libraires et aux particuliers.' *L'Association Bulletin,* January 1990: n. pag.

Ayroles, François. 'Hybridation entre *Placid et Muzo font du judo,* de Nicolaou, et les *Premiers dialogues,* de Platon (*Premier Alcibiade* 107 d).' *OuPus* 1. Paris: L'Association, 1997. 4.

Baetens, Jan. 'Autarcic Comix.' *Frigobox* 5 (1995): 31–7.

– 'Gloria Lopez: Une réflexion sur le langage de la bande dessinée.' *Image and Narrative* 3 (2001). http://www.imageandnarrative.be/illustrations/janbaetens.htm.

'Bande dessinée: Vient de paraître.' *Libération* 26 September 2002: 12.

Bastide, Julien. 'Manga: Le deuxième souffle.' *9e Art* 10 (2004): 69–71.

Becker, Howard S. *Art Worlds.* Berkeley, CA: U of California P, 1982.

Berberian, Charles. 'Une Lettre de Charles Berberian.' *9e Art* 1 (1996): 83.

Bernière, Vincent. 'Comix 2000: Un livre intelligent.' *9e Art* 5 (2000): 129–31.

– 'Genre Peplum.' *9e Art* 7 (2002): 141.

– 'Entretien avec Vincent Fortemps.' (2003). (http://www.fremok.org/
  entretiens/vfortemps.html).

Blanchet, Evariste. 'Pirates!' *9e Art* 8 (2003): 100–7.

Bleton, Paul. 'Piste de signes.' *9e Art* 8 (2003): 88–94.

Boltanski, Luc. 'La Constitution du champ de la bande dessinée.' *Actes de la
  recherche en sciences sociales* (January 1975): 37–59.

Bourdieu, Pierre. *The Field of Cultural Production*. New York: Columbia UP, 1993.

– *The Rules of Art: Genesis and Structures of the Literary Field*. Trans. Susan
  Emanuel. Stanford: Stanford UP, 1995.

Brethes, Romain. 'Bande dessinée et culture.' *Beaux Arts Magazine Hors-série: 32
  bandes dessinées pour 2004* (Paris: Beaux Arts Magazine, 2004).

Bürger, Peter. *Theory of the Avant-Garde*. Minneapolis: U of Minnesota P, 1994.

Bury, Steven. *Artists' Books: The Book as a Work of Art, 1963–1995*. Aldershot, UK:
  Scolar P, 1995.

Canard, Bruno. 'Jean Van Hamme: Autopise d'un succès.' *9e Art* 5 (2000):
  54–9.

Carroll, Noël. *Beyond Aesthetics: Philosophical Essays*. Cambridge: Cambridge UP,
  2001.

Chapple, Steve, and Reebee Garofalo. *Rock 'n' Roll Is Here to Pay: The History and
  Politics of the Music Industry*. Chicago: Nelson-Hall, 1977.

Chollet, Mona. 'En Orbite du monde.' (1998). http://www.peripheries.net/g-
  amok.htm.

Ciment, Gilles. 'Conversation.' *9e Art* 8 (2003): 51–61.

– 'Les Nouveaux Avatars du péplum.' *9e Art* 8 (2003): 95–9.

Classon, Rolf. 1997. 'Cartoons from the Nordic Countries in the 90s.' *Gare du
  nord*. NordiComics, 1997: 2.

'Compte-Rendu.' *Le Rab de lapin* July 1995: 1–4.

Crane, Diana. *The Transformation of the Avant-Garde: The New York Art World,
  1940–1985*. Chicago: U of Chicago P, 1987.

Crow, Thomas. 'Modernism and Mass Culture in the Visual Arts.' *Modernism and
  Modernity*. Ed. Benjamin H.D. Buchloh et al. Halifax: The Press of the Nova
  Scotia College of Art and Design, 2004. 215–64.

'David B.' *Tao* 5 (n.d.): 5–74.

David B. *L'Ascension du Haut Mal*. Vol. 1. Paris: L'Association, 1996.

– *L'Ascension du Haut Mal*. Vol. 2. Paris: L'Association, 1997.

– *L'Ascension du Haut Mal*. Vol. 6. Paris: L'Association, 2003.

Davids, Betsy, and Jim Petrillo. 'The Artist as Book Printer: Four Short Courses.'
  Artist's Books: A Critical Anthology and Sourcebook. Ed. Joan Lyons. Rochester, NY:
  Visual Studies Workshop P, 1985. 149–66.

Dayez, Hugues. 'Blain: Le Détourner de genres.' *La Nouvelle Bande Dessinée*.
  Paris: Éditions Niffle, 2002. 8–31.

– 'Guibert: Le Dessin comme mémoire.' *La Nouvelle Bande Dessinée*. Paris: Éditions Niffle, 2002. 128–51.

– 'Sfar: Le Conteur intarissable.' *La Nouvelle Bande Dessinée*. Paris: Éditions Niffle, 2002. 176–99.

De Gaudemar, Antoine. 'La Nouvelle Bande à part.' *Libération* 25 January 1996: 2–3.

De Man, Paul. 'Autobiography as De-Facement.' *Modern Language Notes* 94 (1979): 919–30.

Deprez, Olivier. 'Entretien avec Pedro Nora.' (2003). http://www.fremok.org/entretiens/pedronora.html.

'Destination Comicon.' (2005). http://bdangouleme.fr/actualites/index.ideal?action=consulter&id=835.

De Tocqueville, Alexis. *Democracy in America*. New York: Vintage, 1990.

Dieck, Martin tom. 'Dada.' *Cheval sans tête* 2.4 (1997): 10–15.

'Donjon People.' (n.d.). http://www.pastis.org/donjonland/news/people/peoplemenu.html.

Dow Adams, Timothy. *Telling Lies in Modern American Autobiography*. Chapel Hill, NC: U of North Carolina P, 1990.

'Du 9 critique.' (n.d.). http://www.pastis.org/joann/filleprof/filleduprof.html.

Dupuy, Philippe. 'L'Année dernière.' *Journal d'un album*. By Philippe Dupuy and Charles Berberian. Paris: L'Association, 1994. N. pag.

– 'Lundi 23 Août 1993.' By Philippe Dupuy and Charles Berberian. *Journal d'un album*. Paris: L'Association, 1994. N. pag.

Dupuy, Philippe, and Charles Berberian. 1994. *Journal d'un album*. Paris: L'Association, 1994.

'Éditorial.' *Frigobox* 2 (1995): 3.

'Éditorial.' *L'Association Bulletin* January 1991: n. pag.

Ellis, Samantha. 'Less of Your Lipgloss.' *The Observer* 7 November 2004. http://observer.guardian.co.uk/print/0,3858,5056926–102280,00.html.

'Entretien avec Olivier Bramanti.' (2004). http://www.fremok.org/entretiens/obramanti01.html.

Everett, Sally. 'Introduction.' *Art Theory and Criticism: An Anthology of Formalist, Avant-Garde, Contextualist and Post-Modernist Thought*. Ed. Sally Everett. Jefferson, NC: McFarland, 1991. ix–xiii.

Foucault, Michel. 'What Is an Author?' *The Foucault Reader*. Trans. Josué V. Harari. Ed. Paul Rabinow. New York: Pantheon, 1984. 101–20.

Fowler, Bridget. *Pierre Bourdieu and Cultural Theory: Critical Investigations*. New York: Sage, 1997.

Gerbier, Laurent. 'Donjon, les 3 âges de l'héroïsme.' *9e Art* 5 (2000): 136–7.

Gerner, Jochen. '*TNT en Amérique*: Jochen Gerner par lui-même.' (2002). http://www.bulbe.com/fr/sous-titres/jochengerner.php.

Gillet, Charlie. *The Sound of the City: The Rise of Rock and Roll.* New York: Outerbridge and Dienstfrey, 1970.

Gravett, Paul. 'Side by Side by Trondheim.' *The Comics Journal Special Edition,* Summer 2002: 46–52.

Gray, Herman. *Producing Jazz: The Experience of an Independent Record Company.* Philadelphia: Temple UP, 1988.

Greenberg, Clement. 'Avant-Garde and Kitsch.' *Art Theory and Criticism: An Anthology of Formalist, Avant-Garde, Contextualist and Post-Modernist Thought.* Ed. Sally Everett. Jefferson, NC: McFarland, 1991. 26–40.

– 'Modernist Painting.' *Art Theory and Criticism: An Anthology of Formalist, Avant-Garde, Contextualist and Post-Modernist Thought.* Ed. Sally Everett. Jefferson, NC: McFarland, 1991. 110–18.

Groensteen, Thierry. 'Petit Manuel d'introspection graphique.' *Ego Comme X* 1 (1994): 2.

– 'Les Petites Cases du moi: L'autobiographie en bande dessinée.' *9e Art* 1 (1996): 58–69.

– 'Genres et séries.' *9e Art* 4 (1999): 78–87.

– *Système de la bande dessinée.* Paris: Presses Universitaires de France, 1999.

– *Astérix, Barberella & Cie: Trésors du Musée de la Bande Dessinée d'Angoulême.* Paris: Somogy éditions d'art, 2000.

– 'Les Années 90: Tentative de récapitulation.' *9e Art* 5 (2000): 10–17.

Harang, Jean-Baptiste. 'Trondheim, du lapin sur la planche.' *Libération,* 22 January 1998: 7.

Hannerz, Ulf. *Transnational Connections: Culture, People, Places.* London: Routledge, 1996.

Hartsock, Nancy. 'Foucault on Power: A Theory for Women?' *Feminism/ Postmodernism.* Ed. Linda J. Nicholson. New York: Routledge, 1990. 157–75.

Harvey, R.C. *The Art of the Funnies: An Aesthetic History.* Jackson: UP of Mississippi, 1994.

Hérody, Dominique. 'En Atelier.' *9e Art* 8 (2003): 76–86.

Hesmondhalgh, David. 'Indie: The Institutional Politics and Aesthetics of a Popular Music Genre.' *Cultural Studies* 13.1 (1999): 34–61.

– *Cultural Industries.* New York: Sage, 2002.

Higgins, Dick. 'A Preface.' *Artist's Books: A Critical Anthology and Sourcebook.* Ed. Joan Lyons. Rochester, NY: Visual Studies Workshop P, 1985. 11–12.

Huber, Markus. *Promenade à Saturnia.* Trans. Waltraud Spohr. Paris: Amok, 2000.

Hume, David. 'Of the Standard of Taste.' *Of the Standard of Taste and Other Essays.* Ed. J.W. Lenz. New York: Bobbs-Merrill, 1965. 3–24.

Huyssen, Andreas. 'Mass Culture as Woman: Modernism's Other.' *Art Theory and Criticism: An Anthology of Formalist, Avant-Garde, Contextualist and Post-Modernist Thought.* Ed. Sally Everett. Jefferson, NC: McFarland, 1991. 228–42.

'Instantané.' *Libération* 12 February 2003: 7.

Internationales Comix Festival – Luzern. (n.d.). http://www.fumetto.ch/main_en.htm.

'Interview David B.: *L'Ascension du Haut Mal.*' (2000). http://www.bdparadisio.com/intervw/davidb/intdavid.htm.

'Interview de Guy Vidal, Directeur éditorial chez Dargaud.' (2002). http://www.bdparadisio.com/intervw/vidal/intvidal.htm.

'Interview de Joann Sfar.' (2001). http://www.bdparadisio.com/Intervw/sfar/intsfar.htm.

Jameson, Fredric. 'The Cultural Logic of Late Capitalism.' *Postmodernism, or, The Cultural Logic of Late Capitalism.* Raleigh, NC: Duke UP, 1991. 1–54.

Kornblith, Gary. 'Becoming Joseph T. Buckingham: The Struggle for Artisanal Independence in Early Nineteenth-Century Boston.' *American Artisans: Crafting Social Identity 1750–1850.* Ed. Howard B. Rock, Paul A. Gilje, and Robert Asher. Baltimore: Johns Hopkins UP, 1995.

Kostelanetz, Richard. 'Book Art.' *Artist's Books: A Critical Anthology and Sourcebook.* Ed. Joan Lyons. Rochester, NY: Visual Studies Workshop P, 1985. 27–30.

– *Dictionary of the Avant-Gardes.* Chicago: A Cappella Books, 1993.

Kuspit, Donald. *The Cult of the Avant-Garde Artist.* Cambridge: Cambridge UP, 1993.

'La BD ne bulle pas.' *Libération* 3 January 2002: 5

'La lutte des cases.' *Libération* 23 January 2003: 11.

L'Association catalogue. Paris: L'Association, 2004.

Lee, Stephen. 'Re-examining the Concept of the "Independent" Record Company: The Case of Wax Trax! Records.' *Popular Music* 14.1 (1995): 13–31.

Lefèvre, Pascal. 'The Importance of Being "Published": A Comparative Study of Different Comics Formats.' *Comics & Culture: Analytical and Theoretical Approaches to Comics.* Ed. Ann Magnussen and Hans-Christian Christiansen. Copenhagen: Museum Tusculanum P, 2000. 91–105.

'Le Frémok: Un dieu vivant.' (n.d.). http://www.fremok.org/fremok/fremok-presse.html.

Lejeune, Philippe. *On Autobiography.* Trans. Katherine Leary. Minneapolis: U of Minnesota P, 1989.

'Le manifeste des nomades.' *Frigobox* 5 (December 1995): 6–7.

Leprévost, Thierry. 'Édito.' *Ego Comme X* 1 (1994): 2.

Le Rab de lapin 15 May 1993.

– 1 December 1994.
– 1 January 1995.
– 1 November 1995.
– 1 April 1996
– 14 July 1996.
– 5 October 1996.
– 8 October 1997.
– 25 November 1998.

'Lewis Trondheim.' (2005). http://www.dupuis.com/servlet/jpecat?pgm=
 VIEW_AUTHOR&lang=UK&AUTEUR_ID=167.

'L'interview! Fabrice Neaud 1/2.' (2001). http://www.bdselection.com/php/
 ?rub=page_dos&id_dossier=9.

'L'interview! Fabrice Neaud 2/2.' (2002). http://www.bdselection.com/php/
 ?rub=page_dos&id_dossier=73.

Lippard, Lucy R. 'The Artist's Book Goes Public.' *Artist's Books: A Critical Anthology and Sourcebook.* Ed. Joan Lyons. Rochester, NY: Visual Studies Workshop P,
 1985. 45–8.

Loret, Eric. 'Collectif Self Service.' *Libération* 7 September 2001: 29.

– 'Hortus sanitatis.' *Libération* 6 July 2001: 31.

– 'L'Ami Sfar cerebral.' *Libération* 25 January 2001: 6–7.

– 'Les Olives noires.' *Libération* 15 June 2001: 31.

– 'Nadia Raviscioni l'affiche bien.' *Libération* 25 January 2001: 11.

– 'Parlez-moi d'Amok.' *Libération* 25 January 2001: 11.

– 'Pince-moi, Genève.' *Libération* 25 January 2001: 10.

– 'L'Art de la guerre.' *Libération* 25 April 2002: 12.

'Marché de la BD en 1994: Légère Reprise.' *Libération* 26 January 1995: xiv.

Martin, Jean-Philippe. 'L'Irrésistible Ascension de l'édition indépendante.'
 9e Art 5 (2000): 22–31.

McCloud, Scott. *Understanding Comics: The Invisible Art.* Northhampton, MA:
 Kitchen Sink P, 1993.

Menu, Jean-Christophe. 'L'Art de tous les paradoxes.' *LABO.* Paris: Futuropolis,
 1990: 91–3.

– 'Foreword.' *Comix 2000.* Paris: L'Association, 1999. ii–iii.

– 'Lapin n'est toujours pas une revue.' *9e Art* 4 (1999): 44–5.

– 'L'Aérophagie, mal des mangeurs d'air.' *Lapin* April 1999: 3–6.

– *Plates-bandes.* Paris: L'Association, 2005.

Mercier, Jean-Pierre. 'Le Vaste Monde du Joann Sfar.' *9e Art* 6 (2001): 114–19.

– 'Christophe Blain: Odyssee loufoques.' *Beaux Arts Magazine Hors Série: Qu'est-ce
 que la BD aujourd'hui?* (2003). 52.

Moliterni, Claude, Philippe Merlot, and Michel Denni. *Les Aventures de la BD*. Paris: Gallimard, 1996.

Morgan, Robert C. 'Systemic Books by Artists.' *Artist's Books: A Critical Anthology and Sourcebook*. Ed. Joan Lyons. Rochester, NY: Visual Studies Workshop P, 1985. 207–22.

Mouchart, Benoît. 'Joann Sfar Debordement Graphique.' *Beaux Arts Magazine Hors Série: Qu'est-ce que la BD aujourd'hui?* (2003). 114.

Murphy, Richard. *Theorizing the Avant-Garde: Modernism, Expressionism, and the Problem of Postmodernity*. Cambridge: Cambridge UP, 1988.

Neale, Steve. *Genre*. London: British Film Institute, 1980.

Neaud, Fabrice. 'Réponses à huit questions sur l'autobiographie.' *9e Art* 1 (1996): 80.

– *Journal (III)*. Angoulême: Ego Comme X, 1999.

– *Journal (4)*. Angoulême: Ego Comme X, 2002.

Negus, Keith. *Producing Pop: Culture and Conflict in the Popular Music Industry*. London: Edward Arnold, 1992.

– *Music Genres and Corporate Cultures*. London: Routledge, 1999.

Ory, Pascal. 'Relecture de *Tintin en Amérique*.' *Lire* December 2002: 27.

'Palmarès des meilleures ventes de bandes dessinées.' *L'Express* 14 July 2003: 33.

Paques, Frédéric. 'Fréon, éditeur de bandes dessinées d'art et d'essais.' (2002). http://www.art-memoires.com/lettre/lm1820/20ulgfreon.htm.

'Persepolis tome 2.' *Libération* 16 November 2001: 12.

Phillpot, Clive. 'Books by Artists and Books as Art.' *Artist/Author: Contemporary Artists' Books*. Ed. Cornelia Lauf and Clive Phillpot. New York: Distributed Art Publishers, 1998. 31–55.

'Planches à billets.' *Libération* 27 January 2000: 5.

'Poisson Pilote.' (n.d.). http://www.imaginet.fr/universbd/dossiers/ poissonpilote/.

Polomé, Pierre. 'Entretien avec Dominique Goblet.' (2001). http://www. fremok.org/entretiens/souvenirgoblet.html.

'Qu'est-ce qui vous manque?' *Amok Catalogue, 1996–1997*. Paris: Amok, 1996. 2.

Ratier, Gilles. *Avant la Case*. Paris: PLG, 2003.

Rice, Shelley. 'Words and Images: Artists' Books as Visual Literature.' *Artist's Books: A Critical Anthology and Sourcebook*. Ed. Joan Lyons. Rochester, NY: Visual Studies Workshop P, 1985. 59–85.

Rommens, Aarnoud. 'Comics & Culture: A Step towards Comic "Absolution"?' *Image and Narrative* 3 (2001). http://www.imageandnarrative.be/illustrations/ aarnoudrommens.htm.

Rosenberg, Harold. 'The American Action Painters.' *Art Theory and Criticism: An*

Anthology of Formalist, Avant-Garde, Contextualist and Post-Modernist Thought. Ed. Sally Everett. Jefferson, NC: McFarland, 1991. 55–64.

Roy, Sandip. 'Back Home, Feeling Homeless.' *San Francisco Chronicle* 29 August 2004. http://www.sfgate.com/cgibin/article.cgi?f=/chronicle/a/2004/08/29/RVGS18B17S1.DTL.

Sante, Luc. 'She Can't Go Home Again.' *New York Times* 22 August 2004. http://query.nytimes.com/gst/fullpage.html?res=9A01E7DF173FF931A1575BC0A9629C8B63.

'Santé, prospérité, bonheur ... et Astérix.' *Libération* 25 January 2001: 4.

Spengemann, William C. *The Forms of Autobiography: Episodes in the History of a Literary Genre.* New Haven, CT: Yale UP, 1980.

Staiger, Janet. 'Authorship Approaches.' *Authorship and Film.* Ed. D.A. Gerstner and Janet Staiger. New York: Routledge, 2003. 27–57.

Stein, Donna. 'When a Book Is More Than a Book.' *Artists' Books in the Modern Era 1870–2000: The Reva and David Logan Collection of Illustrated Books.* Ed. Robert Flynn Johnson. San Francisco: Fine Arts Museums of San Francisco, 2001. 17–45.

'Success Séries.' *Libération* 22 January 1998: 12

Swindells, Julia. *Victorian Writing and Working Women.* Cambridge: Polity P, 1985.

Tassel, Fabrice. 'Spécial bande dessinée.' *Libération* 22 January 1998: 16.

Theokas, Christopher. 'Persepolis Paints Iran from a Kid's Perspective.' *USA Today* 6 August 2003. http://www.usatoday.com/life/books/reviews/2003-08-06-persepolis_x.htm.

Tran, Lionel. 'L'Électron belge.' *Jade* 18 (1999). http://www.pastis.org/jade/cgi-bin/reframe.pl?http://www.pastis.org/jade/avril/freon1.htm.

Trondheim, Lewis. 'Emmaüs.' *Rackham Poutch.* Paris: Rackham, 1991. 39.

– 'Les Gouts et Les Couleurs.' *Rackham Poutch.* Paris: Rackham, 1991. 45.

– *Approximativement.* Paris: Cornélius, 1995.

– *Pichenettes.* Paris: Dargaud, 1996.

– '1987.' *Jeux d'influences.* Paris: PLG, 2001.

– 'Journal du journal du journal.' *Lapin* January 2001: 33–5.

– *La vie comme elle vient.* Paris: Dargaud, 2004.

– *Désoeuvrée.* Paris: L'Association, 2005.

Vadnie, Rebecca Swain. '"Embroideries": Rich Family Yarns Give Rise to Warm-hearted Sampler.' *Orlando Sentinel* 17 April 2005. http://www.orlandosentinel.com/features/lifestyle/orl-livembroideries_bkrv041705apr17,1,2858496.story?coll=orl-living-headlines&ctrack=1&cset=true.

Vanhaesebrouck, Karel. 'Entretien avec Martin tom Dieck.' (2002). http://www.fremok.org/entretiens/tomdiecknouvelles.htm.

Van Hasselt, Thierry. 'Historique du projet *Brutalis*.' (2003). http://
   www.fremok.org/entretiens/projetbrutalis.html.
Ward, John L. *American Realist Painting, 1945–1980*. Ann Arbor, MI: UMI Re-
   search P, 1989.
Yaari, Monique. 'Who/What Is the Subject? Representations of Self in Late
   Twentieth-Century French Art.' *Word and Image* 16.4 (2000): 363–77.

Illustration Credits

Index

STUDIES IN BOOK AND PRINT CULTURE

General editor: Leslie Howsam

David Finkelstein, ed, *Print Culture and the Blackwood Tradition, 1805–1930*

Bart Beaty, *Unpopular Culture: Transforming the European Comic Book in the 1990s*